ECOBLITZ

ECOBLITZ

AN INDIANA FOREST EXPEDITION

Indiana Forest Alliance

Indiana University Press

This book is a publication of

Indiana University Press
Office of Scholarly Publishing
Herman B Wells Library 350
1320 East 10th Street
Bloomington, Indiana 47405 USA

iupress.org

Second printing 2024

Cataloging information is available from the Library of Congress.

ISBN 978-0-253-07107-1 (paperback)
ISBN 978-0-253-07108-8 (ebook)

CONTENTS

Recently retired, John Bacone served as the director of the Division of Nature Preserves with the Indiana Department of Natural Resources for 40 years. *Photo credit: John Bacone.*

FOREWORD

John A. Bacone

As an ecologist (now retired) with the Indiana Department of Natural Resources' Division of Nature Preserves, I was always frustrated with how little time we had to document the flora and fauna of the natural areas we were protecting. Understandably, we had much to do, and we had to be satisfied with a cruise through a natural area, listing the plants and animals we found and putting the list in a file about the site. On future visits, we would update the species lists. But we never had time to really study the site and document what was there. We relied on our experience to decide on the natural qualities of the site and whether it merited protection.

Our overarching goal in the Division of Nature Preserves was to protect at least one example of each of the various types of natural areas found in Indiana and at least one population of Indiana's rarest plant and animal species. Recognizing that our strength was primarily in botany, I asked the state entomologist what we could do to protect Indiana's rarest insect species. He said, "Keep on doing what you are doing. The rarest insects will always be in the undisturbed natural areas."

Another important fact regarding Indiana's natural areas is that they are usually small, surrounded by acres of corn and soybeans, and/or encroached upon by subdivisions. Forested natural areas that are surrounded by forested land are more intact, and all their component plant, animal, and invertebrate species are more viable, with less opportunity to be overrun by non-native species.

And so it is with great respect and appreciation that I read what is contained in this volume. This is the result of the Indiana Forest Alliance's three-year Ecoblitz Forest Census, which enabled an in-depth look into the biodiversity of the Back Country Area located in Morgan-Monroe and Yellowwood State Forests. This was a detailed examination of many of the taxonomic forms of life that occur there, including vascular plants, birds, fishes, beetles, parasitic wasps, and many more. This analysis was carried out over many seasons by experts in all these fields, and what is presented is a very impressive list.

Because the study site is adjacent to a dedicated state nature preserve and within a state forest backcountry area, it has retained its presettlement high-quality condition. Indeed, aerial photographs from 1939, a time of maximum disturbance by clearing and farming, show it to be an intact forest, unlike much nearby cleared and heavily eroded land. It has very few non-native species. Only 15 of the 427 herbaceous and woody species identified in the Back Country Area are non-native. And when the plant list is analyzed and assessed with the Floristic Quality Index recognized and used by regulatory agencies and land trusts to determine protection priorities, it scores as a high-quality natural area. While folks hiking through this area might agree it is a special place, the Ecoblitz documents, in detail, that it is a high-quality natural area.

As extinctions are hastened by the climate crisis, inventories such as these need to be done to establish a comprehensive baseline of biodiversity in Indiana and monitor changes going forward.

Conducting the Ecoblitz with such rigor required significant time and effort from many experts. Thankfully, the Indiana Forest Alliance stepped up to play this role. Hoosiers can be proud of this accomplishment. I hope similar efforts can periodically be undertaken in other natural areas around Indiana.

—John A. Bacone

ACKNOWLEDGMENTS

The Indiana Forest Alliance (IFA) is especially grateful to the following donors and partners who sponsored the Morgan-Monroe/Yellowwood Back Country Area Ecoblitz:

- Nina Mason Pulliam Charitable Trust
- Efroymson Family Fund
- McKinney Family Foundation
- Eleanor F. Bookwalter
- Eleanor D. Bookwalter
- Charles and Julie Bookwalter
- Mary Bookwalter
- Frank Levinson
- Other private donors and IFA members
- Indiana Academy of Science
- Amos Butler Audubon Society
- Knob and Valley Audubon Society
- Hoosier Environmental Council
- Sierra Club Hoosier Chapter
- Indiana Native Plant and Wildflower Society (INPAWS)
- Hoosier Herpetological Society
- Hoosier Mushroom Society
- New York Botanical Garden

IFA also appreciates the cooperation of the Division of Nature Preserves and the Division of Forestry within the Indiana Department of Natural Resources and the U.S. Fish and Wildlife Service, which granted multiple permits to authorize the research of the Ecoblitz.

In addition, we are grateful to the following donors whose support made this book possible:

- Alice and Robert Schloss
- Glory Kulczycki
- Janet Hollis
- Frank Levinson
- Mary Kay Rothert and Tom Zeller

Finally, we acknowledge the work of the team that collaborated to conceive, write, and edit this book:

- Anne Laker, Laker Verbal LLC
- Deidre Pettinga, Ph.D.
- Rae Schnapp, Ph.D.
- Jeffrey N. Stant
- Emma Steele

ECOBLITZ

Anne Laker. *Photo credit: Elizabeth Mahoney.*

PROLOGUE

Toward a Legible Forest

Anne Laker

The birders have gathered at dawn. May's dew will not last long in this old Indiana forest, the Morgan-Monroe/ Yellowwood Back Country Area. Sun rays soon zap the humid chill.

The birders are convened for an urgent project: glimpsing a nesting cerulean warbler. Its presence would prove, in one of a thousand ways, the worth of an undisturbed forest. The birders whisper while sweeping the vaulted overstory with naked eyes and binoculars.

By midday, the warmed forest smells of honeyed mud.

Shades of fresh chlorophyll sting the eye: a golden green vibrating with the sun's potency.

This or that leaf flutters, without wind.

Umpteen beetles seethe.

Moss drapes a fallen giant.

Spotty lichens clothe another.

The whitest beads of fungi beam from a velvety dead log.

Spring beauties and cut-leaf toothwort peek up from fall's brown leaf decay.

The forest is cinematic, hypnotic, bursting with dimension and functional wisdom beyond the perception of most of us. What wisdom do forests know? They know how to live and die productively. They know mutuality, efficiency, utility.

And we must face it: the intelligent beauty of this ecosystem thrives fully without human intervention.

Author Terry Tempest Williams writes that preservation "is the act of loving beyond ourselves, beyond our own species, beyond our own time. To honor wildlands and wild lives that we may never see, much less understand, is to acknowledge the world does not revolve around us."

How easy for us to center our own wills while ignoring what is hard to sense—the slow power of a lichen, the lethal business of a wasp.

Spring beauties are a harbinger of warmer days to come, and their small flowers support several bee species. *Photo credit: Rae Schnapp.*

The irony hurts: humans have zero essential role in the system design of forests, yet we exercise outsized influence on them.

The irony is baked into our Indiana heritage. The Indiana State Seal is an illustration, still in use today, featuring a panicked wood buffalo (a species now extinct) fleeing westward into a dark margin of wilderness as a man chops down a sycamore tree, with the sun setting over his shoulder. The seal's theme was likely conceived by William Henry Harrison, governor of the Indiana Territory, in the early 1800s. The seal is both a documentary of the de rigueur deforestation and an encouragement of human dominance over wilderness.

The cutting and clearing of trees was a relentless 70-year project between 1830 and 1900 that forever transformed the surface of Indiana. By 1920, only 7% of Indiana's forests remained compared to the 87% that early Europeans encountered.

Charles C. Deam, Indiana's first state forester and a member of the Indiana Academy of Science, noticed this profound loss and the widespread erosion that resulted. Deam was moved to draft the Forest Classification Act of 1921, which exempted farmers from taxation of the forested land they owned. In the 25 years after the passage of the law, 2,000 privately owned tracts of forest were set aside.

But the loss of Indiana's original forest was staggering. In 1989, Purdue forest ecologist George R. Parker estimated that only about 3% of the total forest in Indiana was old growth, while the Indiana Department of Natural Resources asserts that fewer than 2,000 acres (less than half of a tenth of 1%) of Indiana's virgin old-growth forests remain.

This loss is derived from a form of illiteracy. As Paul Gruchow writes in *The Necessity of Empty Places*, "A sense of one's standing in the natural

Forest canopy in spring. *Photo credit: Jason Kolenda.*

world is not instinctive, not automatic, and only in the most general way, culturally transmitted. . . . It is, like all learning, a personal acquisition, arrived at only by becoming acquainted with the basic texts, with wild places."

* * *

Charles Deam, also a botanist, was a master reader of wild texts. He traveled the state in the early 20th century and collected more than 78,000 plant specimens, discovering 25 new plant species. The Ecoblitz is indebted to Deam. And Deam was an inspiration to Indiana Forest

Alliance (IFA) executive director Jeff Stant. In 1982, Stant and others moved the U.S. Congress to pass legislation establishing the 12,953-acre Charles Deam Wilderness Area in the Hoosier National Forest east of Monroe Reservoir.

One year before, Governor Robert Orr had designated the Morgan-Monroe/Yellowwood Back Country Area forest that Stant and his colleagues would methodically probe, 33 years later, in IFA's Ecoblitz: an act of science in service of preservation.

Call it an inventory of wonder.

An accounting of life.

A roll call of the wild.

Stant's drive to prove the value of an undisturbed forest—to raise every dollar in support of the project and to recruit knowledgeable people to gather the evidence—is the reason this book exists.

Science sits at the fulcrum of knowledge and mystery. We owe everything to the scientists who do the labors of trying to know. And we owe nearly as much to the environmentalists who awaken nonscientists and political leaders to act on this knowledge.

Metaphors partner with data to expand understanding. So this book is organized into five thematic parts:

1. **Forest as Superorganism.** "Like the work of any given architect, a forest is a gesture uttered in space. It is a collection of heights, dimensions and depths endeared. . . . We can crane our necks to look at the crowns, or genuflect straight to the soil," writes Michael Pollan in *The Botany of Desire*. We begin with the trees and plants that demarcate the green mansion.

2. **Complex Cooperators.** A forest is a study in interdependency. Organisms alive and dead fuel and host one another and, in doing so, transform each other into new organisms. Fungi and lichen are studies in the power of networks and reciprocity.

3. **Forest as Haven.** What flying creatures can only make a home in a forest? What canopy sanctuaries give bats and birds shelter for eating and birthing?

4. **Insect Multitudes.** Predators prey, pollinators pollinate, parasites parasitize, always and forever. An army of insects—beetles, bees, moths, and wasps—keeps the cycle turning.

5. **Forest as Spectacle.** With an affinity for the visual, we bipeds react most readily to the slither of a rattlesnake, the face of a rodent, the speed of a fish. Amphibians, reptiles, fish, and small mammals live larger and higher on the food chain.

Curious readers will find this book to be an unusual weave of data findings and character sketches, packaged for variety as profiles, interviews, and essays. Technical aspects of scientific research are juxtaposed with the personalities of the scientists in pursuit and the flavor of our interactions with them. It is important for the intrepid researchers to speak in their own words. It is vital that their rarely held, hard-won knowledge about Indiana's nature and its workings lives in the broader light of day.

Their quest to ascertain one older Indiana forest is a solving of riddles, a summoning of heritage, a loving reading of a labyrinthine language.

Jeff Stant. *Photo credit: Elizabeth Mahoney.*

INTRODUCTION

Jeffrey N. Stant

It was nearly midnight in the middle of March. I was half a mile into the Morgan-Monroe/Yellowwood Back Country Area with only a flashlight and my own forest wits. I was seeking a vernal pool, where a herpetologist suggested there might be some salamander eggs to take back to the lab. It was the time of year when winter loosens its grip for a day or two, only to get cold again: ideal conditions for spring peeper mating. During the day, most frogs will go mute upon your approach. But shine a light on spring peepers at night and their chorus will break glass. As I approached a vernal pool, my eardrums began to throb. I stared down into the shallow water, shining a light on salamander egg masses coagulated around a branch. A wall of sound engulfed me. I saw the shine in the eyes of these tiny frogs, looking back at me. My ears rang as I hiked back to my car in the darkness, feeling awed.

This is how I regard my interaction with the profound power of spring peepers or any interaction with wild nature: as an entitlement of being alive on this earth.

These connections should be the birthright of everyone. But there are too many walking through their lives without experiencing this benefit. There is an intensity of life—a wealth—that exists in Indiana's hardwood forests. As the executive director of the Indiana Forest Alliance (IFA), it has been my mission to educate the public about this wealth.

That is the point of this book: to tell the story of the inventory of forest biodiversity that IFA undertook from 2014 to 2018 in the heart of the Morgan-Monroe/Yellowwood Back Country Area (BCA).

The idea for organizing a species inventory emerged from conversations with my friend and colleague Tim Maloney, formerly of the Hoosier Environmental Council. After I became executive director of IFA, he and I engaged in many discussions about protecting the state forests from the onslaught of state-sanctioned logging. Tim asked if IFA had considered doing a census of the life that exists in the old forest tracts we were seeking to save. We identified the BCA as a large interior tract of

Executive Director Jeff Stant connecting with the forest. *Photo credit: IFA.*

forest with undisturbed nature in action. After consulting with biologists from the Indiana Academy of Science and Ball State University, we designed the inventory to encapsulate the entire watershed of a creek: the East Fork of Honey Creek in the BCA of Brown and Monroe Counties.

And so the idea for the Ecoblitz was born.

Ecoblitz may sound like some hip idea or hobby, but it is a serious word. Don Ruch, Ph.D. mycologist and botanist from Ball State University, past president of the Indiana Academy of Science (IAS), and coeditor of the IAS journal, suggested the term *ecoblitz*. He said that, rather than the more common *bioblitz*, which provides a snapshot of species identified by experts in a given area usually focused on one or two taxonomic groups over a period of one or two days, the project we were planning would be a much more comprehensive look at many taxa in this forest over several growing seasons. Ruch said that level of census would more appropriately be called an ecoblitz.

The objectives of IFA's Ecoblitz were to characterize the flora and fauna of a southern Indiana mature hardwood forest, document the entire community of life in this ecosystem, and establish a comprehensive baseline inventory of the species living in this relatively undisturbed forest.

Historically, the State of Indiana officially recognized and championed the wild, undisturbed condition of this forest. In 1981, Governor Robert Orr, a Republican, designated 2,700 acres of this forest as a "Back Country Area," one of only three such official designations in Indiana's state forests. In a press release announcing the BCA's creation, Jim Ridenour, the director of the Indiana Department of Natural Resources (IDNR) at the time, stated, "We're extremely pleased to provide this new area for persons who enjoy the rugged primitive areas remaining in Indiana. . . . Work is underway to establish several more Back Country areas to meet the recreational needs of even more Hoosiers."

An article in IDNR's December 1981/January 1982 issue of *Outdoor Indiana* magazine described a visit to the BCA: "The only allowable method of transportation for the user into and upon the backcountry area is by walking. Users of the area should enter with the philosophy that they will disturb as little as possible the natural woodland ecosystem and that it will offer the experience of visiting a forested area looking much the same as it may have appeared a century and a half ago."

The BCA was "to be enjoyed by the wilderness seeker as a place of solitude and repose." As a wilderness seeker myself, the preservation of forests was naturally inspiring to me. I got into the environmental movement in the late 1970s so I could help save forests and the animals that live in them. I grew up tromping the hardwood forests of Indiana, looking at birds with my father and grandfather. I spent a lot of time building bark huts, staying in them overnight, saving fur-bearing animals from traps on Fishback Creek in Boone County, and bushwhacking in the hills of Brown County.

The Indiana Forest Alliance emerged in 1996, founded by environmental leaders engaged in protecting the Hoosier National Forest through a land and resource management plan. These leaders wanted an organization that would remain focused on the fate of the Hoosier National Forest and other forests across the state. I accepted the role of executive director at IFA in 2013, inspired by the mission of conserving the hardwood forests of Indiana and all the life that depends on that ecosystem. To me, our hardwood forest is one of the most underappreciated ecosystems in North America.

For example, while 25 tree species are native to the 71,000 square miles of Washington State, about 100 tree species are native to Indiana's 36,000 square miles, and we found 48 of them within 1.5 square miles in this Ecoblitz. In some respects, the biodiversity in Indiana's eastern hardwood forests rivals that of the tropical rain forests. Case in point: the diversity of salamanders in the hardwood forests of the eastern U.S. is higher than anywhere else on earth; the 24 different salamanders in Indiana are equal to the number of salamanders in all of South America, including the Amazon rainforest. The diversity of warblers also exceeds that of the Amazon, reaching its zenith in our hardwood forests; some 52 warblers are found in North America, and 36 of them migrate hundreds of miles every year to nest in the hardwood forests of the eastern U.S. And where do scientists estimate that as many as 30 million additional species of insects could be discovered? In the tropics and the temperate hardwood forests. In other words, here in Indiana.

Unfortunately, as Indiana moved into the 21st century, the state's political leadership began to view wild nature through a lens that harkens back to the 19th century. In 2004, the election of Republican governor Mitch Daniels ushered in an era of utilitarianism and privatization. The Daniels administration prized the trees in our state forests for their commercial value, ignoring their ecological value. Governor Daniels appointed a new state forester in 2005 who soon more than tripled the logging in Indiana's state forests over previous levels. IFA's board of directors and staff realized not only that we could lose all unlogged tracts of state forest within a relatively short period of time but that we actually did not know what life would be destroyed by this logging.

* * *

Indiana had lost its wild forests before. After European settlers arrived around 1810, some 20 million acres of forest, the vast majority of it virgin, old-growth forest, was reduced to approximately 1 million acres before the end of the 19th century. And nearly all of that remaining forest was being degraded by heavy livestock grazing, intentional burning, and cutting.

Nature is powerful and can recuperate. That is what happened in Indiana in the 20th century as Hoosiers left exhausted farmlands in the southern part of the state; trees slowly grew back, and forests regenerated on eroded landscapes. By 2000, Indiana's forests occupied nearly 5 million acres, about one-fourth of the land they had covered in 1800. Indiana scientists documented and described the most natural remnants of the presettlement landscape that remained in *Natural Areas in Indiana and Their Preservation* in 1969. That volume was followed by Dr. Marion T. Jackson's *The Natural Heritage of Indiana*, published in 1997, which provides hundreds of photographs of Indiana's environmental heritage, discusses its geologic and human history, and examines its natural regions and the biota living in them. It also plainly describes the challenges in protecting what remains.

A Division of Nature Preserves was created in 1967 within the IDNR. This division created the Natural Heritage Database in 1978, now called the Natural Heritage Data Center (NHDC), where the reported locations of rare and endangered species are recorded. However, the NHDC was never designed to provide a comprehensive baseline of what species survive in our forests and cannot be relied on to tell us whether an imperiled species is present in any given tract of forest. Thus, despite the emergence of land management agencies, nature preserves, the NHDC, and myriad books and research programs in colleges and universities, a dearth of knowledge about our forests continues.

Today we generally have no idea about what lives in our maturing second- and third-growth forests before they are cleared for development or logged. In fact, there are no baseline inventories being done by state agencies or other entities on any of the tracts of state forest or the Hoosier National Forest before they are burned, harvested selectively, or clear-cut entirely.

If half or even just one-third of the land in Indiana was protected, this might not be such a concern. However, barely 6% of all Indiana's land is publicly owned, and less than half of that is being managed to protect the flora and fauna that live on it. Furthermore, of the land that is forested, 85% is privately owned. While governments provide incentives to private woodland owners to keep their forests intact, no one has the authority to prevent private owners from clearing their forests. Our public forests, then, have a unique purpose in providing wild places that serve many functions: they allow the native plants, fungi, lichens, and animals that evolved in these forests to survive; they prevent soil erosion and protect water supplies; they capture carbon and clean the air; and they provide Hoosiers with wild places to enjoy.

The need to document what lives in these forests is magnified by the ecological crisis of climate change and the liquidation of biodiversity occurring now. Biologists are calling this the sixth major extinction event on earth and a marker of the Anthropocene epoch, a new unofficial addition to the geologic record marked by severe, unprecedented climate and ecosystem change caused by humankind. Forests and other natural habitats are disappearing as land is continually cleared and cities and suburbs mushroom out into the countryside. This rapid transition of open spaces and rural lands to residential and agricultural uses is happening across

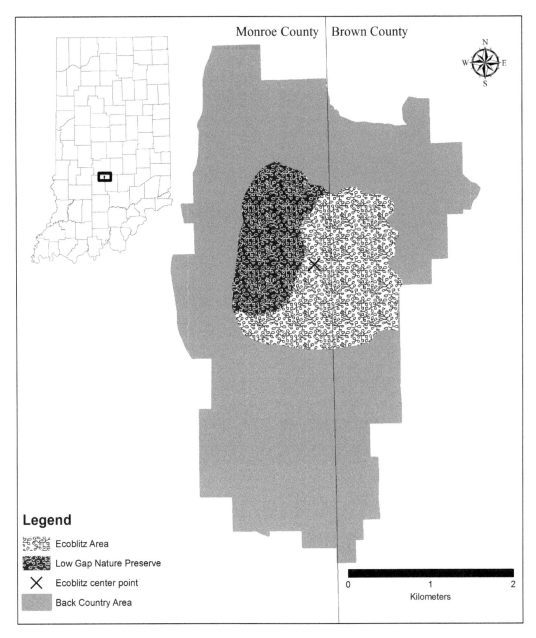

The Ecoblitz study area (patterned) is about 900 acres. Some 320 acres of the study area is designated as the Low Gap Nature Preserve (dark pattern) and set aside from logging by the IDNR's Division of Nature Preserves. The rest of the area is managed by the IDNR's Division of Forestry as the Morgan-Monroe/ Yellowwood Back Country Area (gray) straddling the Monroe County and Brown County line. *Photo credit: IFA.*

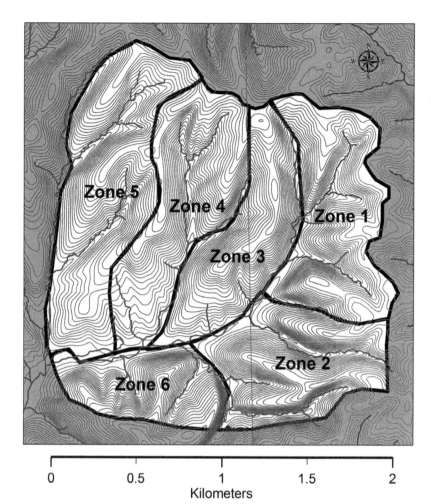

The Ecoblitz study area was divided into six zones to ensure that the entire area was covered. Note the steep topography. *Photo credit: IFA.*

the continent, to the detriment of many wild creatures. Birds that nest in large tracts of forest, such as the wood thrush, Acadian flycatcher, scarlet tanager, ovenbird, and worm-eating warbler, are increasingly unable to raise nestlings to adulthood because of the intensified predation and nest parasitism that occur near forest edges as these tracts are carved into smaller pieces. Birds more adapted to human impacts, such as the yellow-breasted chat, brown thrasher, and prairie warbler, are disappearing because development is eating up their brushy habitats in the suburbs.

Constructing a baseline inventory of the life that exists in the largest tracts of Indiana's maturing second-growth forest provides a yardstick for documenting the species being lost due to the advance of climate change, development, management practices, and disease. Indeed, there has never been a greater need to assess the biodiversity that exists in Indiana than today because we are losing it faster than we are studying it. We need to determine what we have before it is gone.

As of 2014, the 2,700-acre BCA was one of the only places left in the entire state forest system where such an inventory could be done to

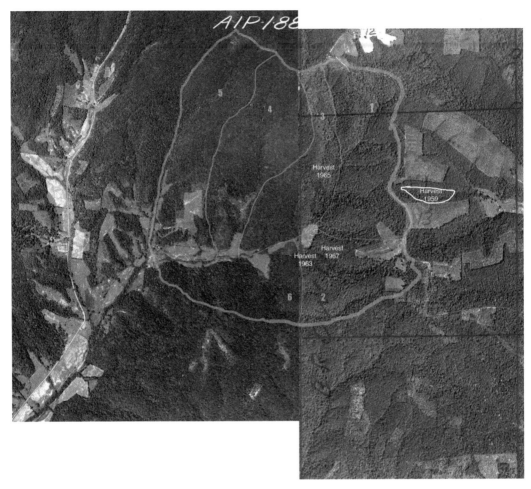

While much of southern Indiana was once farmed and eventually abandoned due to soil depletion and economic hard times, most of the Ecoblitz area was mature forest when the first aerial photographs were taken in the 1930s. After this land became state forest, tract by tract from 1929 to the early 1960s, only a few acres were selectively logged—making it an ideal candidate for the Ecoblitz. *Photo credit: Indiana State Library Archive.*

sufficiently characterize the community of life dependent on the large tracts of undisturbed deep forest that once covered our state. Here, the entire watershed of the East Fork of Honey Creek contains no development and is almost entirely surrounded by state forestland, making it an interior forest with little unnatural edge habitat. The steep topography creates varied microclimates including dry ridgetops, moist slopes, dry slopes, and wet valley floors.

We divided the Ecoblitz area into the six zones to ensure that adequate attention was paid to the entire 900 acres and all the habitat types represented within. Experts recruited from various institutions led 12 teams into each of these zones, identifying species in 13 taxonomic groups, all of which are highlighted in the pages ahead.

* * *

When IFA announced the Ecoblitz Forest Census project in 2014, the excitement was palpable. The IAS helped get the word out to its members and provided some financial support. With help from IAS and the Hoosier Environmental Council, Knob and Valley Audubon Society, Amos Butler Audubon Society, Sassafras Audubon Society, Hoosier Herpetological Society, Indiana Native Plant Society, Hoosier Mushroom Society, and Sierra Club Hoosier Chapter, we recruited volunteers, scientists, and other experts to serve as team leaders and consultants on species identification. We obtained 14 different permits from the IDNR's Divisions of Forestry, Nature Preserves, and Fish and Wildlife and the U.S. Fish and Wildlife Service to conduct the surveys and expended more than $300,000 in staff time, consulting fees, and other costs for this census.

During the inventory, we paid special attention to species listed by the state or federal governments as rare, threatened, or endangered, such as smoky and pygmy shrews, the cerulean warbler, the timber rattlesnake, and several species of bats. These species are symbols of wild Indiana— indicator species of a mature, intact hardwood forest ecosystem and its native biodiversity—no longer found in many places in the state.

A good example was the community of rare shrews identified in the forest in 2015 by Indiana State University mammalogist Dr. John Whitaker and his assistant, Angela Chamberlain. The community included the pygmy shrew, which competes with the bumblebee bat for the title of smallest mammal in the world, and its cousin, the smoky shrew. Both are state species of special concern that were not even identified in Indiana until the 1980s, when they were found in the deep forests of Harrison County. They have since only been found living near or under large logs in deep tracts of undisturbed forests within the south-central region of Indiana.

Another example is the state-endangered cerulean warbler, a forest canopy species that nests successfully only in the deep older forest environments that are dwindling in Indiana. Ceruleans will concentrate their half-to-one-acre territories in some areas of forest while ignoring other areas that are ideal habitat. During the Ecoblitz surveys, ornithologists found a cluster of cerulean territories at the confluence of the East and Main Forks of Honey Creek where the hillsides meet the valley floors. There we studied ceruleans nesting from 20 to as much as 60 feet off the ground in two American basswoods, two black walnuts, two white oaks, a beech, and two sycamores. Later, as spring turned to summer, we followed groups of cerulean parents and fledglings and other warbler families, including worm-eating and hooded warblers, often moving seemingly together across the forest foraging for insects.

The Ecoblitz taught us that sometimes, when you are seeking a certain species, you find another. One sunny day in June 2015, bird team volunteer Derek Coomer and I were scanning the canopy for a cerulean warbler. A few inches from Derek's boot, he spied the deep brown diamonds on the yellow/gold, three-inch-thick, five-foot-long body of a timber rattlesnake. The BCA is one of the only places in Indiana where this state-endangered venomous snake still survives, and we found it thriving there. The large trees in this forest provide ideal denning habitat when they die and fall. Thus, herpetologists were excited to find a mother timber rattlesnake and several of her young in a maternity den in the root buttresses of a downed chestnut oak. Hoosier Herpetological Society leaders found another den in the root buttress of another downed oak nearby. Elsewhere in Morgan-Monroe State Forest, they found two timber rattlesnakes with a copperhead in the same den at one point, and they later found nonvenomous snakes in that log with the rattlesnakes.

Besides the stunning species diversity we found in this old forest, one of the most valuable insights of the Ecoblitz for me was how much we still do not know about the life in our forests. Beyond predation, we observed what appeared to be mutualisms, associations, and synergies that would require much more in-depth study to adequately appreciate. Furthermore, the Ecoblitz did not address fundamentally important creatures like ants, worms, snails, slugs, centipedes, or millipedes due to a lack of available experts in the midwest. And those experts who got involved were amazed and confounded by what they could and could not identify even in the taxonomic groups in which they specialize. They identified more than 150 species of insects, spiders, lichens, and fungi as state records. These creatures had never been found in Indiana before. Yet multiple experts also could not identify more than 400 species and specimens from these taxonomic groups to the species level.

The findings of this survey and many others in the Ecoblitz raise fundamental questions about what species will perish when we indiscriminately disrupt a forest through broad strokes of management. When we burn the forest floor, woody debris, and understory or remove overstory over large areas of our complex temperate hardwood forests, we have no idea what creatures we are killing and what synergies we are eliminating. Ignorance and arrogance are the greatest enemies of our forests.

Conversely, humility and curiosity are what may save them.

Fortunately, the thirst for knowledge of what lives in our forests is contagious. Scientists and forest lovers from all corners of Indiana and beyond volunteered their time to help conduct the surveys:

- 41 scientists
- 13 Indiana colleges and universities
- Indiana Academy of Science
- New York Botanical Garden
- 3 government agencies
- 4 consulting firms
- 10 nonprofit organizations
- 13 interns
- 191 individual volunteers

A flyover provided an aerial view of the BCA tree canopy. *Photo credit: Elizabeth Mahoney.*

This book highlights the character and drive of those who participated in the Ecoblitz and their boundless appetites for discovery. They did this survey work, often in hot, humid weather while bushwacking for miles up and down hills for multiple days. They gave up their weekends. They drove long distances to check insect traps regularly. They dug postholes into hard, rocky soil. They spent many hours back in their labs identifying specimens of plants, fungi, lichens, spiders, and insects and compiling lists and reports. Most donated their time. This book explores how these individuals came to love their subjects so much and what drives them to care. We owe them and many others a great debt of gratitude.

A comprehensive list of the volunteers is found at the back of this book. In addition, a complete list of the species identified in the Ecoblitz, including scientific and common names (where they exist), can be found in appendix 1.

I close this introduction with a story of another of the many wilderness encounters in this Ecoblitz. One day in 2016, near the East Fork of Honey Creek, we spied a shape shifting in the shadows. Its thick legs, husky build, and short nonwhite tail gave it away as a bobcat. Eluding full view or a photograph, the cat jumped out of the brush and trotted off, one of many symbols of wild nature in this forest. We offer this volume in the spirit of knowledge and an appreciation of the unknown.

PART I
FOREST AS SUPERORGANISM

Emma Steele

The history of breathing begins some 2.3 billion years ago with the color green. It was an era of newly birthed continents and warm oceans. The earth was spinning faster. The days were only 17 hours long. The sun was younger and cooler, beating down on the world with 70% of the energy we receive today. Bubbling in the shallow seas of this waking, primordial planet, colonies of blue-green cyanobacteria called stromatolites were about to change everything through one of the most ancient processes of life: photosynthesis. Over the course of hundreds of millions of years, the stromatolites would exhale so much oxygen that the anoxic atmosphere would be irreversibly changed—an era known as the Great Oxidation Event.

The Great Oxidation Event was the catalyst for complex life to evolve on the earth. Before the planet had an oxygen-rich atmosphere, life was constrained to what could survive in the methane-rich conditions of the time—small, single-celled organisms like bacteria and viruses. The explosion of available oxygen in the atmosphere created perfect conditions for the evolution of aerobic metabolism, which serves as the foundation for multicellular organisms to exist. Everything that came after—the Cambrian explosion (known as the "biological big bang," when an unprecedented amount of new life burst forth), the emergence of vertebrate land animals from the sea, the rise and fall of the dinosaurs, the age of mammals, and the first step of *Homo sapiens*—began with this revolution.

The foundation of the forest ecosystem is not the stand of trees but the thousands of small beings threading those trees together, like these mosses, fungi, and lichens. *Photo credit: Jason Kolenda.*

Stromatolites are what is known as a superorganism. They are organisms made up of smaller organisms working collectively to create a unique, functional whole. Today, we recognize structures like ant colonies, beehives, and coral reefs as superorganisms. Pando, the largest organism on earth by mass, is an 80,000-year-old aspen forest superorganism that spans over 100 acres in Utah and is made up of approximately 47,000 genetically identical aspen trees connected to a single root system. Historically, this strange class of life has been defined by the cooperative, social nature of its individuals, the reliance of its individuals on the whole, the division of labor among the superorganism's individuals, and its ability to function as a unified being. In recent decades, more flexible interpretations of the superorganism concept have been proposed, including the idea that the forest ecosystem as a whole functions as a beast of its own.

Perhaps, in order to understand the forest as a superorganism, it is easier to first consider our own bodies, which also have been the subject of another superorganism debate. Look closely, and we might appear as a wall of cells, populated by a collection of microbes. Look at our whole, and we see cells and microbes tied up into organs, organs bound together as systems, and systems performing their unique processes that add up to a human. There is digestion, respiration, nervous system communication, and immune responses. The parts do not function without the whole to inhabit, and the whole does not function without its parts humming along.

To this extent, the forest superorganism is its own breathing body. Look at the edge of a forest, and you may see an indistinguishable wall of green, peppered by insects, birds, and mammals. Look at the forest's whole, and you will see creatures bound together by the systems of the forest ecosystem. There is predation, parasitism, evolution, the cycle of life to decay and rebirth. There is the process where it all began: photosynthesis, the forest's breath. Like our bodies, the forest breaks down when its parts are removed, and its parts cannot survive without the cradle of the forest's body.

In this first section, the forest's structure and complexity are brought into focus. With biologist Leslie Bishop, the first images of the Morgan-Monroe/Yellowwood Back Country Area (BCA) come into view as she provides a landscape view of what makes an old forest tick. We peer at trees through the eyes of dendrochronologist Justin Maxwell, and we probe the subtleties of plant life with botanist Paul Rothrock. Meanwhile, naturalist and citizen scientist Linda Cole leads us through the enchanting world of bryophytes, the microscopic forests within the forest.

As we step into the BCA, it is not the beginning of a journey to simply catalog the life populating an inanimate shell. We are walking into the belly of a living body.

Leslie Bishop. *Photo credit: Jeff Hyman.*

1. PROFILE: LESLIE BISHOP, PH.D.

Prismatic Forest, Prismatic Ecologist

Anne Laker

In the cradle of a ravine, deep in the interior of the Morgan-Monroe/Yellowwood Back Country Area (BCA), there lives an American beech tree (*Fagus grandifolia*), its age an estimated 230 years. For many Indiana forest advocates, a heritage tree such as this is a paean to nature at its most pure. Like a skyward glimpse of a galaxy, an encounter with an elder tree is a portal for imagining before and beyond our limited life spans. Even in the digital age, amid the creeping doom of the Anthropocene, an old tree inspires an honest reverence for its perseverance or a gut punch of grief at its demise.

The old beech's presence also matters ecologically. A forest of uneven-aged trees, with a tapestry of tree species, powers more kinds of life. The healthiest forests are the least one-dimensional. For biologist Leslie Bishop, an old tree is most valuable as an indicator of forest health. Like a thriving forest whose variety breeds resilience, Dr. Bishop is a multidimensional force: an investigator of nature, a feminist, a teacher, a writer, and an activist. "I never thought of them as separate," she says of her identities. "My characteristics are all the same; it's all me. It all has to do with respect."

Whether bushwhacking through Yellowwood State Forest measuring trees, organizing fellow scientists to sign a letter to the governor in defense of wilderness, or presenting to a roomful of colleagues at the Indiana Academy of Science, Bishop attracts respect. After a robust academic career and as a friendly neighborhood biologist to many in her former Brown County community and a consulting biologist for the Indiana Forest Alliance (IFA), she is equally adept at executing scientific inquiry, practicing wonder, and questioning authority.

An accomplished ecologist, Bishop is perhaps best known as an arachnologist. As a professor of biology at Earlham College in Richmond, Indiana, from 1990 to 2013, she taught scores of field biology courses in ecology, biodiversity, and entomology, often taking intrepid students on spider research trips in the wilds of Puerto Rico and Dominica. First

Big beech on steep terrain in the Ecoblitz area. *Photo credit: Samantha Buran.*

summoned by IFA for her arachnid expertise, Bishop led a survey of the 900-acre Morgan-Monroe/Yellowwood BCA for spiders from 2014 to 2017 (see chap. 19). Taxa and species lists of spiders—and many other plants, animals, and organisms—were tallied during the four-year Ecoblitz, as this book chronicles.

Midway through the evolving effort, a natural need emerged for a big-picture backdrop, a characterization of the forest architecture housing all this life. "Most bioblitzes are done in places that are already well known," says Bishop. "But this backcountry area hadn't been studied this way before. Documenting rare plants and animals was IFA's initial goal. But over time, facing lots of questions, we asked ourselves, 'How can we talk about bats and birds without first knowing about the forest structure? Basically, what kind of habitat is it?'"

The answer was needed to help frame the ongoing discussion about biodiversity and the value factor of a mature forest, which happened to be 11 miles from Bishop's Brown County home at the time. The question of the relationship between species richness and a forest's relative age drove her design of the forest characterization study implemented with

Forest as Superorganism

her colleagues—geographer Justin Maxwell, botanist Paul Rothrock, and arborist Jerome Delbridge—and volunteers and IFA staff from July to October 2017.

Their inquiry asked two questions: Is this mature forest developing the ecological attributes of an old-growth forest, thus making it a good candidate for an older forest reserve? And does this forest support the plant community characteristic of natural areas of Indiana? Finding the answers required "looking at the literature, reviewing what others have done, and selecting the scientific methods that help get at the questions you are asking," says Bishop. "At the same time, how do you mold those methods to fit the place where you are?"

The collaborators designed the study to assess six elements: stand density, tree species, tree age, habitat type, quantity of decaying trees, and coarse woody debris. To obtain this information, Bishop's team randomly selected forest plots in each of four different ecological types—ridges, slopes facing northeast (typically the most mesic, or moist, habitats), slopes facing southwest (typically drier), and bottomland. Each plot was geo-located precisely. Within each plot, all tree species were noted, and each tree was measured for diameter and distance to a center point. The measurements were used to calculate basal area and stand density. Within the plots, every dead tree and downed log was also counted, measured, and evaluated. This coarse woody debris contributes to the forest's ability to host wildlife and recycle nutrients as different kinds of fungi and insects aid in the decomposition of the dead wood over time.

Dr. Leslie Bishop (*left*) and (*left to right*) arborist Jerome Delbridge, Dr. Rae Schnapp, Dr. Paul Rothrock, and Samantha Buran of the forest characterization team. *Photo credit: IFA.*

Top, Leslie Bishop and Jeff Hyman measure a tree for forest characterization. *Photo credit: Samantha Buran.*

Bottom, Dr. Darrin Rubino cuts "cookie" slices from a downed log to determine its age through dendrochronology tree ring analysis. Mark Hoard assists. *Photo credit: Samantha Buran.*

The wildness of the forest tested Bishop's methodology and her back-country hiking skills. As the original randomized selection of plots failed to take topography into account, following the most direct route to the plot coordinates sometimes required hiking over extremely rugged terrain, negotiating a hornet's nest, or climbing the steepest slopes. "I spent a lot of time on my rear end," says Bishop dryly.

It was worth it. The tree characterization study painted a prismatic portrait of a maturing forest. The plot surveys revealed a total of 31 tree species, with 66% being red oak, American beech, black oak, tulip poplar, white oak, chestnut oak, and sugar maple. The largest trees were cored to determine tree age. Of these, the average age was 113 years, with 78% of the sample trees clocking in at more than 100 years, and the oldest trees being found in ravines. Of the 428 vascular plants identified, only 5.8% were of non-native origin, reinforcing the high quality of this native forest. The forest exhibited a range of log sizes in each of six stages of decay—a key attribute of mature and old-growth forests.

After all this data was in, Bishop compared the BCA's Floristic Quality Index (FQI) to that of nine Indiana nature preserves known to include old-growth forests. FQI measures a forest's remnant natural quality: What fidelity does a given forest have to a presettlement forest? The FQI ranking of the BCA bested that of Bendix Woods, Hayes Arboretum, Yellow Birch Ravine, and the other six areas already set aside by the state for their outstanding natural quality. Her emphatic conclusion is that the BCA is "developing ecological attributes comparable to Indiana old-growth forest preserves."

* * *

What qualifies a forest as old growth? As Bishop wrote in the fall 2021 Indiana Native Plant Society's *INPS Journal*, "For the central hardwood region that includes Indiana, old-growth usually refers to a forest whose overstory canopy trees are over 150 years old and that has been relatively undisturbed by humans for the past 80–100 years. . . . Throughout Indiana (and the broader Midwest region), most primary forests were cleared for timber, agriculture, and grazing during the 1800's European colonization, leaving old-growth forests rare and fragmented."

In a 1989 paper, Purdue forest ecologist George R. Parker estimated that only about 3% of the total forest in Indiana is old growth. For Bishop, the present moment is a golden opportunity to rectify that rarity. "Given that a significant portion (45%) of Indiana state forests is now in the 80–120-year age class," she wrote in the *Journal of the Torrey Botanical Society* in fall 2021, "reserves within these managed forests could reach old-growth forest status within the next 50 years, in the absence of further timber harvest or high-intensity natural disturbance."

A giant root buttress dwarfs Leslie Bishop and Jerome Delbridge. Root balls of fallen large trees provide great habitat for snakes and other creatures. They eventually decay into mounds of rich humus, contributing to the pit and mound structure of many undisturbed forests. *Photo credit: Samantha Buran.*

More old growth in Indiana's forest system is a valuable prospect for a host of reasons. One is that old-growth forests add to Indiana's landscape-level biodiversity. As Bishop put it in the *INPS Journal*, "A landscape with a mosaic of forests at varying ages can support species of plants, animals, and microbes with varying ecological requirements."

Within a single forest, the presence of older trees and trees of all ages helps the forest function as a full-fledged ecosystem that harbors more plants, animals, and microbes. That biodiversity is "linked to the vertical dimension spanning from the forest floor to the upper canopy. This vertical complexity is high in old forests due to structural features in the form of large snags and fallen dead trees," Bishop wrote in the *INPS Journal*. In other words, an old forest's structural complexity harbors more diverse habitat and, therefore, more diverse species.

Variety of tree ages is an older forest's strength. A key characteristic of old-growth stands is that they include trees of multiple ("uneven") ages and sizes, from seedlings and saplings to pole-sized trees (30–80 years) and trees two centuries old. "If you are looking at the whole forest in terms of successional stages, and ecological changes in each of the stages, you'd want a balance of stages and ages," Bishop says.

Another benefit of uneven-aged forests that include old-growth reserves is greater resilience, meaning these forests have "more pathways for recovery from unpredictable disturbances than do younger forests," as Bishop wrote in *INPS Journal*. Against an invasive pest like the emerald ash borer, an older forest with "a diversity of tree age classes and sizes, one component of a genetically diverse stand, helps ensure that some unaffected [ash] trees remain in the forest."

And then there is climate change. Bishop wrote in the *INPS Journal*, "Recent work shows that older forests remain productive and continue to store carbon in larger amounts compared to younger forests. Further, old-growth forests can be more efficient than younger forests in active fixation of large amounts of carbon as well as in water filtration and nitrogen cycling."

While primary old growth is rare in Indiana, secondary old growth (a forest that is developing the ecological attributes of old-growth forest) can provide similar functions and benefits. Will Indiana's public forest managers wake up to the benefits of allowing more forests to mature?

Bishop referenced this question in the title of her report on the forest characterization study results, published in the *Journal of the Torrey Botanical Society* in April 2021: "Old-Growth Attributes in a Maturing Secondary Indiana State Forest: An Opportunity for Balanced Management." She concludes the report with a compelling, commonsense statement:

> The current management plan of Indiana state forests states that early- and late-successional stages are underrepresented and sets forth the goal of increasing early-successional stages to support shade-intolerant species (oak and hickory). However, the management plan does not include the goal of maintaining state forest reserves that are allowed to proceed to older forest (IDNR 2020). These two goals—increasing early-successional stages and increasing older forest reserves on state forest land—do not need to conflict. But finding a reasonable balance between these goals, and between managing a forest for timber production versus ecosystem services, continues to be a challenge. The creation of reserves of older forests free from timber harvest within the larger managed forest unit can serve to balance these goals.

* * *

So it was especially disturbing when the Indiana Department of Natural Resources (IDNR) decided to log part of the Ecoblitz study site in

Leslie Bishop spoke to the media at the Indiana Statehouse after meeting with the governor about the value of setting aside older forests, 2017. *Photo credit: Anne Laker.*

the fall of 2017, even though DNR leadership was well aware of the permitted surveys IFA was conducting. Right after Bishop and colleagues did their last collection of data, the state harvested trees on one of the ridges. Bishop states, "After spending so much time in the forest, the trees become individuals. You recall having measured certain ones . . . you get to know them."

Bishop's integrated thinking gives unspoken permission for the rigors of forest data collection to comingle with emotional connections to forests. When it came to data, Bishop was determined to publish the results of her forest characterization study and the Ecoblitz inventory as a whole. With the help of the IFA conservation director, Dr. Rae Schnapp, Bishop and many of the scientists and surveyors shared their results at a symposium on the Ecoblitz at the annual meeting of the Indiana Academy of Science in 2018 and published their results in the academy's journal. "The documentation of this Indiana forest is in the scientific literature now," she says. "That was my goal. I felt that way about every aspect of the Ecoblitz. It wasn't going to be useful information unless published in the scientific literature. Now the next round of investigators has a basis for new inquiry."

Then came another opportunity to activate her forest findings. In 2019, backed by IFA and all the Ecoblitz data, Bishop wrote an official proposal nominating the entire 2,380 interior acres that comprise the BCA of Morgan-Monroe/Yellowwood State Forest as a high conservation value forest (HCVF). (For context, these two state forests collectively include 50,000 acres.) HCVFs are forests that receive, as stated on the DNR Division of Forestry website, "added consideration of

Forest as Superorganism

management activities in order to maintain or enhance conservation value attributes. These attributes may be of biological, ecological, or cultural significance."

In the documentation submitted to the DNR, Bishop argues that the area provides a landscape-level representation of old growth absent from the state forest system of Indiana. She points to the site's high-quality plant community, its harboring of threatened and endangered species (from the smoky shrew to the northern cricket frog and many others), and its impressive size compared to most nature preserves. In a section of the document called "Management Considerations and Strategy," Bishop recommends avoiding additional timber harvests to foster the development of secondary old growth. She also recommends controlling invasive species, providing appropriate recreation trail corridors, and leaving standing and fallen dead trees to minimize disturbance to leaf litter and soil, which adds to forest complexity.

If approved, the preserve would surround the existing 320-acre Low Gap Nature Preserve, expanding this protected half square mile to a forest of 2,700 acres, greater than four square miles in size, and allowing it to return to the old-growth condition. Bishop's HCVF nomination was a laudable act of data-informed advocacy. As of this writing, the state has yet to accept or reject the nomination.

*　*　*

On an eerily balmy Saturday in January 2018, Bishop looked out over a sea of livid women outside the Indiana State Capitol. One of two dozen speakers chosen to address the crowd at the Women's March, a global stand against sexism and other tyrannies, Bishop used her time to speak about the right to clean water and air as well as public lands. She said, "I see the forest as an interconnected system. Each one of us has the right to visit a state forest untouched by chainsaws and heavy equipment. We need to ensure that our great-grandchildren can walk in a forest and experience the peace and wildness that a forest provides." She closed her speech with a leading question: "Are there any wild women out there?" The crowd roared, and she concluded, "Wild women need wild places."

Warm passion and cool logic, with a dash of rebellion—this is Leslie Bishop. As a kid, growing up in Chattanooga, on Signal Mountain, before it was developed, young Leslie was ravenous for direct knowledge of nature. Her play was work: "I spent all my time looking at things and studying things, like rotting logs. I had a stack of field guides on the nightstand. I'd make habitats for crayfish in the bathtub and then bring them back to the creek. I was thoroughly engaged. And happy being outside by myself."

Leslie Bishop addresses the crowd at the Women's March on January 20, 2018. *Photo credit: Samantha Buran.*

She majored in botany at the University of Tennessee (UT) as an undergraduate. Then, for her master's degree in biology at Western Carolina University, she wrote her thesis on the pollination ecology of two spring wildflowers of the Blue Ridge Mountains, Dutchman's breeches and squirrel corn. She then returned to UT for a Ph.D. with a focus on ecology and evolution. Her dissertation explored the mechanisms and effects of spider dispersal on ecological communities and included a study on how spiders can serve as biocontrol for insect pests in agricultural systems. An early piece of Bishop's research on spider migration glides from science into poetry: "The importance of long-distance dispersal is recognized in the recolonization of disturbed habitats, but little is known about how migrating spiders respond to the various features of their atmospheric environment. Many spiders balloon by silken threads on wind currents for long distances and thus disperse to new habitats."

Bishop has always respected the power of the well-written word. For years, she was a member of a Bloomington group called Women Writing for (a) Change. She looks to nature writers Terry Tempest Williams, Mary Oliver, Robin Wall Kimmerer, and Rebecca Solnit as models for literary activism. Bishop also knows the value of sharing scientific knowledge with the general public. She did so for nine years running in a folksy monthly column, "Nature Notes," which she pitched to the editor of the *Brown County Democrat* in 2012.

Forest as Superorganism

"I lived in Brown County and was observing things in nature across the seasons," she says. She channeled her reflections into short, accessible pieces, written with a big helping of affection and a dash of philosophy. Column topics ranged from the intelligence of crows and the wonder of muddy burrowing crayfish chimneys to spiders as "nature's fiber artists" and colorful, quirky spring ephemerals as the best companions during a pandemic lockdown.

"[The column] was really fun and connected me to the readers," Bishop recalls. "People would stop me in the grocery store and say, 'I never thought about turtles before, but now when I see one in the road, I move it.' People read the column and I got great feedback. It was a fun way to share things I was enthusiastic about in a pretty benign way." Her enthusiasm overflowed. Bishop wrote at least three columns in praise of rotting logs over the years. "Some of the most decayed logs have literally returned to the earth, and I can crumble what used to be an ancient tree between my fingers," she wrote.

Her handy proximity to the Morgan-Monroe/Yellowwood BCA kept her in close contact with the same trees she had studied through the lens of science. She and her dog, Bee, were especially intimate with "distinctive characters in a community of trees," as she put it in one of her *Democrat* columns. "Forestry had marked this tree to cull," she says from afar, referring to an American beech in Yellowwood State Forest behind her house. "I begged them to spare it and they did. I hope it is still standing."

Like a spider on silk in the wind, Bishop has dispersed to a totally new habitat. In 2021, she traded the humid, deciduous Indiana forests for the mountains and deserts of New Mexico to be closer to her grandchildren. Her new home is one hour from the famous Ghost Ranch retreat center, a convenient writing getaway where she was recently working on a piece about coyotes and their role in the ecosystem. She reports that she is doing a spider survey at New Mexico's Valles Caldera National Preserve. And, no surprise, she is already politically engaged . . . with prairie dogs. She says, "People hate them, and yet I see them as ecosystem engineers . . . the beavers of the west."

Another gratification for Bishop these days is staying in touch with former students. "I am so proud of them and their accomplishments," she says. Bequeathing her love of nature and science is heartening. "If I can pass on that enthusiasm and appreciation, that's the best I can hope for these days. I'm pretty pessimistic about the future," she admits.

"But I'll always be grateful for the chance to do the Ecoblitz," she continues. "The Ecoblitz, the data analysis, the journal articles, and the personal connection to the forest consumed me for those years." She gave her all.

Her scientific assessment of the BCA echoes through the ravines and ridges: "Forest reserves should be promoted across the state to increase the representation within Indiana's state forest system of late-successional secondary forest exhibiting ecological attributes of old-growth forests, thereby enhancing the role of state forests in biodiversity protection and climate mitigation."

If any portion of the Morgan-Monroe/Yellowwood BCA is eventually set aside, Hoosiers can be grateful for the data, the heart, and the nerve of Dr. Leslie Bishop.

Highlights

The steep topography of the study area creates diverse habitat types, including:

- Dry ridgetops

- Mesic (wet) slopes, northeast facing

- Xeric (dry) slopes, southwest facing

- Extensive valley floors, wet bottomlands

Generally, slopes facing northeast tend to be more moist and those facing southwest tend to be the driest due to differences in exposure to sun and wind.

Key Findings

The Ecoblitz area is a high-quality mixed hardwood forest in late successional stage developing old-growth attributes including scattered big old trees, high volumes of late-decay woody debris, numerous snags, and standing dead trees. A Floristic Quality Assessment has determined that the remnant undisturbed condition of the plant community in the Ecoblitz forest surpasses that of Indiana nature preserves known for their outstanding natural qualities.

Forest as Superorganism

Fire pink (*Silene virginica*) among spicebush. *Photo credit: Karen Smith.*

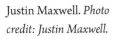
Justin Maxwell. *Photo credit: Justin Maxwell.*

2. ESSAY: STANDING SENTINELS

Observations on the Art of Tree Dating

Justin Maxwell, Ph.D.

I have one of the best jobs in the world. I am a dendrochronologist: *dendron* meaning trees and *chronos* meaning time. I study forests using the tree's growth rings. I travel to forests all over the country to find the oldest trees and determine their age.

I do this using an instrument called an increment borer, which takes a pencil-sized sample out of the tree. This tree core sample allows us to see the growth rings of a tree without harming it. The core is polished with fine-grit sandpaper in my lab so that the number of rings can be counted. In locations where the winters are cold and trees go dormant, a tree produces one growth ring per year; therefore, counting rings is a way to assess a tree's age.

Once people discover what I do for a living, they often tell me of some huge tree that is special to them. When I first started my job at Indiana University, a staff member was excited to tell me about a huge black walnut tree that grew at the forest edge of their grandparents' property. As a child, she remembered playing with the green billiard ball–sized walnuts of this huge tree.

It always brings me joy to hear these types of stories. I have even been invited to take core samples from some of these notable trees. Many of these giants are in a yard or field. These open-grown trees have a lot of resources and not much competition; thus, they are happy. When trees are happy, they grow very fast. The core samples from these types of trees typically have very large rings, indicating that they grow a lot each year. Often these trees are 50–75 years old, which, for a tree, is actually fairly young. If the same tree were in a forest, competing for light and resources, it would grow more slowly. Thus, a forest tree that is similar in size to a field tree is much older.

So, the size of the tree does not indicate its age. The soil, slope, and many other environmental aspects determine how quickly a given tree grows. Climate is one of the most important factors that controls a tree's growth rate. During favorable climate conditions—typically cool and

The dendrochronology team looks up at a giant tree as they prepare to core it to determine its age. *Photo credit: IFA.*

wet growing seasons—trees will grow a lot and produce large growth rings. During hot and dry growing seasons, resources (water, sunlight, soil nutrients) are limited and trees have to find a way to survive, which leads to a low-growth year. This means that tree growth rates can reveal the climates of the past. Using this information, we can compare droughts we experienced, like the one in 2012, to droughts that occurred before such weather events were recorded.

This climate sensitivity is critical in determining a tree's age, especially one growing in a forest, where competition is high. Determining a tree's age is often not as simple as counting the annual growth rings. Some trees grow very asymmetrically, and this can lead to two or three rings merging into one ring on one side of the tree. We refer to this as the pinching of rings. If we take a core sample on the side where rings were pinched, we will miss a few of the annual rings. Similarly, there are features in the tree core that can look like rings but are not; these are known as false rings.

While having a trained eye helps with discerning these variables, we can ensure the accurate dating of a tree through cross dating. It consists of measuring the width of every growth ring for every sample we collect. We usually collect two samples per tree from 15 to 30 trees of a given species. We then see how well the pattern of growth from one core sample matches up to all the other samples through a correlation analysis. This process can indicate if a ring was missing or false by comparing the growth patterns of the surrounding trees.

　　　　　　　　　　　　Forest as Superorganism

I have been fortunate enough to visit many of the oldest forests in
Indiana, some protected as nature preserves by the Indiana Department
of Natural Resources or the United States Forest Service and some privately protected. I have found many trees that date back before European
colonization. Old-growth forests are rare in all the eastern U.S., where a
massive amount of logging occurred in the 19th and early 20th centuries
due to the high demand for wood and the expansion of agriculture.

Coring a giant
northern red oak in
the Ecoblitz forest
to determine its age.
*Photo credit: Saman-
tha Buran.*

In those days, forests that survived the axe did so because landown-
ers at the time made the decision not to log. Many farmers had small
woodlots, and while it was financially lucrative to log, some families did
not need the money or enjoyed the forests so much that they did not
want to log them. Thus, most of the old-growth forests in Indiana are
named after the families who opted to protect them. It has been a great
joy of mine to determine the ages of the trees in these small patches of
old-growth forest.

In the early 1900s, across much of the eastern U.S., farmers began
to abandon their acreage due to the westward shift in desirable farmland. This is particularly true for southern Indiana, where the soils are
thinner and less suitable for agriculture. With farm abandonment came
reforestation. This occurred both naturally and through strategic tree
planting to reduce erosion. Naturally, reforestation occurred faster at
farms with some trees already on the land. These trees were useful for
shade and were often oak or hickory as these nut-bearing trees attracted
wildlife. Such secondary-growth forests are now becoming an important

part of forests in the eastern U.S., including Indiana. Many of these forests are now over 100 years old but have individual trees that often exceed 250 years. These older forests are particularly meaningful for Indiana because most of our true old-growth forests are very small in size, often under 100 acres.

The Morgan-Monroe/Yellowwood Back Country Area (BCA), site of the Indiana Forest Alliance's Ecoblitz, is an interesting case study. In each ecotone (a transition zone between two adjacent ecological communities), I sampled trees with a 4.3 mm diameter increment borer at breast height on one side of the tree parallel to the slope. I sought trees with a morphology that indicated older age: narrow crowns, a very high lowest branch, crooked stems, and other clues. Each sample was taken to my lab and sanded using progressively finer-grit sandpaper (from 120 grit to 600 grit) to make the ring boundaries visible under a microscope. The growth rings from each sample were counted and measured using a joint Velmex measurement stage and a software program called J2X.

While determining the ages of the trees in the Morgan-Monroe/ Yellowwood BCA, I found that many along the ridgetops were established around the mid-1800s, thus making it a secondary-growth forest. The average age of trees in the BCA (in 2018) was 114 years old. However, in the bottomland forests, I found a few individual trees that were established in the mid- to late 1700s, including a 233-year-old American beech growing during the Revolutionary War.

These ages and species reveal an important history for this part of the forest. First, our documented tree dates indicate that the valley bottoms were not clear-cut in the past. Second, the species of beech is an important indicator of what kind of forest existed here in the past. Many forest management plans work under the assumption that forests in Indiana are

Forest as Superorganism

Tree core up close.
Photo credit: Samantha Buran.

going through a transition in species makeup. These management plans assume that many Indiana forests were dominated by oak and hickories, largely due to more frequent fires—part of the land use practices of some Indigenous peoples. Fires in the eastern U.S. are less frequent today than in the past due to active fire suppression. While this is certainly true for regions in Indiana, the forest demographics are more complex and have high spatial variability.

At Morgan-Monroe/Yellowwood State Forest, the presence of old beech and maple indicates that this forest has harbored these species for several hundred years. The valley bottoms in the area are very wet, and thus fires have likely been infrequent for centuries. Understanding this history is important as we try to manage our forests to increase oak and hickory. Areas that have been dominated by beech and maple for centuries are unlikely to respond to management practices geared to increase oak and hickory because the environment is wet and thus not conducive for oak regeneration.

The secondary forest of the ridgetops is very common throughout the eastern U.S., including Indiana. These maturing secondary forests are developing characteristics of old-growth forests, including a similar sensitivity to climate. Older Indiana forests are an underrepresented protected forest type in Indiana. Wood production can be a renewable resource, but it is also important to maintain and increase the area of forests that can become old growth.

In Indiana, we do a great job protecting the small patches of old growth that we have throughout the state. However, now we have an opportunity to make a similar decision to those that early Hoosier farmers made when they set aside older forests to allow them to become old growth for future generations to enjoy. This also can create and expand old-growth habitat for many animals and plants that is currently very limited in the state.

One of the biggest lessons I have learned from working with the oldest trees in Indiana is that our preservation decisions today can be appreciated and enjoyed for centuries in the future.

Key Findings

- The average age of cored trees was 114 years old.

- Dominant canopy trees on ridgetops are 120 years old.

- The oldest tree was an American beech, aged 233 years.

- Remnant bottomland trees are from 150 to 233 years old (American beech, sugar maple, and pignut hickory). This shows that at least portions of the valley bottoms have not been clear-cut.

- Over 40% of cored trees were more than 130 years old.

- Some of the largest trees are more than 200 years old, predating the establishment of the state forest in the 1930s.

- The morphology of the trees and the number of very large trees with very high lower limbs and narrow crowns are typical of old-growth characterizations.

The forest in the Ecoblitz study area compares favorably with other old-growth forests in the state, which are primarily found in nature preserves.

Comparing the BCA with Nature Preserves

Nature Preserve	Oldest Tree	Average Age
Pioneer Mothers	301	161
Hemmer Woods	318	173
Wesselman Woods	127	115
Hoot Woods	179	105
Oppenheim Woods	188	162
Meltzer Woods	199	116
Ecoblitz study area	229	113

Bloodroot (*Sanguinaria canadensis*). *Photo credit: Karen Smith.*

Paul Rothrock. *Photo credit: Paul Rothrock.*

3. PROFILE: PAUL ROTHROCK, PH.D.

Finding Floristic Quality

Anne Laker

As I have personally observed in Morgan-Monroe State Forest, our old-growth forests provide unique habitats . . . a greater variety of ecological niches in the form of snags, fallen branches, deep soil organic matter, and tip ups of earth that favor a different suite of species than harvested forests. . . . These [mature and] old-growth forests . . . are sources of seed and spores that spread to nearby areas thus sustaining the health of future forest generations. These forest systems preserve plant populations that are large enough to maintain genetic diversity important for future [adaptation] to changing conditions and disease. . . . [Mature] forests are a research tool, they support the complex mosaic of nature necessary for vibrant animal populations, and they are tools for [biological] restoration and renewal.

—DR. PAUL ROTHROCK, TESTIMONY TO THE INDIANA SENATE NATURAL RESOURCES COMMITTEE, FEBRUARY 13, 2017

To enter the Morgan-Monroe/Yellowwood Back Country Area is to time travel to an Indiana of yesteryear, where native species reign supreme. In 21st-century Indiana, such a historically intact plant ecosystem is as rare as it is precarious—in a way that both breaks the heart and stiffens the resolve to defend this ecological treasure.

Thanks to Dr. Paul Rothrock, we possess a good deal of knowledge of the floral richness that persists in Indiana. As associate curator emeritus at the Indiana University (IU) Herbarium and an associate research scientist emeritus in the biology department, Rothrock is perhaps the premier expert on the taxonomic variety of plant life in the Hoosier state. His plant knowledge is broad, but his specialty is sedges, an often-overlooked family that contains more than 2,000 grasslike species that thrive in a wide range of natural habitats and serve as food for insects and birds.

Rothrock's work curating IU's preserved plant specimens means he is a primary steward of the pioneering work of Indiana forest scientist

Charles Deam (1865–1953). The relentless Deam discovered 25 new species and collected over 63,000 specimens, most archived at the Herbarium.

When Rothrock arrived at IU in 2014, his charge was to curate the specimens and assist in leading the digitization of the collection, now available virtually to the public and to scientists around the country and the world—an enduring gift of knowledge and access. He says, "When I am doing taxonomic work, I can compare what I collect with historical samples of those same specimens. In some cases, one can even extract DNA for genetic analyses. There is value in historical benchmarks and our ability to see what's changed."

Are certain plant species moving northward or southward in response to changing climate conditions or other pressures? What was once plentiful that is now gone? Are flowering periods shifting? Is this puzzling specimen a previously unknown species?

Rothrock's virtual database helps scientists answer these questions and more. We should all want to know.

* * *

As one of the leaders of the Indiana Forest Alliance's Ecoblitz vascular plant team, Rothrock's key contributions were to construct a complete inventory of plant species within the Ecoblitz area and apply the Floristic Quality Assessment, or FQA, to the inventories.

FQA is a protocol for assessing the quality of plant communities based on their similarity to pre–European settlement plant communities. How telling that the presence or absence of European settlers is the primary determinant of nature's integrity: colonization was a turning point when many native species began a steep decline and new species were introduced, some intentionally and some accidentally.

The idea for the FQA grew out of a system designed by Gerould Wilhem and Floyd Swink of the Morton Arboretum in Chicago in the 1990s. Chicago, always a leader in urban green space preservation, needed a way to prioritize land acquisition and preservation. An unbiased system for ranking properties would prove to be invaluable. The FQA requires every plant species to be assigned a "coefficient of conservatism," or C value, ranging from 0 to 10. If a plant species gets a ranking of 10, it has a high likelihood of occurring in a relatively unaltered native landscape. Japanese stiltgrass, on the other hand, which thrives in disturbed sites—like recently cultivated fields—gets a ranking of 0.

Through field experience, scientists like Rothrock assign C values based on their understanding of the responses of individual plant species to habitat modification. The most conservative species, with the highest

Forest as Superorganism

C values, are intolerant of disturbance and require narrow, special ranges of ecological conditions.

In 2004, during his 33-year tenure as Taylor University professor of biology and environmental science, Rothrock saw a need for an Indiana version of the FQA. So Rothrock and his colleagues "sat in a room, with a lot of onion rings and sandwiches from Ivanhoe's Restaurant, and evaluated each of the 2,700 vascular plant species occurring in Indiana, and assigned them C values."

"Once a plant is ranked, then you can average the values of, say, 100 plants on the same site to get the mean C," explains Rothrock. "A mean C of 3.5 or higher means that you have a natural community with moderate to high remnant value, with the highest theoretically being 5," although a few sensitive wetlands rank a 5.6.

Another of the FQA metrics is a Floristic Quality Index (FQI). FQI adds a weighted measure of species richness by multiplying the mean C by the square root of the total number of native species. As with mean C, higher FQI numbers indicate higher floristic integrity and a lower level of disturbance impacts to the site. Explains Rothrock, "FQI provides a numerical picture of a habitat's ecological integrity based on its plant species composition." Forests that are the most like mosaics have the most integrity: the more pieces, the more artful—and valuable—the mosaic.

Rothrock and the Ecoblitz plant team compiled a list of all the plant species within the Ecoblitz area and applied the FQA protocol. They found that the species richness of the Ecoblitz area is comparable with the most botanically rich forested sites known in the state. Rothrock's analysis found that "the FQA of the herbaceous community in the Ecoblitz area shows that this forest has very high remnant natural value, with portions that are clearly remarkable and likely are unmatched in other forest ecosystems in the state."

* * *

There is botany in Paul Rothrock's blood. His people, from the Moravian line of original German Protestants, migrated to the U.S. from southern Germany in the 1740s.

Growing up in Scranton, Pennsylvania, Rothrock was aware of a distant, somewhat famous relative: Joseph T. Rothrock (1839–1922), Pennsylvania's "father of forestry." Joseph Rothrock joined exploratory missions to the American southwest in the 1870s to study plant species. He also advocated for conserving and reforesting depleted land, led an education program for state foresters, and helped start Pennsylvania's system of state forests and parks. To wit, there is a Rothrock State Forest smack in the center of the state. "We're connected on some mystical level," says the latter-day Rothrock.

Like many future botanists, Paul Rothrock "liked to mess around in whatever edge was nearby and pretend it was the frontier." Some of his fields of play were degraded by coal mining; others were untamed. He had a family that prioritized flowers and vegetable gardening, and the whole family of five was expected to help. "I remember sitting under the apple tree, paring out the rotten parts, collecting the good parts so my mother could turn them into applesauce for the deep freeze," he says.

Gardening was beloved in his extended family, too. Rothrock's "Uncle Doc" was a country doctor. Rothrock says, "I was impressed that he could name all the plants, and the fact that all plants had names, and belonged to certain groups. This enthralled me."

In 1961, the Rothrock family got its first car, a stripped-down Plymouth Valiant ("We didn't need and couldn't afford one before," says Rothrock). Suddenly, visits to national parks were possible. He recalls, "Ultimately, I got to see the broader world and was particularly absorbed by the ecological lessons of western states. Once I saw nature at its best, I began to understand the destruction of it in and around the industrial city of Scranton."

Rothrock attended a state university branch campus because it was inexpensive and ultimately received his advanced degrees from Pennsylvania State University, majoring in botany with an emphasis in plant ecology and plant taxonomy. In 1981, he landed a position at Taylor University in rural Northern Indiana. The new physical geography, and mindset, were shocks.

"It was a tough adjustment because Taylor is in Upland, the flat lands, with acre upon acre of corn and soybean fields. Grant County has scant public green space. And there was no history of conservation there; it wasn't in the blood," he laments. "The Indiana approach was to remove and replace natural landscapes with industrial animals and agriculture, to push nature in that direction. Increasingly, there was no allowance for hedgerows or weeds or natural areas to be present."

Rothrock contrasts that approach with that of the Indigenous peoples: "Native peoples also made a lot of modifications to the landscape, transitioning it from deciduous forests to tall grass prairie. But they proved it's possible to have productivity of the land without compromising ecological health."

Says Rothrock solemnly, "In my Appalachian experience, I could find mountain folk, and even people on the street, with a sense of admiration and pride in their natural heritage. I fear that Indiana has never quite developed a deeper conservation ethic that regards broader questions

of human life, quality of life, long-term well-being, and the incredible beauty that the state had historically."

*   *   *

The Ecoblitz vascular plant team was determined to document the bounty of natural wonders. One of the delights of the Indiana Forest Alliance's Ecoblitz is that it invites collaboration among forest lovers, trained experts, and academicians. The plant team included self-taught enthusiast David Mow, Kevin Tungesvick (hired by the ecological restoration firm EcoLogic in 2018), Steven Dunbar (leader of the Indiana Native Plant Society), Karen Smith (see her essay in chap. 7), Scott Namestnik (hired by the Indiana Department of Natural Resources as the state botanist in 2019), and leaders Dr. Rothrock; Dr. Don Ruch, professor of biology at Ball State University and former president of the Indiana Academy of Science; and Dr. Collin Hobbs, associate professor of biology and curator of the Huntington University Herbarium.

Across the seasons from 2014 to 2016, the plant teams visited each of the six zones in the 900-acre Ecoblitz area several times. Their 20 or more forays involved walking portions of the Low Gap, Tecumseh, and Possum Trot Trails while blazing new pathways into the heart of the area during different seasons.

The Ecoblitz vascular plant team at work (*clockwise from top*, botanists Kevin Tungesvick, Paul Rothrock, Scott Namestnik, and Steven Dunbar). *Photo credit: IFA.*

Rothrock states, "I remember the first time we went out. Coming in from Possum Trot Road, it was drop-dead beautiful . . . a natural cathedral. We went down a slope, descending into a glade of greenness. The number of fern species we were seeing was amazing. Two-foot-tall ones! It was like being transported into another dimension."

"We came in on the east side down a deep ravine, following the topography, down a valley, up some slopes, catching different exposures and plants specific to those sites," he continues. One zone had north-facing slopes, with more mesic, or moist, elements, where the team found a large contingent of species that required those conditions. Other zones had more upland, drier qualities. "Each zone had a different story to tell," says Rothrock.

Rothrock's specialization in sedges, and his ability to recognize them in the field was a key contribution. Sedges typically have triangular stems forming grasslike fronds, and they are legion—with almost 250 species in Indiana. Because they are wind pollinated, their flowers are tiny but the pollen is abundant. The fruits too can be small and yet are critical for identifying the species.

Rothrock has spent a good deal of time with sedges in the genus *Carex* and beyond. He is the author of *Sedges of Indiana and the Adjacent States: The Non-Carex Species* (2009, Indiana Academy of Science). His study

Forest as Superorganism

Figure 4

Indiana Natural Regions

LAKE MICHIGAN NATURAL REGION

NORTHWESTERN MORAINAL NATURAL REGION
- Lake Michigan Border Section
- Valparaiso Moraine Section
- Chicago Lake Plain Section

GRAND PRAIRIE NATURAL REGION
- Grand Prairie Section
- Kankakee Sand Section
- Kankakee Marsh Section

NORTHERN LAKES NATURAL REGION

CENTRAL TILL PLAIN NATURAL REGION
- Tipton Till Plain Section
- Entrenched Valley Section
- Bluffton Till Plain Section

BLACK SWAMP NATURAL REGION

SOUTHWESTERN LOWLANDS NATURAL REGION
- Plainville Sand Section
- Driftless Section
- Glaciated Section

SOUTHERN BOTTOMLANDS NATURAL REGION

SHAWNEE HILLS NATURAL REGION
- Crawford Upland Section
- Escarpment Section

HIGHLAND RIM NATURAL REGION
- Mitchell Karst Plain Section
- Brown County Hills Section
- Knobstone Escarpment Section

BLUEGRASS NATURAL REGION
- Scottsburg Lowland Section
- Muscatatuck Flats And Canyons Section
- Switzerland Hills Section

BIG RIVERS NATURAL REGION
- Ohio And Wabash Rivers

Michael A. Homoya
1985. Proceedings Of The Indiana
Academy Of Science, Volume 94,
Plate 1.

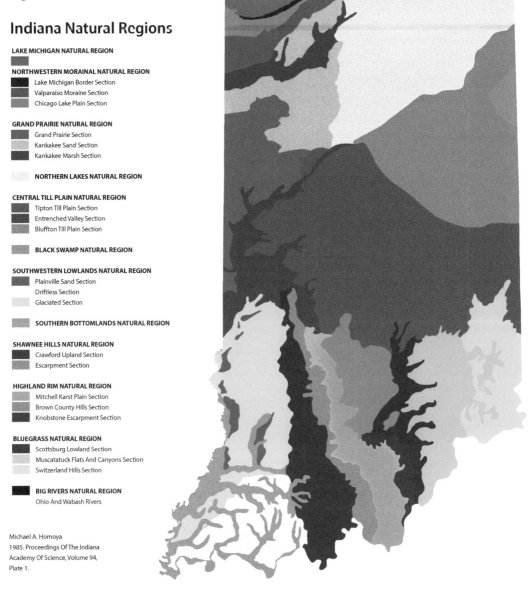

reveals the subtlety, diversity, and curiosity of these common, dutiful plants. In 2022, Rothrock published a second volume: *Sedges of Indiana and the Adjacent States: The Genus Carex* (Indiana Academy of Science). Sedge species are a full 10% of Indiana's native flora.

Rothrock takes a special interest in contextualizing these plants in the precise ecological systems in which they exist. "Take the genus *Carex*, to which the tussock sedge belongs," he says. "The tussock sedge has a symbiosis with an ant species that co-occurs with it. Similarly, there's the Penn sedge—if you have that sedge, you have a world of ants." And the ants are major dispersers of a wide range of seeds from woodland herbs. So, sedges are faithful contributors to the ecological structure of the forest community, providing material for nesting and food for a variety of animals. "To make a forest floor, you need ants, and you need sedges," Rothrock says. Sedges also play a starring role in wetland systems, supporting food webs and creating habitats for animal diversity.

But not all forest floors are created equally. Geography and geology are responsible for the diverse concentration of plant species in the Ecoblitz tracts. "In the southern third of Indiana, you have an old geology that has not been affected by glacial ice," says Rothrock. "That allows for a totally different expression of the plant community to be present."

"There's even a difference between what you'd find in Brown County versus Monroe County," says Rothrock. While Brown County has low fertility soils, Monroe County's limestone layers beget more nutrient-rich soils, especially along stream corridors, and dense growth. He continues, "That's why I consider the Ecoblitz project so fascinating. You have such a richness of species within a few square meters."

He points to botanist Michael A. Homoya's definitive 1985 paper on the natural regions of Indiana, a map of which is reproduced in the first volume of Rothrock's sedge book, as "so useful for understanding the distribution plants in the state." The Ecoblitz zone is the epitome of the mature deciduous forest of the Highland Rim natural region.

* * *

Off and on over several growing seasons, Rothrock and the vascular plant team combed the backcountry zones. They identified a whopping 427 herbaceous and woody species. Of these, a mere 15 were non-native. The forest teemed with 40 different sedges, 29 shrubs, 51 trees, 28 grasses,

American ginseng (*Panax quinquefolius*), a rare species on the state's watch lists for Brown and Monroe Counties, has been found in the Ecoblitz area in multiple locations. *Photo credit: David Mow.*

17 vines, 15 ferns, and 243 wildflowers, or "forbs" (herbaceous flowering plants that are not grasses or sedges).

Forest-literate Hoosiers harvest and sell American ginseng (*Panax quinquefolius*), with its flamboyant red berry clusters and hairy fingerling roots, for medicinal properties. It is against Indiana law to harvest ginseng before the plant is five years of age, since it cannot reproduce until it is three or four years old. Ginseng can be sustainably harvested, allowing those with permits to return to the same site after enough years have elapsed.

The large yellow lady's slipper (*Cypripedium parviflorum* var. *pubescens*) is another watch list specimen identified by the vascular plant team. These sunny orchids light up the forest in May. Other sensitive species of note found in the Ecoblitz include the red-fruited goldenseal (*Hydrastis canadensis*), the lavender-budded showy orchis (*Galearis spectabilis*), and the three birds orchid (*Triphora trianthophora*), named for its triple-petal design.

Rothrock also devoted time to working with Dr. Leslie Bishop, professor emerita in the Department of Biology at Earlham College, to examine the 51 tree species found in the area and the infrastructure they lend to the forest. Was the forest approaching old growth? This means not only asking whether the trees are getting old enough but also if the forest contains a diversity of tree ages, standing snags, and sufficient woody debris good for burrows and dens. Do these results, combined with other FQA measures, confirm that the Ecoblitz area is rapidly approaching the status of secondary old-growth forest?

The answer is yes. The Ecoblitz forest had not only a well-aged woody structure but also diverse herbaceous cover. A mean C value above 3.5

Showy orchis
(*Galearis spectabilis*).
Photo credit:
Paul Rothrock.

suggests a high-quality remnant forest. All six zones assessed in the Ecoblitz area had a mean C higher than 4; the mean C of zone 6 was 4.85, and the mean C of zone 2 was 4.74. "This is maxing out what you could expect to be there," Rothrock says. "You had sensitive ferns, you had conservative sedges, you had orchids, and glamorous flora like ginseng and trillium."

Areas with an FQI higher than 35 have species quality and richness that make them floristically important from a statewide perspective. Areas registering in the 50s and higher are extremely rare and represent a significant component of Indiana's native biodiversity and natural landscapes—that is, they are nature preserve quality. All the zones in the Ecoblitz area had FQI values ranging from 62.2 to 77.1. Although invasive Japanese stiltgrass (*Microstegium vimineum*) muscles out the native plants in many Indiana forests, in the Ecoblitz zones, Rothrock's team "did not see it at all except near heavily traveled hiking paths."

The numbers led Rothrock to conclude that "the forest community in the Ecoblitz area of Morgan-Monroe/Yellowwood State Forest is one of superlatives. It is a biological hotspot that deserves only the most sophisticated management protocols and the highest conservation priority. It retains the historic diversity of vascular plants characteristic of a mature deciduous forest of Indiana's Highland Rim natural region. The species richness of the Ecoblitz area is comparable with the most botanically rich forested sites known in other bioregions of the state."

* * *

Rothrock remains frustrated that the exacting, data-driven, impartial measurement of the quality of the Ecoblitz forest is subject to capitalism-inspired power machinations . . . otherwise known as politics.

When the Division of Forestry announced a timber sale in the eastern portion of the Ecoblitz area in 2017 after the division had received the plant team's results, it was a slap in the face. "They're not hearing the opportunity," Rothrock entreats. "This area is special, in its own category." Rothrock finds it hard to understand the resistance to allowing more old-growth forest to be restored within a small portion of state forestland when the agency enthusiastically creates young forest habitat.

Another unfortunate example of the challenges to conservation was evident in the delineation of the Low Gap Nature Preserve that is a part of the Ecoblitz region. Rothrock states, "On one of our trips, we surveyed a sizable area included in the Low Gap Nature Preserve that had been cleared of trees in the late 19th century and planted with conifers during the Civilian Conservation Corps era. Including a chunk of a derelict pine forest in a nature preserve is a way of cheating the nature preserve," especially since the delineation failed to include a highly desirable section further south.

Despite these experiences, a 2018 meeting among Governor Holcomb, the Indiana Forest Alliance, and Professors Rothrock, Bishop, and John Whitaker, premier mammalogist from Indiana State University, proved encouraging. They urged the governor to have the Department of Natural Resources set aside the Ecoblitz area as a high conservation value forest. Rothrock recalls, "I felt very affirmed and welcomed. He gave us a full hearing. It was a wonderful experience. Our concern was, 'Is there a place for an old-growth forest within the portfolio of state forestland?' Old-growth forest is underrepresented. We're trying to present an opportunity where leaders could say, 'This a special place, and it should

Forest as Superorganism

have a refined, particular kind of management that enhances its old-growth characteristics.'"

Rothrock continues, "The 900-acre Ecoblitz area is rugged country. Logging would require road building. Invasive species will come right in. Then this uniqueness is gone forever, no matter how long you wait."

*   *   *

The Indiana that pioneering botanist Charles Deam explored in the early 1900s was still "a very wild place," Rothrock reminds us. Towns had railroads, but there were no highways. As the first state forester, Deam was already seeing big changes take place in the Hoosier landscape between 1905 and 1935.

"When I think about how much the state has changed in a little more than 100 years, and I try to visualize where we'll be in the next 100 years, it scares me," says Rothrock quietly. "We're going to see a lot of changes due to the shifting climate. I wish the state as a whole could find a conservation ethic that takes into account values beyond mere extraction."

What does Paul Rothrock know that everyone else needs to know? "There are species yet to be discovered," he says with light in his eyes. "The fear is that we will not know them before they are gone."

Key Findings

In total, the plant team recorded 428 species of vascular plants. These plant species fall into the following categories: 51 trees, 29 shrubs, 15 ferns, 17 vines, 40 sedges, 3 rushes, 28 grasses, and 245 forbs. Only 15 non-native species were found.

At least 24 species are sensitive species, with a C value (coefficient of conservatism) of 8–10, meaning they are found in relatively unaltered, native landscapes. Sensitive species of note include winter green, cranefly orchid, American ginseng, Indian cucumber root, Virginia snakeroot, large yellow lady's slipper, goldenseal, and showy orchis. American ginseng and goldenseal are on the state watch lists for Brown and Monroe Counties, and large yellow lady's slipper orchid is on the watch list for Monroe County.

Two of the forbs—ginseng and lady's slipper—are on the state Division of Nature Preserves' watch list of "plant or animal species existing in such small numbers that they are in danger of becoming extirpated from Indiana, this includes species that are in jeopardy as a result of human activity."

A diverse community of some 15 different species of ferns, one of the most sensitive plant groups, was pervasive throughout the Ecoblitz forest.

FQAs are measurements of a natural area's ecological integrity based on their plant species composition. "Floristic assessment demonstrates that the study area (Ecoblitz forest) has very high 'remnant natural value,' among the highest in the state," concludes Dr. Paul Rothrock, associate curator of the Indiana University Herbarium.

Plant Categories

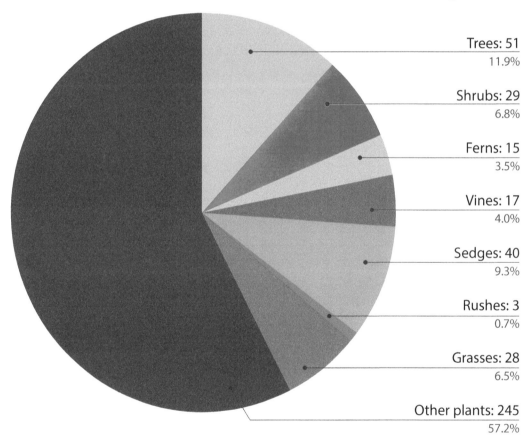

Trees: 51
11.9%

Shrubs: 29
6.8%

Ferns: 15
3.5%

Vines: 17
4.0%

Sedges: 40
9.3%

Rushes: 3
0.7%

Grasses: 28
6.5%

Other plants: 245
57.2%

TOTAL: 428

Forest as Superorganism

Non-Native Species

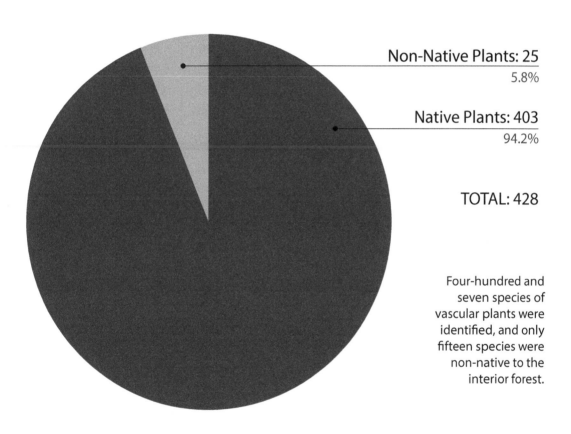

Non-Native Plants: 25
5.8%

Native Plants: 403
94.2%

TOTAL: 428

Four-hundred and seven species of vascular plants were identified, and only fifteen species were non-native to the interior forest.

Linda Cole, bryophyte team leader. *Photo credit: Myron Cole.*

4. Q AND A: LINDA COLE

The Forest within the Forest

Anne Laker

Naturalist Linda Cole reveres mosses and invites us all to do the same. Why? Preceding the existence of forests, "mosses basically set up the nutrient chain on the terrestrial earth," she explains. The plush, fairy-tale beauty of mosses belies their intricate function and structure. And especially in this era of climate change, we all owe mosses a heavy debt of gratitude, as they store more carbon than any other plant on land.

A periodontal therapist by trade, Cole was accustomed to assessing the fine details of microbial activity inside her patients' mouths. Today, as a self-taught naturalist, she applies the same observational acumen to the enchanting mini-forests belonging to the bryophyte family: mosses. Cole, a Hoosier native, has devoted years to understanding mosses, cultivating them in her Brown County backyard, depicting them in the art medium of printmaking, and traveling the globe to explore them.

For as many as 500 million years, mosses have punched above their weight in the ecosystems in which they operate: fixing carbon, processing toxins, modulating air temperature, feeding fauna, and housing microbial goodies that rebuild soil. They even rival rushing water for the ability to break down rock.

Three high-performing nonvascular plant groups belong to the bryophyte family: mosses, liverworts, and hornworts. Like vascular plants, bryophytes use chlorophyll to photosynthesize and produce sugars from sunlight. Unlike vascular plans, bryophytes have no roots and do not produce flowers or seeds. Rather than soil, bryophytes obtain their nutrients from atmospheric deposition on their leaves. While mosses have tiny leaves and a radial design around a stem, liverworts have a stem (i.e., thallus) and lobes, and hornworts have narrow pipelike horns. They all enrich a forest, from Ireland's oceanic woods to the cloud forests of the Andes and our own Indiana woodlands.

In the springs of 2015 and 2016, Cole and a team of seven volunteers surveyed the Morgan-Monroe/Yellowwood Back Country Area (BCA).

Cole reported that the team's 2015 trek "revealed an interesting and diverse population of bryophytes typical of a healthy intact hardwood forest ecosystem." After their 2016 survey, Cole reported,

> This year's bioblitz covering zones 3, 4, 5, and 6 proved fairly impressive in bryophyte richness. The diverse topography and deciduous stands of trees that contain old logs and generally higher amounts of standing and downed biomass on the forest floor definitely contributed to our findings. These positive effects might probably be explained by characteristics of old trees that make them better habitats for bryophytes. Robust growth of well-established, successional bryophytes can only occur on older trees in various states including downed biomass. Therefore, the retention of mature to overmature trees in forests appears to be important for maintaining species richness. Many of the specimens came from tree bark which shows that trees act as population centers for diverse species.

Over three treks in these two years, Cole's team collected samples of 53 species from 30 genera of mosses from various substrates and habitats, including "sandstone rock, bark from living and dying trees, tree roots, rotting logs downed for various periods of time, forest soils of mesic slopes, ridges and bottoms, creek beds and seeps."

Among those identified were six mosses that Cole characterized as "rare," although she sees the complex community they belong to as more important. These include goose egg, cord glaze, goiter, beaked comb, feather comb, and tassel mosses. Three species of leafy liverworts were also found, two on rotting logs and a third on rotting bark in the wet forest bottoms. As Cole wrote in her 2015 report, "This inventory, representing healthy moss diversity, clearly indicates there is much to see beyond the trees and illustrates the mutual interdependence of all life in a healthy forest ecosystem."

What follows is an interview with a self-made bryologist and believer in the connectedness of all living beings.

LAKER How did you first fall in love with bryophytes?

COLE By accident. I started really young by being in nature a lot of the time; my dad was in the landscaping business. I started my career in the dental field treating periodontal disease. I was studying oral biofilms, integrating this into my practice in order to understand the mechanisms of microbiomes unique to individuals being treated. So I was always looking at small things. What initially inspired me was the scientific work of [evolutionary biologist] Lynn Margulis in endosymbiosis [a symbiotic relationship where one organism lives inside the other] and her study of early microbial mats [multilayered sheets

of microorganisms that are among the earliest forms of life on earth, called stromatolites in fossilized form].

I worked 40 years in the dental field, retiring in 2013. But after so much of that—when the patient is leaning back in the chair and you're doing something they really don't want you to do, that can be stressful. I got my relief by retreating into nature. I would put on my backpack and go. My husband loves hiking too. We've hiked in Labrador, in the Pacific Northwest. We are always exploring forests, so I am pretty strong on forest ecology.

LAKER How did you educate yourself on mosses?

COLE I spent a lot of time in boreal forests over the years. I read about a study that found 80 species of tardigrades [eight-legged micro-animals about one millimeter long], which is what I initially started out researching. Tardigrades' habitats happen to include mosses, lichens, and damp organic litter. They are thought to have specifically evolved along with mosses. Like mosses, tardigrades are extremophiles and assume a "tun" state, which is a form of suspended animation that allows them to survive desiccation. Tardigrades in this tun state have been recovered from moss herbariums 100 years old and been brought back to life. Tardigrades are what led me to first view mosses and lichens under the microscope, and I was smitten.

Beaked comb moss (*Rhynchostegium serrulatum*) was found in the Ecoblitz forest. *Photo credit: Linda Cole.*

I can remember the first moss sample I looked at under my dissecting microscope. I was just blown away by it. The light coming through these organisms, only one cell thick. It was so beautiful, a sublime experience to see. It was not the way I imagined that moss looked up close.

Mosses are complicated, they're a lot more complex than I realized. When I was just starting to explore bryophytes, I contacted a biologist who worked for the DNR [Department of Natural Resources], Bill McKnight. He helped me out by referring me to a good book. He said, "You know, if you haven't had any training in biology, you're going to have to learn all the lingo." Bill told me that I would be able to become a bryologist if I had enough passion, that being the most important asset. This was just the inspiration I needed to hear. So I bought every book that I could get, but mainly what I was doing was putting lots and lots of specimens under my microscope and really looking to see where they were growing, in what circumstances, and in what conditions. So, lots of observation. I was letting the bryophytes be my mentor. I had no expectations, no biases. I found out that being an "amateur" is not a deterrent. An amateur is a person who engages in a pursuit out of love for the subject, without monetary reward as motivation. This lends itself to a wonderful freedom that helped me develop an intimate relationship with mosses, gradually transforming my perception of the living field and the purpose of human beings as part of nature.

LAKER Beautiful. You mentioned light and mosses. How do they work together?

COLE The light travels right through the leaves because they are so thin, and you can see all the definition and interesting morphology that they use on their leaves to collect and reflect light for photosynthesis, so there's all different kinds of shapes of cells and you could see all of that definition, which was something I had been blind to before. Now I see it in a whole different perspective than just looking at it on the ground. It was like looking at something sacred—so exquisitely designed, capable of so much for such a tiny little plant. The moss is always responding to its immediate environment, almost as if the environment was an extension of its own physiology. So this was an incredible new way to look at life, and it made me start looking at my own life in a different way.

LAKER You mean the way we're all a product of our environments?

COLE Yes, mosses are impacted by physiological stimuli from the environment that they convert into their beings. We do the same thing. Right now, all the challenges and changes in our environment

Forest as Superorganism

Train tracks moss (*Thelia hirtella*) growing on a tree trunk in the Ecoblitz forest.
Photo credit: Linda Cole.

really bring about a lot of genetic activity in plants and animals, including us.

Mosses are nonvascular plants, so they get most of their nutrition through atmospheric deposition and other feedback systems constantly. They have no cuticle on the leaf like vascular plants do. They just have pores, so they're always taking in all kinds of signals from the environment and converting that into their metabolism.

LAKER Is it correct that mosses thrive in low-nutrient environments? Which is sort of a superpower.

COLE Yes, they take the rain from the atmosphere directly through their pores . . . they don't take water up their rhizomes, which kind of act like Velcro, attaching them to the substrate. All their nutrition mainly comes from atmospheric deposition, and it goes directly into the pores. They take in toxins, too.

LAKER Do mosses prefer older trees?

COLE There are definitely more species of mosses associated with older trees. The reason is that young trees with small crowns and tight bark have limited stem flow and storage. They are usually colonized by a small group of pioneer bryophyte species that make thin mats and dense tufts. As the crown increases, bark roughens and storage and flow increase. The pioneer species are supplemented by successional species that tend to make fringes and shaggy mats on the trunk and thick skirts covering the base.

I am often asked if mosses do damage to trees, and the answer is no. There are complex symbiotic relationships going on here that involve all kinds of benefits for both organisms. In big old mother trees, mosses may extend high into the crowns, and their bases accumulate soil, becoming extensions of the forest floor, where other genera of mosses move in and occupy this area and exposed roots. Old-growth forests are important for the maintenance of genetic variation in clonal colonies of mosses. Some grow on mature trees, fallen logs, or decaying stumps. Some mosses are dead wood specialists, usually thick mat species which colonize decaying, moist woody debris on the forest floor. In our Indiana deciduous woodlands, old trees and logs are especially important as substrates that lift bryophytes above the leaf litter, helping to build a richer biome. For me, mosses represent a primordial link in old-growth forests where they flourish and are allowed expression over the long term. Old trees and mosses just naturally go together—a complex mutualism full of secrets we have yet to discover.

It's important to remember that bryophytes don't just clothe the landscape in visual beauty but are integral to its function, playing a vital role in creating it. And I feel that is why we intuitively notice

and sense that venerable quality of old growth forests covered with a diversity of mosses: We sense that it's an expression of our ancient and primordial source.

LAKER Powerful! How did you approach a survey like the Ecoblitz?

COLE I am looking at everything high and low, tuned into the geology and niches. Because the mosses tell you a lot about the land and soils. Then I collect samples. It's not like walking around and seeing a certain flower. A clump of moss may have multiple species that are so tiny and intertwined. It's not a race to see the species. You want to look at the landscape and evaluate to look at as many substrates as possible.

Every moss is unique. When I go in and I see mosses, I'm not really trying to see how many species I can get in the shortest amount of time. I'm just trying to get as good a random sample as I can get in the amount of time that I have. What I remember about the Ecoblitz survey is that we did go at an excellent time of year. It was before the canopy was on the trees, and I remember the color of the mosses really showed up a long distance away. That's when they're getting a lot of sunlight and photosynthesizing in that time of year without shade. Those ultraviolet-absorbing compounds were showing up in the mosses, and they were just striking against the humus and the leaf litter. I think mosses always look more beautiful in the winter. They form protective compounds in full sun: an orange-yellow color you wouldn't see at all if it were really shady.

A golden *Thuidium* moss against a clump of *Dicranum* moss with lance-shaped, thin-curved leaves. These two mosses are commonly found in Indiana woodlands and, unlike many mosses, are easily identified without a microscope. *Photo credit: Myron Cole.*

LAKER In your report on the Ecoblitz in 2015, you described mosses as "miniature forests within the greater forest helping to support many types of organisms and healthy soils that underpin the dynamics of our entire ecosystem." Can you elaborate?

COLE Mosses protect the soil and microbes, and they reflect the microclimate of the forest. They are their own tiny forest, modulating temperatures and harboring mycelia beneath them.

LAKER Within the forest ecosystem, what would happen if mosses weren't there?

COLE We would lose so much biodiversity. Because mosses protect the metabolism of the earth by covering it. They provide habitat for a ton of arthropods and microorganisms. A moss clump looks like a forest to these beings. They use it to raise their young, they store pollen and seeds there. It would affect everything if mosses went away. You'd have fewer spiders, fewer birds, and less of everything because mosses are right at the bottom of the food chain. They basically set up the nutrient chain on the terrestrial earth.

LAKER Also in your report of Ecoblitz results, you called bryophytes an "undervalued group of pioneer plants." What do you mean by that?

COLE Most people are not aware that bryophytes are the evolutionary first step toward terrestrial existence and the greening of the land. Cyanobacteria may be what made it possible for mosses, for bryophytes to move from water onto land earlier than what we thought, when earth was like a lunar landscape with water. This movement of life to land is probably one of the greatest transformations the world has ever known, and it has made our life as heterotrophs [organisms that rely on other plants or animals for food] possible. Forests are the legacy of mosses.

LAKER What is the role of liverworts?

COLE They have a really interesting biochemistry, with high concentrations of UV-protective chemicals. They were probably the first bryophytes to move onto land. It took a long time for leaves to form on plants. A great diversity of mosses expanded when forests started emerging on the earth, creating ecological niches for bryophytes to grow in. The earliest bryophyte was a liverwort.

LAKER What are the functional differences between mosses and fungi . . . and mosses and lichens?

COLE There are so many similarities. Bryophytes and lichens are found along with fungi in cryptobiotic soils [the word *cryptobiotic* refers to them being hidden and small in size]. Both mosses and lichens exhibit desiccation tolerance and use anabiosis as a strategy, which is a temporary state of suspended or greatly reduced metabolism. Both lichens and bryophytes can survive in extreme environments because of this

Goose egg moss (*Arrhenopterum heterostichum*), another notable moss found in the Ecoblitz forest. *Photo credit: Linda Cole.*

trait, along with other unique biochemical strategies for withstanding extreme temperatures, tolerance to toxins, etc. That is also why both are good bioindicators and have also been used in bioremediation along with fungi. There is much ongoing study in this area involving the restoration of environments that suffer from pollutants of many kinds. I was once called about doing a study in northern Indiana about using these organisms where it was suspected that environmental pollutants from a factory were contributing to high rates of cancer. Bryophytes and lichens absorb directly from the atmosphere and also help filter our watersheds. Basically, they are both extremophiles that live in ecological niches that many organisms could not survive in.

LAKER My husband and I once hiked an alpine mountain in Washington State. There were so many moss-draped boulders and trees . . . it was otherworldly. What do bryophytes need to thrive?

COLE Bryophytes have a consummate relationship with humidity and moisture. And cooler temperatures, or a low-temp condensation point. Mosses can photosynthesize at lower light levels when other plants can't. One habitat they really like that is typical of our mesic forests in Indiana is a log in a state of decomposition. A rotting log exists in the boundary layer with a rich environment of carbon dioxide, where conditions are going to stay nice and damp. Imagine a place rich in moisture, with sun flecks coming through the woods.

LAKER How do mosses respond to changing temperatures or interact with their environments?

COLE The optimal temperature for mosses is 68 degrees. Above 77 degrees, they will slow down or shut down. It may be below zero, but they can still photosynthesize. They can transfer water to the tips of their tiny leaves, but they do much better in colder temps. In tundra areas, they insulate permafrost. Mosses are the largest carbon sink in the world. Once a glacier has melted, bryophytes move in immediately to cloak it. They also perform bioremediation by sucking up oil from an oil spill. I see them everywhere: city sidewalks, in cracks, and on asphalt. There's a bryophyte for every ecological niche. I can't name a place I haven't seen mosses. They are accessible, so there is always something to study! In Newfoundland, on the northeast Canada coast, the mantle of the earth is exposed. It was torn up, it's full of heavy metals. Mosses are growing even there.

LAKER Were your findings in the BCA remarkable or notable? How did they compare to other surveys you've done?

COLE In that forest, I found a robust community of mosses. The conditions were such that the mosses were especially beautiful because they were well hydrated and full. I did find what I might have expected: species perfectly adapted to the topography, geology, and other conditions of the terrain, integral to the landscape and its function—offering vital ecological services.

I was with a herpetologist, and so we were not only looking at mosses, but we were looking for salamanders, which actually use mosses and logs. We found one spotted salamander, with algae growing in its eggs. That's a unique find. On this property [the BCA], there are creeks, ponds, low-lying ravines, embankments: an excellent area for mosses in the watershed, abundant and prolific.

I did not particularly find what I would really call "rare species" and feel that we often have too much fixation upon so-called rare species while omitting the importance of how all these organisms relate to the whole. This is something we can learn from participating in an ecoblitz that goes beyond collecting data and statistics. Symbiotic relationships are not only necessary for a forest but are necessary for evolution—this is the way of connection, collaboration, and communion. Some of the most important clues can be beautifully small, considered mundane and easily overlooked. One of our major stumbling blocks is that we have been conditioned into breaking the living holistic biosystem into parts, which is a limited way of seeing.

LAKER What do you believe needs to happen to protect, preserve, or conserve forests in Indiana?

COLE When I hear people say, "I can't do anything about climate," you know they're waiting for the politicians and the companies and leaders to do something about it. To me, the main thing is not climate change or loss of biodiversity or ecosystem collapse. The main problem is the size of our egos. We need to downsize our egos and pay attention to small things. To solve our problems, our awareness and education is really important starting at the youngest age.

And there is a spiritual aspect to our lives when we see our part in the whole creation. I hope we learn that we are part of nature, instead of trying to override it. We don't understand that everything is connected. We don't understand the benefits. The Purdue forest management graduates are taught to measure board feet . . . not alignment with the ways of nature. We need a radical consciousness shift and to reach children as young as possible. Your data and scientific information only go so far in trying to advance the truth.

LAKER What have bryophytes taught you?

COLE Being small does not mean being unsuccessful. It just means we pay very little attention to them, since we are unfamiliar with their ancient history and the important ecosystem services they have evolved to provide. We generally have become dismissive of that which requires no advanced technology but only time, patience, and attentiveness to perceive. More attention is given to larger, more charismatic species and so-called keystone species. How many people nowadays would take time to get down on their hands and knees and realize they are peering at something sacred in these tiny paragons of adaptive flexibility that have so elegantly enlisted the forces of nature into their simple designs, diversity, and nonlinear ecological dynamics?

There is a universe under our feet that we are ignoring. Becoming intimate with small creatures in our forests and our own backyards can serve as portals to the unseen, innermost weave of life. The first time I gazed at a moss under my microscope, the words of Thoreau instantly came to mind: "How can we expect to understand Nature unless we accept like children these her smallest gifts?"

Highlights: Characteristics of Bryophytes

- Very sensitive to chemical and physical surfaces
- Many grow only on older trees and woody debris

Key Findings

Bryophyte surveys revealed:

- "Diverse population of bryophytes in this forest are typical of a healthy intact hardwood forest ecosystem," according to Linda Cole in 2015.
- "This year's bioblitz covering zones 3, 4, 5, and 6 proved fairly impressive in bryophyte richness. The diverse topography and deciduous stands of trees that contain old logs and generally higher amounts of standing and downed biomass on the forest floor definitely contributed to our findings.... Robust growth of well-established, successional bryophytes can only occur on older trees in various states including downed biomass," stated Linda Cole in 2016.
- 53 species from 30 genera
- Six "rare" mosses (some pictured), five "infrequent" mosses:
    - ◊ Goose egg moss
    - ◊ Goiter moss
    - ◊ Beaked comb moss
    - ◊ Tassel moss
    - ◊ Cord glaze moss
    - ◊ Feather comb moss
    - ◊ Three leafy liverworts

Devils urn fungus (*Urnula craterium*) is one of many saprotrophs in the BCA
that decompose organic material, processing nutrients back to the soil.
Photo credit: Karen Smith.

Lichens and fungal fruiting bodies on a tree trunk. *Photo credit: IFA.*

PART II
COMPLEX COOPERATORS

Emma Steele

There was a time when the earth's continents were nothing but rock. There were no animals, no trees, no grasses, and no flowers. In this prehistoric time, there was not even dirt. Life was simmering in the unrecognizable sea, but on land, the colonization of the continents was just beginning with the creep of fungi. The exact timing of this emergence is still up for debate, but geoscientists have used fossil evidence to date the bloom of terrestrial fungal life as far back as one billion years ago. This is where soil begins.

Fungi crawled along the barren rock by way of mineral mining. Relying on their unique ability to break down rock for mineral nutrients, fungi were the impetus for life's evolution out of water. The procession went something like this: following fungi came the liverworts and mosses some 470 million years ago (mya), partnered by the evolution of the first insects, in the geologic period known as the Ordovician; then came the ancestors of ferns and the first vertebrate to crawl on land before the second mass extinction of the Devonian period 360 mya that led to the golden age of sharks and the evolution of trees as we know them; rudimentary seed-bearing plants like conifers developed during the Carboniferous period 300 mya as the great supercontinent, Pangea, began to take shape; with the dawn of the dinosaurs in the Triassic period following the earth's third mass extinction circa 252 mya came great forests of cycads, ginkgoes, conifers, and other now-extinct seed-bearing trees; then came the first of the flowers 130 mya and the diversification of angiosperms, the precursors to hardwood trees, just 20 million years after the slow birth of the Atlantic Ocean and the evolution of the first sequoia trees.

After the fifth mass extinction that ended the dinosaurs' reign, the age of mammals began, which culminated in the evolution of humanity. Then, the world started to look like the one we know, with its forests, prairies, savannahs, and swamps growing out of the rich soil that blankets the ancient bedrock.

Along with their role in the genesis of life on land, fungi bear the duty to usher the earth's ephemeral creatures through their end. Just as fungi create fertility from stone, they dismantle the compounds of once-living bodies, leaf litter, and fallen snags, sending the atomized fragments of dead cells on a dreamlike trajectory, rising again, alive. Fungi are the divine connection, the nexus, in the transitional space between decay and regeneration. From them, terrestrial life began, and only with them does the cycle continue.

In this second section, we examine some of the most mysterious relationships within the forest. Steve Russell, an Indiana mycologist, explores the intricacies of mycorrhizal fungi, the forest's underground nutritional conveyor belt and communication highway. And James Lendemer introduces us to an ancient partnership: the lichens.

Steve Russell. *Photo credit: Steve Russell.*

5. ESSAY: IDENTIFYING BACK COUNTRY AREA FUNGI

A Baseline for Healthy Forests

Steve Russell

Imagine you overhear a conversation in an Indiana café: someone describing a trip they are planning to find and document hundreds of vibrant, charismatic species that are currently unknown to science. Where might they be venturing? You may envision a tropical destination with dense rainforests or a mountainous region with unexplored valleys. Most people would not consider Indiana a likely location to encounter that level of novel biodiversity. However, for mycologists—who study mushrooms and fungi—novel species abound in this state, and the Ecoblitz in the Morgan-Monroe/Yellowwood Back Country Area (BCA) was an attractive opportunity for exploration.

Varied in color, shape, and size, fungi can be subtle or flamboyant. Most of us cannot help but notice the snow-white mushrooms that pop up from the dark soil after a moist night. But the mushroom is merely the fruiting body of a much larger, more complex fungal network thriving underground.

Indiana is not unique for the abundance of novel mushrooms that are left to be documented in the scientific literature. The primary difference with other geographies is that Hoosiers are actively looking for them at a large scale, under the auspices of the Hoosier Mushroom Society, the Indiana Forest Alliance, and others. Understanding what exists, where it exists, and when it exists is foundational knowledge for all future lines of scientific inquiry about the role of fungi—as a remediator of toxins, a nutrient-rich food, a source of medicinal compounds, and more. Penicillin, after all, was originally derived from fungi.

It is generally accepted that fungi are vital components for forest ecosystem health and are key components of healthy soils, but there is a need to understand the specific patterns of fungal biodiversity and indicator species within different environments to help assess the health

Right, Calocera cornea, a saprotrophic fungus. *Photo credit: Ron Kerner.*

Below, Boletus bicolor. Photo credit: Ron Kerner.

and functional dynamics of a forest. Systematic biodiversity surveys like the Ecoblitz are a necessary first step toward this end.

To examine the impact of fungi on forest health, we can start by examining specific nutritional strategies that different groups of fungi employ and how changes to their occurrence levels can impact the health and biodiversity of a forest overall. Some groups of fungi, called saprotrophs, decompose organic material to grow. Other fungi, called mycorrhizal, form a mutualistic association with the roots of live trees to get their energy.

Both of these fungal nutritional strategies play important roles in forest health. The vast majority of land plants worldwide (over 90% of plant families), as well as most of the dominant tree species of Indiana, form relationships with mycorrhizal fungi. These plant-fungal associations play an essential role in the nutrient cycling and transport of phosphorus, nitrogen, and/or water; provide drought and pest resistance; promote vigorous growth of both plant and fungi; assist with plant seedling establishment and survival; and positively impact soil chemistry. Without fungi, the functional diversity of a forest is severely diminished.

Healthy Indiana forest soils contain hundreds of species of mycorrhizal fungi buried under every footprint in the woods. The benefits these fungi bring can be compared with soils that have been deprived of mycorrhizal fungi, such as monoculture farmland. One reason why farmers need to apply so many synthetic "nutrients" to their fields is that generations of traditional soil management have yielded a substrate that is limited in the diversity and biomass of mycorrhizal fungi that can help plants unlock hidden nutrients.

Clear-cutting forests, or even selective logging, has been shown to have a negative impact on soil health and healthy forests by altering mycorrhizal communities. Selective logging has been shown to reduce the species diversity and biomass of these beneficial mycorrhizal fungi. Clear-cutting, logging trails, and the soil compaction caused by heavy machinery can bring about similar reductions in the species diversity of these fungi. As there is a mutualism between specific species of mycorrhizal fungi and specific species of trees and plants, the high host specificity of these interactions means that removing a dominant species from a forest stand will reduce or remove entire fungal communities, in turn reducing the ability of forest soils to support future stands of those tree species.

Mycorrhizal species diversity tends to increase when both the age and plant diversity of a forest grow. Thus, the abundance of mycorrhizal fungi found in the Ecoblitz, including 28 species of *Amanita* mushrooms, 20 species of *Lactarius* mushrooms, and 18 species of *Russula* mushrooms identified in the field, should not be surprising in this old forest. Many species of mycorrhizal fungi are successional generalists—they can associate with young and old trees alike. However, there are many other species of mycorrhizal fungi that are only able to associate with trees after they reach a certain level of development. Succession in fungal communities occurs through time, just as it does in forests. Early colonizers are replaced by late colonizers, both bringing an essential ecological function to forested environments.

Underground mycorrhizal fungi are not the only category of fungi that are impacted by selective logging and the removal of large-diameter trees from the forest. Managed forests show a significantly lower species diversity of decomposer fungi (saprotrophs) operating on downed wood than in less disturbed, old-growth stands. Many species of saprotrophic fungi have a growth preference for large-diameter logs on the forest floor and do not colonize and reproduce on small-diameter logs or branches. There are also successional patterns of saprotrophic fungi

Hemioporus betula, an example of a mycorrhizal fungus. *Photo credit: Ron Kerner.*

on these large-diameter logs to consider; some species are only found on recently fallen large-diameter logs, while other species only occur on well-decomposed large-diameter logs. Removing trees of a certain age from the forest outright diminishes species diversity of saprotrophic fungi in these environments by removing an entire successional step in the chain of organisms that recycle nutrients in the forest. The long-term result is a less diverse and less resilient forest ecosystem.

Ecological impacts aside, the significant economic value that can be produced from forests managed for mushrooms is largely ignored. Mushrooms make substantial economic contributions to communities around the world. There are at least two groups of mushrooms—truffles and matsutake—that each have a multibillion-dollar market globally. In 2015, the Hoosier Mushroom Society, in conjunction with the Indiana State Department of Health and Purdue Extension, started a wild mushroom training and certification program, with the goal of beginning to develop a safe and profitable market for Indiana wild mushrooms. Indiana is home to many abundant and financially important species of mushrooms. These include morels, chanterelles, boletes, and many other choice edible species. All these species generate a premium price (from $40 per pound) in local markets and are sought by fine-dining establishments around the country. For this emerging market to continue to develop, healthy forest habitats are essential.

Another focus of the Hoosier Mushroom Society is to document all the mushrooms and macrofungi that occur in the state to establish a full catalog of our state's macrofungal biodiversity. Volunteers around

Complex Coordinators

the state are taking part in a large-scale, citizen science–based survey combined with DNA sequencing of dried specimens. The initial phase of the project was completed in 2022, with more than 2,000 species of macrofungi documented across more than 10,000 DNA sequenced collections. This gives our state a fungal biodiversity database unparalleled worldwide.

To continue documenting new species at a high rate, the Hoosier Mushroom Society's project often seeks out unique habitats around the state. Most of Indiana's forest stands on state and private lands fall between 40 and 100 years of age, so it was a pleasure to survey woodlands on the far end of this spectrum: the old forest stands of the

Left, Porodiculous pendulus, named for its pendulous discs, is a saprotrophic fungus that grows on newly dead branches. *Photo credit: Ron Kerner.*

Below, Callistosporium purpureomarginatum, a rare fungus first officially described in 1996, is a saprotrophic fungus that grows on decaying oak.

Morgan-Monroe/Yellowwood BCA that were the subjects of the Indiana Forest Alliance's Ecoblitz.

Because the Ecoblitz took place early in the Mushroom Society's DNA sequencing program, a significant majority of the Ecoblitz specimens represent the first Indiana sequence of the species. Nearly half, or 36 of the 74 sequenced species, received temporary or provisional names, as they could not be fully identified using currently available DNA reference data. We do not yet know what species they are. They could be new to science, or more likely they are species for which there are DNA sequences that have yet to be matched up with the sequences of these specimens.

A majority of the Ecoblitz specimens that received temporary/provisional names represent first records for the state of Indiana (the first time a species has been documented in the state). An additional seven of the specimens that were definitively identified from DNA sequencing were first records for the state of Indiana. These novel data are vitally important for ongoing research worldwide—because once a species is documented for the first time, we have a chance to understand its role in the environment and how it might help humanity. Since they function as miniature chemical factories, fungi harbor great biotechnological potential to combat disease in humans and plants or transform agricultural waste into fuel.

There is so much more work to do to relate the presence and diversity of various species and functional groups of fungi to the ecological health of Indiana forests. The fungi survey of the Morgan-Monroe/Yellowwood BCA is a first step toward that goal. The quest to document the biodiversity of Indiana's fungi continues because it is in the best interest of forests, and humans, for fungi to flourish.

Highlights: Fungal Types

- Saprotrophs (aka decomposers): Some fungi decompose organic material to grow. These saprotrophs recycle carbon, minerals, and nutrients for use by other organisms and contribute to the quality of soil. They also provide food for many species, including microbes, arthropods, nematodes, and mammals.

- Mycorrhizal: Other fungi form mutualistic associations with the roots of vascular plants. Mycorrhizal fungi have very specific host associations and are important to the health of a forest ecosystem. They get their energy from the plant, but they also play an essential role in cycling nutrients to the trees and other plants and can help provide drought and pest resistance. At least 66 species of mycorrhizal fungi were identified in the Ecoblitz forest. Mycorrhizal diversity tends to increase as the age of a forest stand increases and may be important in species regeneration.

Key Findings: Fungal Diversity

- A total of 334 species of fungi were identified in the field.

- DNA sequencing was performed on 94 specimens collected from the Ecoblitz, aggregating 74 species across 43 genera.

- In total, 36 of the 74 sequenced species could not be identified using currently available DNA reference data and received temporary or provisional names. A majority of these specimens were first records of a fungi species in the state. An additional 7 specimens that were definitively identified from DNA sequencing were first records for the state.

- Two species—*Porodisculus pendulus* (whitish discs about four millimeters long that affix to freshly dead branches) and *Callistosporium purpureomarginatum* (a two-toned purple-capped fungus found on well-decayed oak)—were among the rarest finds. *Callistosporium purpureomarginatum* was first officially described in 1996.

James Lendemer. *Photo credit: James Lendemer.*

6. PROFILE: JAMES LENDEMER, PH.D.

Learning the Lessons of Lichens

Anne Laker

James Lendemer, Ph.D., interprets lichens as if reading a history book. "They are a window into the past, present and the future," says the roving lichenologist and associate curator at the New York Botanical Garden. "If you know enough about them, you can go into a forest, and with a pretty high degree of certainty, infer what has happened there in the past based on what is there, in what quantity and variety."

Whether expressed as flat lacy white scabs, tiny orange ruffles, hairy green threads, or many other iterations, lichens adorn rocks, soil, or tree bark in every kind of biome on land, from alpine to arid. The word *lichen* derives from the Greek word meaning "licker," or "that which eats around itself." Deftly defying categorization as either animal or plant, a lichen is as much an *idea* as it is a living organism.

That idea is the magical, resilient might of mutualism. As Lendemer explains, a lichen is a partnership, a site of interactions. It is the pairing of a fungus with a photosynthetic partner, such as an alga or a cyanobacteria. The alga or bacteria provides energy through photosynthesis. In return, the fungus provides a protective base and gathers moisture and nutrients. Sometimes a yeast even gets in the act. Just as our guts have microbiomes based on our genetics and diet, a lichen is a complex mini-biome that lichenologists are still striving to understand on its own terms.

Dr. Lendemer likes to say that lichens "host the party in the forest." The party or partnership or mutualism that is a lichen results in creative, site-specific combinations that give us the 5,800 (and counting) species of lichens in North America. The cooperation they harness is so powerful a survival tool that it is said that lichens could be immortal, under the right conditions. How convenient, since lichens play key roles in air pollution mitigation, soil formation, temperature maintenance, moisture regulation, and wildlife subsistence, referring to food and shelter for mammals, birds, and insects.

At the New York Botanical Garden, Lendemer oversees the largest lichen museum collection in the Western Hemisphere. His respect and affection for lichens are based on his profound scientific intimacy with these humble tufts, patches, and growths. "Lichens are underappreciated by people and by scientists," says Lendemer. "If you go to any science museum, the lichens, much like the fungi, are often relegated to second-class-citizen status, with the fewest people studying them. They are 'othered' in science and in society," he continues, with a whiff of indignation. "That rings true with me. It's certainly something that I can identify with in any number of ways, and so maybe that's what drew me to them. I love lichens. I love going out into the forest and seeing them in places new to me." Namely, Indiana, and the Morgan-Monroe/Yellowwood Back Country Area (BCA).

* * *

When organizing the Ecoblitz of the BCA, Indiana Forest Alliance (IFA) executive director Jeff Stant committed to a comprehensive census of biological life. Without active lichenologists in the state, he turned to New York–based Dr. Lendemer. Lendemer reports that he has studied "lichens all over the Atlantic Coast from New Jersey to Florida." For a recent federally funded project, he and his colleagues surveyed the diverse lichen community across Appalachia. When Stant called from Indiana in 2016, a few factors captured Lendemer's fancy: "It sounded like a great opportunity to help fill a gap in knowledge. Jeff said to me, 'We know nothing about the lichens of Indiana.'" The relatively small scale of the project was attractive as well.

"I was also personally interested because Indiana's eastern deciduous forest is related to the Appalachians, where I have worked a lot, and to the Ozarks, where my Ph.D. adviser did a lot of work," says Lendemer. A third factor that attracted Lendemer was the conservation and forest management implications underpinning IFA's research approach. He says, "I care deeply about the conservation of these organisms, and it was exciting to inventory lichens in a mature forest stand, especially in a place that doesn't have that data."

A fourth reason was an exciting historical connection between the New York Botanical Garden and Indiana, thanks to a 20th-century scientist ahead of her time. Dr. Winona Welch (1896–1990), born in Jasper County, was a bryologist (moss specialist) at DePauw University in Greencastle and, in 1948, the first female president of the Indiana Academy of Science. Like Lendemer, Welch was drawn to study normally neglected species and collected widely, in all 50 states, amassing 133,500 lichen specimens. Over many years, she and her DePauw colleague Dr.

James Lendemer
examines lichen on
a tree trunk. *Photo
credit: IFA.*

Truman Yuncker added specimens to an herbarium begun at DePauw
in 1891.

As Welch's career drew to a close, she knew that DePauw lacked the
resources to care for the collection, so in 1987, she donated it to the New
York Botanical Garden. "I didn't know her personally," says Lendemer,
"but she, and her colleagues, did an amazing job documenting the baseline of biodiversity in Indiana at the time, and it's the only real information we have to compare to the present day." Welch's work resulted in
one of the best historical collections of Indiana lichens. "So I thought it
would be helpful and interesting to improve that area of our collection
and get some comparative material and draw some conclusions from
that," says Lendemer. Dr. Welch would have been delighted.

* * *

So, for five days in April 2017, Lendemer lived and breathed Indiana
lichens in the backcountry area. Why April? "Well, lichens are very 'year-
round.' To do their research, many of my colleagues here at the botanical
garden have to time their work to, say, be in a swamp in the deep south in
the height of summer to see a certain flower get pollinated. But I can go
out anytime, whenever the nice time to be out is wherever I am working.
That said, it's hard work looking for tiny or big things for hours on end, on
your knees and bending over. It's very intensive mentally and physically
and difficult to do under less than ideal conditions."

With a wiry frame and speedy speech, Lendemer approaches his fieldwork with precision and appetite: "You're just basically going out into the
forest and trying to find at least one representative of every single species
that you can find within a given area. For me, that's usually one hectare.
But I want to know everything that's growing in one place, so I have to

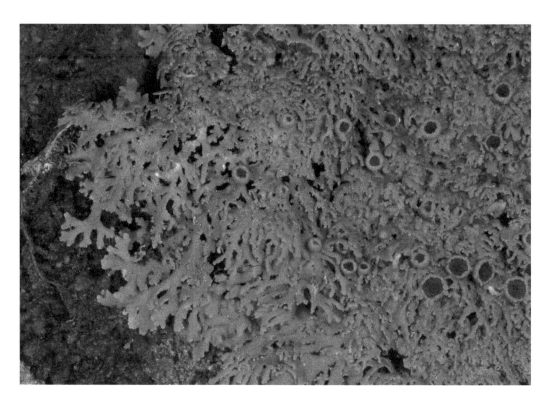

ta, a foliose lichen.
Photo credit: James
Lendemer.

collect a piece of each distinct species. The species can look similar; it can be difficult for lay people to tell them apart even though it's easy once you know them. It's a steep learning curve."

Lendemer describes himself as "an evangelist for the kind of standardized sampling that allows you to infer more about a place than just what's growing there. You can make inferences about what's going on in one part of a forest and also what's going on in those forest stands compared to anywhere else in the country where you've sampled the same way. So, we are using the data generated from standard sampling to untangle and discover a lot of really interesting things about lichens that we did not have the ability to study before because we lacked comprehensive data, or data from large land areas."

One thing sampling lichens does not require is pricey equipment. Think peanut butter jars, razor blades, a mini chisel, a mini hammer, and a pair of garden clippers. Lendemer says, "I basically take a piece of bark, rock, or soil back to the lab that has the lichen on it. Then I look at it under a microscope and section it and look at spores and anatomy and drop some chemicals on it, and sometimes run chromatography to determine exactly what chemicals are in it, which helps to identify it."

Subtleties abound, because lichens are microhabitat specific, says Lendemer. "One species will be on the twigs of the tree, one will be on the base of the tree, one will grow only in the cracks of the bark of this one species of tree. Knowing that allows you to go into the forest and say,

'This is what I see, this is what I expect to see here.'" In the Morgan-Monroe/Yellowwood BCA, Lendemer was sure to sample on the edges of the forest, near parking lots or roads, and in places further afield, in less disturbed spots.

Stant describes Lendemer as a "real mountain goat," willing to seek samples at some risk. Among the April bluebells, Lendemer climbed, scooted, crawled, and wriggled up ridges and near creeks. He states, "In the past, most lichens have been collected at a trailhead or along the road, and that's appropriate, because at times it's physically impossible to travel across a varied landscape. So you have to do what is possible."

With a single-minded quest for lichen varieties in this Indiana forest, Lendemer experienced the gift of deep focus. "Being alone in the wilderness allows me a certain experience of what we think of as wilderness qualities," he says. "That's one of the reasons why we legislate forests' existence in the United States."

When asked for a metaphor for how lichens operate in a forest, Lendemer compares them to corals on the land: "They are as sensitive and symbiotic as corals." But unlike corals, which occur in narrow spaces in the ocean, "lichens can and should be everywhere on the land," says Lendemer. The symbiosis of corals is a "one-to-one relationship. But lichens have evolved many different times, and they partner with many kinds of entities. They are dynamic and diverse and so much more amazing than coral, if you ask me." Part of the amazement comes from all that is not known about lichens and the suspicion that they are much more important to our quality of life than anyone has bargained for.

* * *

Thanks to Lendemer's acumen, Indiana's lichen picture is much richer. In five days, he collected 406 lichens and, from these, identified 108 distinct species; 64 of those species were new distribution records (species not previously documented) in Indiana, illustrating the paucity of field research on lichens in the state. To be fair, Indiana is not alone in relative lichen ignorance. "In most states, there's often not a modern updated checklist," he says. Lendemer's work in the 900-acre BCA was the first in-depth study of lichens in an Indiana forest in 74 years and the first ever carried out with modern standardized sampling protocols.

What he found was a smorgasbord of lichens that hint at the history of the forest. All 108 species found fit into one of the three taxonomic groups of lichens: 65% crustose (the flat, grainy kind), 29% foliose (roseate, with cups or holes), and 6% fruticose (with fingerlike upward growths). Among the plentiful crustose specimens, a great diversity shone through; 55% of the species Lendemer collected were found fewer than three times. And yet, 80% of the crustose lichens found shared a

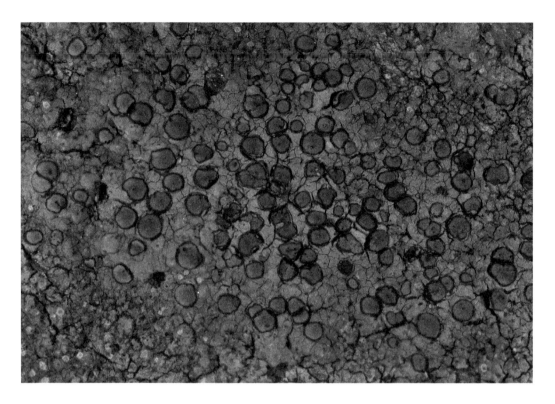

Porpidia albocaerulescens, a crustose lichen. *Photo credit: James Lendemer.*

predictable profile: that of green coccoid photobionts, a type of algal partner popular with fungi in the temperate forests of the eastern U.S.

For unknown geological and meteorological reasons, lichen variety in this forest turned out to be highest on ridgetops and lowest in riparian corridors. Lendemer surmises that ridgetops might provide the alternating wet and dry conditions that lichens love, as opposed to creek banks, where humidity and flooding reign. But in all cases, each site within the BCA hosted unique species not found elsewhere in the study area. Lendemer found that areas outside the Low Gap Nature Preserve, situated within the Ecoblitz study area, were as rich as areas inside the nature preserve, "although many species rare in the study area were found only outside preserve boundaries," he writes. This implies that a lot more of the Morgan-Monroe/Yellowwood BCA is of a similar caliber to the nature preserves.

Thanks to the Lendemer's participation in the Ecoblitz, the latest checklist of Indiana lichens now includes 222 species—though 72 of the oldest reported lichen finds need to be double-checked for accuracy, he says. When he stepped back to look at lichens in the context of all the total taxa found in the Ecoblitz, "insects and spiders together with lichens and other non-lichenized fungi comprise more than half of the total biological diversity," Lendemer wrote in a 2018 paper for the Indiana Academy of Science.

What, if anything, astounded Lendemer about his findings? "I was surprised that many of the things I found hadn't been reported in the state before, yet this is not so surprising given how little published literature there was," he replied. His honed radar for certain species made it easier for him to find some outliers: "But at the same time, this lichen quantity and variety in such a small area was pretty amazing. Even if those species occur in many other places in the state, it is still amazing to go into one tract of forest and find that more than half of the lichens are new reports to the state."

One surprise for Lendemer was finding fewer pollution-sensitive, disturbance-intolerant lichen species. Intact, unpolluted forests can be used as a reference to determine the approximate number of lichens that should be in a given place. That the lichen community here evolved to handle pollution may point to a history of such pollution in the region. He surmises that industrialization across the Ohio River valley has affected the lichen community, although the Clean Air Act of 1963 gradually helped turn the tide on air pollution, along with a 1988 amendment to the act that curbed acid rain. This is how, Lendemer says, "you can have a forest that's quite old but it can be lacking certain [lichen-based] indicators of old growth" as lichens catch up to cleaner air.

Lendemer's take on the Ecoblitz study area is this: "The forest itself has been relatively undisturbed, so you get a relatively natural community of species that's lacking the most sensitive lichens, but some are still there, along with subsets of things that need older trees or more stable microhabitats to grow." To date, the relationship between lichens and older trees has not been deeply studied in the temperate forests of the eastern U.S.

Nor have crustose lichens been given their due, much to Lendemer's chagrin. He says, "With plants, you have trees, you have shrubs, and you have herbaceous plants. Lichens are the same deal: there are shrubby ones [fruticose], leaflike ones [foliose], and then you've got the crusty ones [crustose] that are completely attached to whatever surface they're growing on. The shrubby and the leafy are bigger and more frequently studied, so they are the ones that get inventoried. Most of our knowledge about lichens in general comes from those two types. Crustose lichens are generally considered harder to identify, and so they're often excluded from studies." Yet this is the taxa he found in high abundance and highest variety in the Ecoblitz study area.

In Lendemer's experience, crustose lichens make up half or more of lichen diversity. He states, "If you were to just walk into the forest and ignore the crustose, you're losing so much information. Crustose lichens have very specific ecologies and a huge amount of diversity that actually has great importance to it." By virtue of being a lichenologist, Lendemer is already a supporter of the underdog. Waving the flag for crustose lichens makes him a dogged defender of a double underdog.

Because they are a rare species of their own, every lichenologist needs a mentor. One of Lendemer's is Dr. Isabelle Tavares, an expert on *Laboulbeniales*, an order of fungi that grows on the legs of beetles and the wings of flies. While still in high school, Lendemer met Tavares when he was taken to a scientific conference at the University of California, Berkeley, and ended up attending a lunch with her, along with an algal specialist and a fungal specialist. A correspondence commenced, as Lendemer went on to earn a B.A. in biology at the University of Pennsylvania and his Ph.D. at City University of New York. Lendemer also learned at the elbows of Alfred "Ernie" Schuyler, the former curator at the Academy of Natural Sciences of Philadelphia, and lichenologist Richard Harris, whom Lendemer succeeded at the New York Botanical Garden.

"The thing that I learned from Dr. Tavares was to never accept anything at face value and don't necessarily think that you know something just because something is written down or printed in a book," he says. Not to assume that everything is wrong, but that scientists should be very open to possibility and should investigate, well, their own investigations. Says Lendemer, "If a piece of data or an idea is good and valid, it can stand up to criticism."

* * *

Lendemer came to science through a wide-ranging sense of place. He recalls, "I grew up in a lot of different locations that were very starkly different from each other. I'm from inner-city Philadelphia, and my mother's family were farmers in eastern Maryland. So I would spend a lot of time with my grandparents in a much more rural setting where there were lichens, compared to the city where I lived. My father's family was from Germany, and they had a farm as well."

Through the lens of place, Lendemer teases out the lives and fates of lichens. "I'm less interested in the lichens of one family all over the world," he confesses. "What I'm interested in is all the lichens that are in a place and also what's going on across big or small areas." That angle makes it easier to see short-term human alterations to the environment that affect lichens. His sampling often reveals the relative rarity of so many lichen species and how many appear to have declined over such large areas. "Many of these changes are largely irreparable or effectively permanent" for lichens, he says. "Radical environmental changes have a direct negative correlation with lichen diversity and, typically, abundance. It's striking. We see that in every dataset that we look at." Think

Complex Coordinators

industrial pollution, dense auto emissions, clear-cutting, and climate change.

Young Lendemer also observed this with the hyperurbanization of the East Coast in the 1980s, leaving endless sprawl in its wake, from Washington, DC, to Boston. "I knew certain places as farmland or forests, and then I saw them being converted, and so from a very early age, I was cognizant of the fact that there had to be some impact on the environment, right?" he asks. Witnessing loss made Lendemer into a guardian of biodiversity today. "I do my best to make sure that the things that I study are still here in the future given the current trajectories of where we're going," he says with a fascinating combination of devotion and foreboding.

Lendemer has found a fertile ground, a high road between the objectivity of science and the application of data to the obvious crisis of a degrading environment. "That's what draws me to all of this," he says. "We intuit a lot about what's going on in the world, but I like that research is a way to empirically test what's happening. My work is apolitical in the sense that I go out and seek increased knowledge and find out what's actually going on in nature. Whatever it may be, could be good or bad, could be A or B. I stay open to all the possibilities."

But what if a scientist's findings are that everything is falling apart and dying? "You kind of have to do something about that," Lendemer says. His data-informed activism includes building grassroots networks and interfacing with agencies that normally do not prioritize lichen conservation per se. He states, "For example, I work with those responsible for land management or species management. I try to get to know them and convince them to do something. I don't want to be someone from New York City traveling to eastern Tennessee to say, 'Y'all need to fix this stuff and do this or that.' I need to become part of the community, become a known quantity and build long-term relationships that result in people recognizing that I care about the things for the same reasons that they do. That's a lot of the kind of work I do in the 'political' realm."

Lendemer hopes that his Indiana Ecoblitz findings provide the fundamental basis to protect and conserve these incredibly important organisms in Indiana. He says with a nervous laugh, "Knowing about ecology, evolution, biodiversity, and the patterns and processes that underlie them is hugely important to knowing what to do to protect and conserve life on earth and our continued existence! But I don't believe in catastrophizing. It's more: 'This is what's happening, here's the information. And let's try and do something about it.'"

In Indiana, Lendemer prepared a paper about his findings and delivered it at the Indiana Academy of Science annual conference in 2018. His

Cladonia macilenta var. *bacillaris*, a fruticose lichen. Fruticose lichens are the rarest type of lichen in the BCA. *Photo credit: James Lendemer.*

paper notes the surprising number of lichens for such a small area, that more than half of these appear to be rare in the study area, the almost total absence of fruticose lichens, and the observed lack of lichen cover on many tree boles. He wrote, "These observations must be placed in the broader context that the study area comprises a significant area of intact core-forest surrounded by a dense, complex matrix of lands fragmented by agriculture, development, infrastructure, and forests managed for resource extraction. This core-forest likely functions as an essential reservoir for lichen diversity that has been substantively impacted elsewhere in the region."

* * *

As independent lichenologist Trevor Goward puts it, "I doubt there's a lichen anywhere that couldn't teach us something about where it grows: the frequency of dew fall, the strength of the wind, the depth of the winter snow, the chemistry of the soil, the places where birds like to perch." Also, ethnobotanists report that lichens have been used by traditional cultures from six continents to treat skin disease, digestive disorders, infections, and more.

What will humans do with our evolving knowledge about lichens? James Lendemer is waiting for the world to catch up with lichen intelligence. "In my short lifetime of studying them," he says, "I've seen it go from this very strict interpretation and simplistic view to this really open-ended, dynamic, interactive-based framework. It's really cool to live in a period when we cannot only appreciate and understand lichens but actually have the tools to start untangling their role."

Just because we have not understood how and why lichens matter does not mean they do not. "In our culture, we're forced to monetize and justify the existence of things whose existence really shouldn't have to be justified," says Lendemer. If we were buying the services of lichens to fix nitrogen—that is, to supply plants with a vital nutrient they cannot otherwise obtain—how much is that worth? Or, if lichens regulate humidity in a way that limits temperature extremes, how valuable is that function in the face of climate change?

Thanks to Lendemer's work and that of other national lichen experts, we may come to understand a link between lichens and our own survival. What is the consequence if lichens further diminish?

"That's the billion-dollar question," says Lendemer. "We don't have great data from before we started really changing the environment. We just have little snapshots of what used to be before industrialization. It's hard to extrapolate to answer a question like 'What would the temperature and humidity in this forest have been like a 100 years ago versus today?' At that point, the lichens would be present on every surface, covering everything, probably dripping from trees. So what happens when you lose these abundant organisms? Of course there's going to be an impact, in combination with a whole constellation of other factors."

And while there is so far no such thing as a lichen factory, once we agree that the survival of lichens matters, conversations could be had about what parts of the country to focus on, how to promote their growth, and how to revegetate areas with them. Citizens could take part in lichen-restoration parties by painting lichen growth formulas on trees—a mixture of milk, flour, yeast, spirulina, fertilizer, gelatin, and existing lichen thalli (or bodies). Imagine the state's great science minds coming together to figure out how to re-lichenize Indiana at scale to—who knows?—save our own lives.

* * *

It is poetic justice that James Lendemer's hobby is long-distance running. Near the research station in the Great Smoky Mountains where he works each year, there is a lichen he likes to check on every time he goes for a run on the nearby nine-mile-loop trail. "I look under the rock.

There it is again," he says. "*Rockefellera crossophylla*, known as old gray crosslobes." It is a small, dark-gray lichen studded with tiny orange pearls that grows on rock faces, and it is listed as endangered by the International Union for Conservation of Nature. He continues, "It's the same rare species that I've been seeing there for the last 15 years. It's delightful to see that these things are persisting—or that they do change. I have watched populations get bigger and smaller and all of that. To me, it's like visiting old friends."

By any measure, a lichen makes an excellent friend—if we can catch up to them or await them. There is human time, and there is lichen time. Their evolutionary history is spotty because they do not fossilize well, but for at least 140 million years, lichens have been omnipresent. But their sensitivity means they are all too easy to extirpate. Once gone, their comebacks require a kind of patience we humans lack. Some species grow only one millimeter per year, most actively in atmospheres with rain and fog.

Humidity plus humility. Persistence plus cooperation. All are the lessons of lichens. Are we ready to learn?

Highlights

Lichen are obligate symbionts formed between fungi and algae or cyanobacteria. A few reasons why lichens are important:

- They contribute to soil formation.

- Some fix nitrogen, making it available to plants and other organisms.

- They provide shelter for numerous arthropods, mollusks, and microbes.

- They provide food for animals and nesting material for birds.

Intact, unpolluted forests can be used as a reference to determine the approximate number of lichens that should be in a given place.

Key Findings

Dr. James Lendemer, lichenologist from the New York Botanical Garden, conducted the first comprehensive lichen survey in Indiana since 1943:

- 108 species were identified:
  - ◊ 65% were crustose (flat, grainy).
  - ◊ 29% were foliose (roseate, with cups or holes).
  - ◊ 6% were fruticose (with fingerlike upward growths).
- 49% of known Indiana species were found in the study area.

- 64 species were not reported in Indiana before.

Lendemer states, "This lichen quantity and variety in such a small area was pretty amazing. Even if those species occur in many other places in the state, it is still amazing to go into one tract of forest and find that more than half of the lichens are new reports to the state."

Each site within the BCA hosted unique species not found elsewhere in the study area. Areas outside the Low Gap Nature Preserve, within the Ecoblitz study area, were as rich as areas inside the nature preserve. Many species rare in the study area were found only outside preserve boundaries.

Lichen variety in the Ecoblitz forest was highest on ridgetops and lowest in riparian corridors. Dr. Lendemer surmises that ridgetops might provide the alternating wet and dry conditions that lichens favor, while humidity and flooding reign in creek-bank areas.

Despite the "relatively undisturbed" condition of the forest, fewer pollution-sensitive, disturbance-intolerant lichen species were found than in other undisturbed eastern hardwood forests. Lendemer surmised that the lichen community in the study area evolved to handle pollution from industrialization across the Ohio River valley. Reduced air pollution from the Clean Air Act of 1963 and 1988 amendments to the act to curb acid rain may be allowing lichen-based indicators of old growth to gradually return to "a forest that's quite old."

PART III
FOREST AS HAVEN

Emma Steele

Deciduous forests as we know them began some 33 million years ago with a great chill at the end of the Eocene. The Rocky Mountains were new, and Antarctica had separated from the rest of the continents, creating the circum-Antarctic current, which persists today as the strongest oceanic current on the planet. It was around this time that a drop in carbon dioxide sent the earth into a period of cooling that brought forth the Antarctic ice sheets, larger mammals, and broad-leaved deciduous trees as the dominant force in North American forests.

There are many ways to consider the age of a forest. The most straightforward way may be to defer to its oldest standing trees. This way is concrete and tangible, but how do you date a forest ecosystem? How do you age a structure that supersedes its individual parts? You could trace your way back to the oldest point in time when the species assemblage of an area looks like the one we know—the same types of trees, the same mix of birds, the same chorus of insects. You could consider how many generations of forest you have to trace back before the forest becomes unrecognizable. You could walk further back in time to the abstract origins of forests: the first rudimentary tree canopy on the earth. Though the deciduous forests that rose after the Eocene would be altered for millions of years to come by the ebb and flow of ice ages, this is the point when the global deciduous forest ecosystem began to take a recognizable shape. In the centuries following the most recent ice age, North American deciduous forests continued on the dynamic path of evolution. Tree species

dominated, subsided, then dominated again, the forest bending to the will of an ever-shifting global climate. Landscape-level transformation is how the forest ecosystem survives.

No matter the moment chosen to represent the metaphysical dawn of the eastern hardwoods, it is beyond doubt that the ecosystem existed in its contemporary form in Indiana for hundreds of years relatively unchanged until European colonizers arrived to begin the era of aggressive timbering, burning, clearing, and draining. Well before that, however, as the deciduous forests waxed and waned across the continent, retreating from glaciers and then stretching out again in their absence, animals evolved within each generation of forest, as tightly knit into the ecosystem as the trees themselves. Species slowly morphed to time their emergence from hibernation to that of their prey or the bloom of their food plants. They evolved camouflage to mimic a tree species' bark or blend into leaf litter. They adapted their metabolism to specialize on the sustenance available in the forest. They bestowed upon their young instinctive paths of migration. Animals of the eastern hardwood forests are not bound to any forest. They are bound to this forest.

In this third section, we dance along the ribbons of evolutionary ties with some of the forest's most mobile canopy habitants. Ecoblitz bird team volunteer Karen Smith guides us through the Morgan-Monroe/ Yellowwood Back Country Area (BCA) with the awe of a citizen scientist. With career birder David Rupp, we hunt for one of the forest's most elusive birds, the cerulean warbler, which migrates thousands of miles and across the Gulf of Mexico to return to the eastern hardwoods of Indiana to nest each year. Naturalist Angie Dämm focuses our minds on what the future holds for Indiana's forests and the birds that evolved to rely on them. Bat biologist Dale Sparks turns the clock to the dead of night with a discussion of Indiana's remarkable flying mammals, the imperiled bat species surviving in the BCA. Finally, in dialogue with Ecoblitz coordinator Samantha Buran, we interrogate humanity's relationship with the forests that took root in Indiana far before we did.

Twinleaf (*Jeffersonia diphylla*) has white flowers about one inch across that quickly mature into leathery, pear-shaped capsules that turn from green to yellow-green as they mature. A suture near the top opens like a hinged lid when the capsule is ripe to release oblong, shiny brown seeds that are dispersed by ants. *Photo credit: Kevin Tungesvick.*

Karen Smith. *Photo
credit: Karen Smith.*

7. ESSAY: LETTERS FROM THE BACK COUNTRY

An Amateur's Passion

Karen Smith

The word *amateur* is borrowed from French and rooted in the Latin *amātor*, meaning "lover, enthusiastic admirer, devotee." In this sense, I have been an amateur of nature all my life, but I trace my special interest in forest ecology and preservation to my 2007 internship at the Highlands Nature Sanctuary/Arc of Appalachia Preserve System in southern Ohio. Of my wide-ranging duties, I especially enjoyed leading weekend visitors on interpretive nature hikes: through majestic beech-maple climax forest; along dolomitic cliffs harboring rare, white-flowering *Sullivantia sullivantii*; and past the "Seven Caves," a former tourist attraction being restored as habitat for hibernating bats, salamanders, and other sensitive species. I think gratefully of the sanctuary staff and associates who shared with us interns their reverent appreciation and intimate knowledge of local plants and animals—the truly amazing biodiversity resulting from a confluence of glacial till plains, the Appalachian Plateau, and the Kentucky Bluegrass region.

Fast-forward to 2014: When I learned that the Indiana Forest Alliance (IFA) was seeking volunteers for a comprehensive survey of flora and fauna in the Morgan-Monroe/Yellowwood Back Country Area (BCA), I was eager to sign up. I had previously enjoyed IFA-sponsored hikes in various southern and central Indiana forests, but here was a not-to-be-missed opportunity to hone my plant identification skills while participating in major fieldwork with botanists, biologists, and other experts. My subsequent involvement in the BCA Ecoblitz surveys over the next four years stands out in my memory and features prominently in correspondence with family and friends. All told, I went out on 15 surveys—10 with the vascular plant team and 5 with bird teams, including those focused on cerulean warblers in 2017.

Ecoblitz plant team, September 13, 2015, featuring (*left to right*) Kevin Weinburg, Audrey Moore, Steven Dunbar, and David Mow. *Photo credit: Karen Smith.*

Sunday, June 8, 2014, was my first day volunteering and the second day of Ecoblitz project surveys. Since I do not own a car, Collin Hobbs, assistant professor of biology at Huntington University, who was heading up the plant and fungi team, kindly gave me a ride from Bloomington to our base camp at the Weaver Plantation on Low Gap Road. There we met fellow team members and determined which of the six survey zones we would be working in. Because several teams were present for this Ecoblitz kickoff, there were tents and chairs set up for the lunch break, stations for cleaning off our boots (to prevent the spread of invasive species), and even portable restrooms. What luxury! We also enjoyed plentiful food and beverages provided by staff and volunteers, including some scrumptious and colorful veggie wraps with hummus.

In a letter to a friend written June 12, I described this initial plant team foray: "We divided into two groups and each covered a zone in the Back Country Area. Our group cataloged over 100 species in the two and a half hours that we were out hiking." In another letter dated June 18, I remarked, "Apparently this is the first such survey to be conducted in an Indiana state forest, which seems almost incredible to me. There are other groups cataloging mammals, birds, fish, amphibians, etc. It's sort of a pioneering event."

That first weekend, the two plant teams recorded a total of 246 species!

Looking back on the three years I surveyed with the plant team, I remember several encounters with challenging terrain—steep and slippery slopes, thick vegetation, fallen trees to clamber over—along with easy comradery, plenty of humorous moments, and the rich diversity of BCA flora. For me, scanning the forest for species not yet included on the survey list had the thrill of a treasure hunt. For example, during our last outing of 2015 (September 13), I noticed a pale, leafless stalk with small green flowers, purple tinged, rising from the leaf litter right behind team member David Mow's shoe. I warned him not to step backward. As I related in a letter to my family, "I didn't know exactly what it was, but I knew it was *something*." Of course, David, a naturalist and curator of the herbarium at the Brown County State Park Nature Center, and team member Steve Dunbar, with the Indiana Native Plant Society, recognized the plant in question as an autumn coralroot orchid (*Corallorhiza odontorhiza*). This was a species we had not yet documented in zone 2 and, for me, an exciting find.

Indeed, prior to my Ecoblitz involvement, I was unaware that Indiana is home to so many native orchids—more than 40 species, several of which I got to admire for the first time on our hikes, including the glossy-leaved purple twayblade (*Liparis liliifolia*). After a survey on May 31, 2015, I noted in a letter, "I spotted a single orchid which turned out to be a twayblade orchid, something we hadn't yet seen in Zone 4." I later added, "My only disappointment was not seeing a timber rattlesnake. Two other groups that have gone out recently have spotted them. Otherwise, an excellent outing."

It was also near the end of this hike that I noticed a tall, solitary plant with a smooth stem and white umbellate flowers growing along the trail, one I knew from description and photos but had never seen in person. "*Cicuta maculata*," I announced, "the most toxic plant in North America." I then looked at David, who smiled and nodded, confirming the identification. Do most people get excited about a "noxious" native plant like water hemlock? Maybe not, but it certainly made *my* day.

In 2016, I went out once with the bird team and twice with the vascular plant team. Following the latter's July 10 survey, I shared with a friend, "I got some good pictures of the downy rattlesnake-plantain orchid that we spotted. It was in flower, but it's the leaves that are really spectacular. . . . I think the white veining on the leaves is so striking. What a weird name, though. I've read that the Native Americans used the plant to treat snakebite, burns, and other ailments."

Twayblade.
Photo credit:
Kevin Tungesvick.

The plant team wrapped up its BCA surveys in 2016, so in 2017 I hiked out four times with bird teams to document cerulean warblers and their nesting activity in the area. Unlike the birds, I am not really a morning person; however, those Sundays I was up and ready to meet my ride as early as 5:45 a.m., fortified with coffee.

For the May 22 survey, local bird expert David Rupp coached us on what to listen and look for: distinctive buzzy songs and calls and a small cuplike nest atop a branch, often high up in the canopy. We would typically spread out and stand in one spot, craning our necks, hoping to zoom in on a well-camouflaged nest with the aid of binoculars. I also joined the knowledgeable Angie Dämm for three surveys. She brought a big scope that enabled excellent views of these tiny warblers, the males especially attractive with their blue-and-white upperparts, black "necklace," and streaking. As I enthused to a fellow bird lover, "We had wonderful views of females sitting on the nests and even of the nestlings. I saw one tiny

Left, Downy rattlesnake plantain orchid, named for the pattern on its leaves. *Photo credit: Karen Smith.*

Below, Downy rattlesnake plantain orchid flower stalk. *Photo credit: Karen Smith.*

Female cerulean warbler on nest in an American basswood. *Photo credit: David Rupp, IndiGo Birding Nature Tours.*

face peeking over the edge of a nest. . . . The nests are probably 80 or 90 feet up in the trees."

Since completion of the 2014–2017 survey project, I have had additional opportunities to participate in Ecoblitz bird team surveys in the Combs Creek Upper Watershed in Hoosier National Forest. On my own, I enjoy wandering the trails in Griffy Lake Nature Preserve in Bloomington, Indiana, a relatively secluded place to immerse myself in forest sights and sounds and view the succession of wildflowers from season to season. For example, on one late April hike, I entered a ravine to find a meandering display of dwarf larkspur (*Delphinium tricorne*), the flower clusters ranging in color from white to lavender and deep purple. Gorgeous! In addition, my Ecoblitz experience has motivated my ongoing study of forest plants, including memorization of the scientific (Latin) names for all 175 flowering species highlighted in Michael A. Homoya's *Wildflowers and Ferns of Indiana Forests: A Field Guide* (2012). The ferns are next . . .

Above all, my hope is that ongoing study and analysis of published results from the Morgan-Monroe/Yellowwood BCA surveys will lead to fuller awareness that all forest life—from nestlings to 200-year-old trees—persists and thrives in complex communities of mutual support; that the inherent wisdom of biological processes far surpasses our

species' shortsighted attempts to manage and control; and that we humans, in order to survive and flourish, must remember our own place within the natural world and rejoin its conversation.

May our teams' collective work documenting the biological richness of this state forestland inspire deeper appreciation of its beauty and further efforts to protect its wholeness.

Ferns under tulip poplar in the Back Country Area. *Photo credit: Jeff Stant.*

Ecoblitz bird team leader David Rupp. *Photo credit: David Rupp.*

8. ESSAY: RARE CERULEAN WARBLERS RAISE YOUNG ALONG HONEY CREEK

David Rupp

Once a common nesting bird throughout the Ohio and Mississippi River basins and the mature forests of eastern North America, cerulean warblers are now rarer than needles in haystacks due in part to habitat loss. Their populations have declined 63% in the last 50 years, making the cerulean warbler a species of concern in eastern forests, an endangered species in Indiana, and the focus of numerous forest management studies.

Cerulean warblers are tiny, weighing 8–10 grams (about the same as two nickels). These birds are beautiful—the male is sky blue with a white belly and blue necklace, and the female is a light greenish yellow that makes her difficult to spot in a leafy forest. Ceruleans favor large tracts of forest with mature trees and openings in the canopy. As neotropical migrants, they spend their winters in the Andes Mountains of South America. Upon arrival in the U.S. each April, they spend the majority of the next three to four months high in the canopy of remote, contiguous forests before returning again to the tropics in late summer.

Our team's assignment, as requested by the Indiana Forest Alliance (IFA), was to find these birds and document their use of the Honey Creek Ecoblitz area during the spring and summer of 2016 and 2017. It took a village—birders, nature enthusiasts, photographers, and IFA supporters—to survey the area. It also takes a trained ear to hear the variations in the songs and calls that a pair of ceruleans use to communicate while they court, build their nest, and raise their offspring. And it took time . . . field technician Angie Dämm and I combined to spend 52 days in 2017 out in the elements peering into the canopy searching for and monitoring nests.

Over the course of three field seasons (2015–2017) that I spent in this remote section of the Morgan-Monroe/Yellowwood State Forest, I became well versed in the topography of the landscape, the easy (and the

One of many male cerulean warblers seen in territories clustered in the southwestern portion of the Ecoblitz area. *Photo credit: Scott Evans.*

difficult) routes from one place to another, and the seasonality of the natural events occurring in the forest. The succession of the spring wildflowers often distracted me from the birds as I traipsed off trail. I delighted in the arrival of bird species that had spent the winter in the tropics, now full of raging hormones and ready to defend their preferred nesting territories against their neighbors. And I learned to navigate steep ravines and flooded creek beds after big rains. This truly is a wild area.

We were excited to learn how cerulean warblers were distributed in this natural landscape. Our survey strategy included locating territorial males by sight or sound, finding the females associated with the males, and trying to track them back to a potential nest site. A territory is an area that a bird defends because it contains the resources necessary for survival and reproduction. A male bird sings to help announce to his neighbors that he has claimed a territory . . . and to attract a mate! Cerulean warbler songs are buzzy and bouncy, usually increasing in speed as the phrase rises in pitch at the end. Females will stay in contact with their partners by giving a metallic *zeet* call in response. We recorded GPS points where we consistently found males singing and confirmed the presence of females. We listened for irregularities in male song and female response calls to help us key in on mated pairs, thus upping our

Forest as Haven

chances of finding nesting behavior. We made special note of any encounter between a male and a female or any nest-building behavior.

The territories we found were clustered in the southwest corner of the Ecoblitz survey area—largely riparian bottomlands along Honey Creek and the mesic slopes directly adjacent to them. Most of the Ecoblitz area, particularly the uplands to the north and east, did not have any cerulean warblers present. In 2017, we estimated that there were 20–25 territorial males claiming areas along the drainages and low slopes ranging from the Low Gap parking lot to the heart of the Ecoblitz area. These clustered territories are to be expected; for reasons unknown, ceruleans usually nest close together. Our search efforts paid off, too, as we found five cerulean nests in 2016 and two more in 2017. The well-camouflaged nests are works of art and science, woven out of thin strips of bark, grass, and spiderwebs and placed on top of forks on horizontal branches with leaves strategically protecting the nest from the elements above.

Each year had its own puzzle. In the middle of May 2016, we revisited the five nests that we had found and discovered that three of them had disappeared and two had been abandoned. It was a good reminder that nests fail more often than not and that constant vigilance would be needed to come to some conclusion about what had happened. So,

The bird team at work with a spotting scope in the Honey Creek area. *Photo credit: David Rupp.*

Female cerulean warbler feeding fledglings in a nest in the Ecoblitz area. *Photo credit: Angie Dämm.*

in 2017, when we found nests, we monitored them quite closely. It was good that we did, because one of the nests where we had observed the cerulean adults feeding their newborn chicks was suddenly empty on June 12, days before the young ones should have been ready to fledge. We surmised that a larger bird (maybe a blue jay or red-bellied woodpecker) had preyed on the chicks.

Then something fascinating happened. The female systematically dismantled this empty nest over the course of three days and rebuilt it in another white oak about 50 feet from the original nest. By June 27, she was brooding another clutch of baby ceruleans. As best we could tell, she and her partner successfully raised this clutch to the point of fledging. In a basswood tree further up the creek, we also monitored another cerulean family to the point that the babies fledged the nest.

While we did not get to witness the actual fledging event at any of the nests we monitored, we did find numerous cerulean family units in the days and weeks after the young had left the nests. Most of these observations would start with our team finding an adult with a caterpillar; it would soon fly down into the underbrush to feed and hush a begging young bird. On one occasion, a fledgling even popped out of the shadows and seemed to pose for a photo! We hypothesize that cerulean parents are attracted to wide creek basins for the lush understory that effectively hides the young ones after they fledge the nest.

The uniqueness of this thriving cerulean warbler population is certainly worth noting. Forest tracts like this one—mature, diverse, and wild—can contain clusters of ceruleans, but not all of them do.

Forest as Haven

The Morgan-Monroe/Yellowwood Back Country Area appears to be ideal habitat for this tiny warbler to live out its reproductive destiny, from high in the hardwood canopy to the cover of the creek-side understory below.

Key Findings

We identified 79 species of birds, including scarlet tanager, summer tanager, red-eyed vireo, yellow-throated vireo, Acadian flycatcher, wood thrush, Louisiana waterthrush, ovenbird, Kentucky warbler, and four different woodpeckers, as well as the following state-listed species.

- State endangered:
  ◊ Cerulean warbler (*Dendroica cerulea*)
  ◊ Species of special concern:
  ◊ Worm-eating warbler (*Helmitheros vermivorum*)
  ◊ Hooded warbler (*Setophaga citrina*)
  ◊ Black-and-white warbler (*Mniotilta varia*)
  ◊ Whip-poor-will (*Antrostomus vociferous*)

Nesting success was documented in the following forest birds:

- Cerulean warbler (state endangered)

- Worm-eating warbler (species of special concern, abundant in Ecoblitz area)

- Hooded warbler (species of special concern)

- Louisiana waterthrush

- Blue-gray gnatcatcher

- Ovenbird

- Wood thrush

- Acadian flycatcher

- Scarlet tanager

- Blue-winged warbler

- Yellowthroat

Angie Dämm. *Photo credit: Angie Dämm.*

9. UP CLOSE: ANGIE DÄMM

Young Birder in an Old Forest

Emma Steele

The birder's day begins before dawn. Every spring, when millions of birds are making journeys of unfathomable lengths across oceans and continents, birders across the country are setting alarms for four in the morning and trekking through fields and forests to witness the incredible show of the spring migration.

For Angie Dämm, peeling herself out of bed and bundling up for the dark drive from her home in Bloomington, Indiana, to the Morgan-Monroe/Yellowwood Back Country Area (BCA) survey site was anything but a hassle. She made this trek at least four days per week from April through July in 2017 to find state endangered cerulean warblers, track them through the forest, and document their nesting and fledging activities as a field technician for the Ecoblitz bird team. Layered up with jackets and rain gear to protect her from the chilly morning dew, Dämm arrived at the BCA armed with binoculars and bright-eyed excitement for what the day would bring at such an early hour that most of the residents in her hometown, a college town, had yet to open their eyes.

As the first dim glow of sunrise breaks over the horizon in the forest, the sounds of night are replaced by overlapping chips and trills, seemingly instantaneously. Like a switch has been flipped, an unbelievable amount of life seems to appear out of thin air. The intense peak of bird activity during the earliest hours of sunlight makes this window one of the best times for birding. Species that hunker down during the hotter parts of the day can be spotted bouncing across the forest floor. Species that are hard to spot, like the tiny ovenbird on the forest floor or cerulean warbler high in the canopy, are singing with a frequency and vigor that are unmatched at other times of the day.

"Witnessing the forest waking up each morning—the changing light and color, little bits of fog, the morning chorus of birdsong, echoes of thrushes when things got still, and absolute showers of pollen stirred up when a group of us would walk through a tall area of vegetation where it had settled—was absolutely a gift every moment," Dämm recalls. "We'd

119

relocate corners of impressive spiderwebs as we walked the trails. Having the permit for the study meant we were all good to thoughtfully venture off trail, which is not something you get to do often. It was exciting, and it felt very satisfying to learn the landmarks and topography of the study area so intimately and know exactly where I needed to go or hadn't been and could still search."

When Dämm talks about her time combing through the BCA looking for cerulean warblers with the bird team, her passion for the natural world shines through. It comes as no surprise that she was one of the most active Ecoblitz participants during the 2017 bird survey of the BCA. After Dämm finished college, she had hoped to transition into professional biological fieldwork, but finding a good fit proved hard. At the same time that Dämm was looking for her next step after moving to Bloomington for her husband's job, she met David Rupp, owner of IndiGo Birding Nature Tours, during a local birding event. David was the leading bird expert on the Ecoblitz team, and this time, everything was right for Dämm to say yes to heading into the field as an Ecoblitz survey technician.

With David and the rest of the bird team, Dämm spent weeks marching through the BCA and meticulously cataloging the movements of the cerulean warbler and the overall wealth of bird species living in the forest. The team recorded species diversity, individual species abundance, nesting and fledging, courtship displays, and territory fights. Dämm spent many more hours coming back to locations where she and the rest of the bird team had located male cerulean warblers singing and defending their territories. Exerting much effort and patience, staring upward, scanning the canopy—sometimes with the help of David Rupp and a few other team members and sometimes alone—Dämm often located the females along the boundaries of two territories contested by males, observed male-female courtship behaviors, and then watched the nest building and arrival of nestlings, which in some cases would survive to fledge and, in others, might disappear due to storms or predation. From late June through mid-July, the bird team found cerulean fledglings in six instances, usually foraging in lush understory with their parents near the main branch or East Fork of Honey Creek. As spring progressed into summer, the bird team was continually welcomed into the BCA by the reverberant morning chorus of birdsong. Beneath this vibrant display of life, however, a hard truth lurked: the skies are emptier than they once were.

A landmark study published in 2019 made waves in the conservation community when it revealed that North America alone has lost three billion birds since 1970, a figure that equates to the disappearance of one in every four birds in less than 50 years. If that number alone was not damning enough, the study documented declines in bird species across all North American ecosystems and of the most common and historically abundant species, like the white-throated sparrow, which has lost 93 million individual birds alone. The severity of this widespread disappearance points to a chilling conclusion: our ecosystems are being degraded to a point at which they can no longer support their most common, hardy species.

For younger people, like Dämm, the vanishing of the earth's wildlife is nearly impossible to grasp in its totality. Biodiversity has been declining since before any of the millennials or Gen Zers were born. This creates what is known as shifting baseline syndrome—the phenomenon in which younger generations think of the degraded conditions they grew up with as the norm. They are more accepting of lower environmental standards because they lack the memory or experience of what the world was like when the baseline was higher. For example, North American children born in 2020 may see empty skies as normal, even though older generations now consider this a shocking revelation of environmental destruction. Shifting baseline syndrome, also known as "environmental generational amnesia," creates an enormous barrier to engaging younger generations in the fight against biodiversity decline. Simply put, it is hard to get people to miss something they never knew.

Reflecting on these grave reports of global biodiversity loss, Dämm says, "People protect what they love, and love what they know." It is a beautifully succinct description of how shifting baseline syndrome and the ever-growing disconnect between society and the land that sustains us are feeding into the progressive butchery of American nature.

Dämm herself is a glowing example of what it looks like for older generations to pass the torch on to their children and instill a reverence for the natural world. She was raised birding alongside her father—a man who can remember a world with millions more birds than his daughter ever knew. Now, when Dämm speaks about the BCA, you can sense an undercurrent that resists the normalization of a decayed natural world. It is a force that feels akin to a bite of sweet fruit, the perfectly humid moment before rain, or a mother describing her child. It is an overflow of all that life is made of: sugar, water, and love.

Ultimately, love is why Dämm said yes to the strenuous demands of the Ecoblitz bird surveys. It was her love for being in the woods, for the plants and trees themselves—a love for the birds, the science, and what conservation means in the context of today's world—that coaxed her into the old forest of the BCA week after hot summer week. For Dämm, conservation means protecting the wilderness she has loved since childhood. For the world, it means halting the greatest threat to life on earth since the extinction of the dinosaurs.

Among the bird team's goals was to identify at-risk bird species living in the BCA, particularly during the spring and summer months, when migratory species return to North America to nest from their winter grounds in South and Central America. The incredible feat of identifying and documenting successful cerulean warbler nests was one of the highlights from the team's surveys. Adult cerulean warblers average just over four inches long—about the length of your palm. They stay high in the leafy canopy, sometimes nesting more than 100 feet above ground. Because they are so difficult to spot, a primary method of identification is by their trilling, high-pitched song. Dämm, though an experienced birder, noted the difficulty of tracking this species in the BCA.

"Before we determined their territories, one of the hardest parts was the 'tricky' northern parulas, which can sing a very similar song—albeit a bit more buzzy," she says. "In general, even ceruleans have some variation in their vocalizations. We became familiar with certain individuals, as we observed them in their territories or spent time where those territories were still being determined or overlapped. Keeping in mind that there was another kind of bird that has a similar song at times, we'd have to take some time to keep listening or look up and wait for a good view to be sure what species we were hearing. There was also a learning curve when it came to distinguishing the chip notes—quick, single syllable calls—of cerulean females versus other birds.

"Finding nests of cerulean warblers is especially challenging," she continues, "because they are masters of hiding their tiny nests perfectly in the crook of branches or along a branch and shaded by leaves. They have very specific preferences for where they build a nest, and they are very good at being stealthy when they come or go to avoid drawing the attention of other creatures. They even vocalize more quietly or stop entirely when they are near the nest to protect its location."

The documentation of cerulean warblers in the BCA underscored the determination and skill of the Ecoblitz bird team and also gave key insights into the forest itself. Cerulean warblers are picky nesters that overwhelmingly prefer large, mature trees in deep, undisturbed forest to fledge their young. Pressure from development, agriculture, and logging on Indiana's historical forestland over the past two centuries has pushed undisturbed old-forest habitat toward its own type of extinction. The presence of successful cerulean warbler nests in the BCA indicates that, while the great majority of Indiana's land now appears, to deep forest species, a barren and unforgiving shadow of the ancient forest that used to exist, the BCA is a place where these creatures can find refuge.

The presence of these striking, delicate warblers speaks volumes about the quality of the forest, but they are only one of many bird species that echo calls through the BCA every morning. While the cerulean

warbler's fate as a species is intrinsically tied to the fate of our forests, so is the fate of thousands of other species that evolved exclusively in the ancient eastern hardwood forest that once blanketed nine-tenths of Indiana's acreage.

Dämm writes, "When you search for cerulean warbler nests, you also find all kinds of other nests: American redstarts, Northern parulas, fly-catchers, indigo buntings, broad-winged hawks, and so many others . . . all those other puzzle pieces that make up the whole of the forest. There were the familiar paths we'd take to get to certain cerulean territories, and we got familiar with 'those cardinals' or 'that feisty indigo bunting after the creek crossing.'"

Some 79 bird species were documented in the Ecoblitz survey area by the bird team in the spring and early summer months of 2016 before the team turned its focus to cerulean warblers. These species included the cerulean warbler and 10 other species of migratory warblers, as well as numerous at-risk or declining species, such as the state-listed worm-eating, hooded, and black-and-white warblers and the eastern whip-poor-will. The value of recording the success of a species in danger of extinction in Indiana—the cerulean warbler, in this case—cannot be understated. For such species that are declining due to habitat loss, identifying key habitat where the species is having success should enable land managers

The American redstart was a frequent sighting in the Ecoblitz area. *Photo credit: Scott Evans.*

The worm-eating warbler, a state species of special concern, is prolific across the Ecoblitz area. The bird team identified 22 worm-eating warblers in a single trek through one hollow in 2015. *Photo credit: Scott Evans.*

to protect those areas from degradation. Habitat that supports listed species can receive legal protections from the federal government under the Endangered Species Act or under state laws that prevent harmful activities like development and logging that could further compromise the habitat. But in this era when biodiversity is declining so widely and rapidly, protections originally established on the premise that wildlife extinctions would be rare and extraordinary events simply are not adequate.

The truth is that many of the 79 species identified by the Ecoblitz bird team not currently listed as at-risk species are likely represented in the three billion birds North America has lost since 1970. Regulatory protection that runs on a species-by-species basis has delayed the outright extinction of many creatures, but it has been unable to slow the jarring collapse of wildlife populations across the board. Addressing biodiversity loss on an individual-species basis is itself inherently flawed. It attempts to heal a gunshot by treating the pain but letting the wound fester. Species do not function as individuals that can be removed from their whole.

Each species is inseparably bound to another, a single brush stroke in a landscape-level ecological portrait. Until the wound is treated by confronting the drivers of habitat loss and climate change, endangered species lists will continue to grow at staggering rates, regardless of current regulatory measures. To repopulate the skies with cerulean warblers, the entire ecosystem on which the warbler depends—from the underground fungi that break down nutrients for the trees birds need to nest in to the

Forest as Haven

The black-and-white warbler, another state species of special concern, is found in the Ecoblitz area. *Photo credit: IFA.*

weevils they eat and the hawks that prey on the warblers themselves—must be intact. For the ecosystem to be intact, entire swaths of land, thousands upon thousands of acres, must be intentionally preserved to exist as that ecosystem in perpetuity.

"Indiana has much less forest than it did historically, and a lot has changed in the forests that are left, but even still, they are home to the sum of all the natural and geologic history of our area . . . and human history!" Dämm says. "These forests are so rich and beautiful, because they have built on the lives of every past tree and plant and bird and animal and every soaking rainstorm and frozen winter and heavy summer. Some species, like the moths endemic to only this forest, literally came from this very bit of earth."

"The ecosystem has persisted, because all its parts have continuously been present, interacting and stabilizing each other and the land itself," she says. "All the parts belong, coexist, live and die, react, use, care for, and thrive together. We're so lucky to have the plant and animal biodiversity that exists in Indiana, and to live and spend time in a place with such obvious and beautiful seasons. You can see the greater purpose of each piece. It's rare and unique, valuable, and more than worth protecting."

The BCA is one of the only places left in Indiana where an old, expansive forest stands relatively undisturbed. Left to heal and return to the ancient rhythm of forests millennia ago, it has blossomed into a natural haven unmatched by anything made by humans, a guiding light on a path forward from unprecedented loss.

Dale Sparks. *Photo credit: Dale Sparks.*

10. Q AND A: DALE SPARKS, PH.D.

Chasing Bats in the BCA

Emma Steele

As the sky blooms orange in the evening hours, the sun over the Morgan-Monroe/Yellowwood Back Country Area (BCA) is replaced by the pale rocky moon, and the birds quietly hunker down into the crevices of the forest as they wait for tomorrow's dawn. During these transitional hours between day and night, birdsong is replaced by the croaks and chirps of the forest's night shift. For Dr. Dale Sparks, a career biologist and principal scientist at an Ohio-based environmental consulting company, Environmental Solutions & Innovations Inc. (ESI), bats are the star of the show.

Sparks "got the bat bug" early in his academic career when he took a summer job as an assistant zoologist with the Kentucky Nature Preserves Commission during his undergraduate years at Murray State University. The position entailed surveying the Jackson Purchase region west of the Tennessee River. "This area is geographically and geologically part of the Gulf Coastal Plain that extends all the way up the Mississippi River from New Orleans," says Sparks. "It's this weird area where you've got a wide variety of animal and plant species that are typically associated with Louisiana, Mississippi, Arkansas, and yet they appear in western Kentucky." Sparks worked to locate protected species of bats, especially Indiana bats, as well as northern long-eared bats, evening bats, and southeastern bats, which typically are not found in other parts of the state.

After finishing his undergraduate degree in wildlife management, Sparks earned a master's degree in ecology at Fort Hays State University in Kansas and then a Ph.D. in ecology from Indiana State University in 2002 with a thesis that evaluated the impacts of urbanization on bats. In 2016–2017, Sparks oversaw the Ecoblitz bat team during the search for rare and at-risk species in the BCA. With a mix of Indiana Forest Alliance (IFA) staff, citizen volunteers, and biologists from ESI, the team spent weeks combing through the midnight forest to catalog a version of the landscape few people get a chance to experience.

Surveying for nocturnal species has all the challenges of surveying during the day—bushwhacking in unfamiliar terrain, hiking to remote survey sites with cumbersome equipment on your back, fighting the humid heat of southern Indiana summer—with the extra factor of near blindness. If you live in a city, it is easy to forget how dark the world can be. Surveying the BCA at night is a reminder. Every summer, bat biologists engage in bat surveys for clients ranging from construction companies to the oil and gas industry to nonprofit organizations like IFA. To these researchers, the cloak of nighttime becomes a second, familiar home.

The night yielded an active community of bats. The Ecoblitz bat team identified eight species of bats in the BCA, including four species that are listed as federally endangered or in the process of being listed or assessed for this designation. Most notably, the team netted two federally endangered Indiana bats and tracked them both back to maternity roosts in the BCA. Additionally, the team netted two lactating female northern long-eared bats, then listed as federally threatened and now federally endangered, and a juvenile male tricolored bat, a species proposed for federal endangered status by the U.S. Fish and Wildlife Service (USFWS) at the time of this writing. Acoustic data also indicated the presence of state endangered little brown bats and evening bats in the Ecoblitz forest. The little brown bat is also undergoing status assessment by the USFWS for federal endangered listing.

While the fungal disease white-nose syndrome (WNS) has been a major driver for the catastrophic collapse of bat populations across multiple species—including the northern long-eared bat, little brown bat, tricolored bat, and, to a lesser extent, Indiana bat—wind farms, habitat loss, and the slow rate of reproduction for many bat species are compounding factors. Most bat species only produce one offspring per year. If a pregnant bat is stricken by WNS or unable to find summer roosting habitat, she can lose her pup, and the chance to add to the new generation of bats is lost for another year. Finding all these imperiled species in the BCA in 2017 well after their populations began to plummet from WNS underscores the importance of this forest as habitat for these flying mammals, symbols of the wild forests of the eastern U.S. Several of the species were found successfully reproducing in this forest. The following discussion with Dr. Sparks highlights the delicate relationship between bats and their forest habitat.

STEELE There are two main options when it comes to surveying for bats: acoustic monitoring and netting. The monitoring in the BCA included both of these approaches. Why?

One of two lactating female northern long-eared bats (NLEBs) caught in the Ecoblitz area in 2016 and 2017. The presence of the females indicates that these animals have been using this deep forest for maternity roosting while their numbers have plummeted by more than 90% across the state from the disease white-nose syndrome. The status of NLEBs was changed from threatened to federally endangered in 2022, making the protection of maternity roosts a top priority for the survival of this species. *Photo credit: IFA.*

SPARKS Yes. Most of the surveys we do are presence/absence surveys for the purpose of environmental compliance, so companies will hire us [ESI] to go out and determine if protected bats occur in the area where they're looking at doing some kind of a project—and the vast majority of those are, of course, development projects, whether that's a transmission line for electricity, natural gas pipeline, or even liquid product lines, all the way to land development projects like neighborhoods. Those surveys can be done with either acoustic bat detectors, or you can go out and net. For most of my time both in academia and consulting, I have really chafed at the idea that you have to use one approach or the other. Both of these tools have real strengths and real weaknesses. They do much better when they're used in combination, and they tend to fill each other's gaps relatively well.

First, looking at acoustic monitoring, when you run an acoustic bat detector, you capture the sound of every single bat that flies past the microphone. The issue we deal with is that bats can sound a lot alike. To demonstrate what I mean, let's compare this to birds. They are relatively easy to identify by their calls because those calls specifically evolved for the purpose of species recognition. When a male bird calls, he is advertising what species of bird he is to both females and to males in surrounding territories. On the other hand, the bat calls we're looking at with acoustic monitoring evolved as echolocation to help bats find their way through the environment and find prey. There wasn't the pressure for calls to end up as unique as bird calls. There's an enormous amount of variables that can complicate these analyses, so we use computer analysis. Our software is able to identify the species most likely to have produced the call.

At the end of the day, acoustics allow you to get information about all of the bats that are flying through your area, as well as indicators of species abundance and where these species are located. Another plus that comes with acoustic monitoring is that one person can run multiple acoustic bat detectors on their own every day, versus only one net site. Acoustic monitoring gives you a huge opportunity to see the big picture of what's out there. It's like a big dragnet.

Conversely, when you go out there to net, bats can "see" and avoid the nets, so you may have bats flying through the area but never catch them in your net. A second challenge with netting: you have to physically go over to your net every few minutes to check for bats with a flashlight, carefully remove any bats from the net, and then spend time handling the bat to make your notes and identify the species. There's always a risk of injury and stress to the animal. We are also wary of spreading disease among the bats we handle, particularly now with COVID, which was originally thought of as a bat disease. We already have white-nose syndrome that has hit North American bat populations hard, so we're very nervous about introducing another disease.

Finally, another challenge with netting comes if you've got multiple bats in the net all at once. If you have ten bats in your net, which can happen, you may have one escape while you're getting the others out. You've got the opportunity to miss individuals. You also have the tendency with netting to simply get the most common bats in the immediate area. After all, you're not sampling a vast area like you would with a microphone during acoustic monitoring.

Once we catch something in the net, however, we can verify its identity and check its health. We can take photos of the bat and, in some cases, collect DNA, which comes from fecal material. The

Researcher removes bat from mist net. *Photo credit: IFA.*

certainty of what you have in your hand is much greater with netting. You can also do things like place a radio tag on the bat to see where it goes after you release it.

We used both of those techniques in the BCA, because they fit so well together. The approach we used in the Ecoblitz was to place acoustic bat detectors in advance of the netting and use the data from the bat detectors to identify the best areas for netting.

STEELE Your survey turned up several exciting finds in the BCA, including a maternity roost of the federally endangered Indiana bat. Can you tell me about the process of finding that maternity roost?

SPARKS When we capture a species of interest, the typical process is to use surgical glue to attach a tiny transmitter—only about half the weight of a thumbtack—to the bat's back, which we use to track the

Researcher weighs bat in a paper bag. The bag keeps the bat snug and secure. *Photo credit: IFA.*

bat for several days after netting. The glue is designed to wear off in about a week or so, but in the hot, humid conditions of the Indiana summer, transmitters tend to be lost quickly. It's not unusual to have one that falls off after three or four days.

So, we'll catch the bat late at night and glue the transmitter to it. Then, we take the bat to a tree, where we let it climb up the trunk and fly away. Once the bat is loose, we take the telemetry gear to do a quick check to make sure that everything is working and get some information about the direction the bat flew off in. In most cases, what these bats do is fly a little distance away and then take a half hour or so to try to chew that thing off their back. Eventually, they either give up or get accustomed to it and fly away.

As early as possible the next day, the biologists get out there to track the bat. The initial search is usually done from nearby roads in a vehicle, because we can cover a big area. We usually have what's called a whip antenna on top of the truck and somebody with a directional antenna that will lean out the window of the truck to search for the transmitter's signal. If things go well, you'll start getting some beeps with the directional antenna, which gives you an idea of where to look for the bat. After that initial search, we head to some high ground, remeasure the signal, move a bit, measure the direction of the signal again, and so on. We do this to get several readings. After that, we plot the signal readings on a map and use triangulation to find where the readings overlap. The middle of this overlap is the area where your bat is.

At this point, we have to find reasonable access to the area identified during the triangulation process so we can hike into the forest with the telemetry equipment to search for the bat. In theory, the bat should be just right there, but typically what happens is that you have to do some serious searching. Especially in an area like the BCA that doesn't have many accessible roads, it can be a challenge to narrow down the search area during the initial readings. On top of that, the signal from the tags attached to the back of the bat are relatively weak, so once you start walking into the forest, you can lose the signal pretty easily. You can lose it behind a hill, behind the trees. The signal can also be picked up and rebroadcasted by other things in the environment, like fences, power lines, even buried gas lines, which can give you a false reading. Even fog can push the signal around.

It's always exciting when you catch an endangered species and when you can track it to a roost tree. You get a much better understanding of how the bats are using the landscape, which is always a very valuable thing. In the case of the Indiana bat maternity roost in the BCA, the signal got lost several times in the initial drive-bys. IFA volunteer Jim Jean took the telemetry equipment into the forest and eventually picked up the signal. We were then able to track it to the roost tree. After the roost was located, we had one of our biologists sit under the tree and count the number of bats that emerged each night. It's not perfect, but this technique does give you an idea of how many bats are in a roost at any given time.

The pattern for this species [Indiana bat] is that while you'll have 150 or 200 bats living together for much of the summer, by the time you get later in the summer—late July and early August—the bats start to spread out and occupy multiple trees. Even when you have a tree that has only a handful of bats in it, there is value associated with

Researcher examines bat with a light to note details about gender and condition. *Photo credit: IFA.*

the fact that they have picked that tree out of a forest of possibilities. Primary roosts are those trees where you have a large proportion of the colony that uses it on a regular basis. Alternate roosts are less intensively used, and it's not unusual to have several alternate roosts out there, especially later in the season. Loss of these big trees that are being used all the time can have significant impacts on the bats. That being said, you have to remember that Indiana bat species have evolved using big dead trees as their habitat, and the remarkable thing about big dead trees is that they tend to fall down.

STEELE Other vulnerable species were found in this forest too. The team netted a lactating northern long-eared bat, which is now a federally endangered species, along with a tricolored bat, and there is acoustic evidence that indicates state endangered little brown bats

Forest as Haven

may be out there as well. How common is it for you to find these im-periled species in Indiana, especially all in one place?

SPARKS Several of the species that are now really uncommon, like northern long-eared bats, were relatively common just a few years ago. For example, when we were consulting on a major highway proj-ect in Indiana a while back, we were catching hundreds of little brown bats every summer at first. We were catching these bats nearly every night, sometimes 70 or 80 in a single night. By the end of that work, the species' decline was to the point that there were only a couple of places out of many netting sites where you could still reliably catch little browns.

I've seen similar patterns with the tricolored bat. When I was doing my Ph.D. work, finding a site where you had little browns, tricoloreds, and northern long-eared bats all together was not unusual in Indiana. If the site you picked had all three of those species plus Indiana bats, it was a little bit more exciting, but now, it's pretty rare to be able to find sites where all four of these species occur.

STEELE What does it say about the BCA habitat to have all of these vulnerable species present at one site?

SPARKS Having all four of these species co-occur indicates that there are enough different types of habitat in the Back Country Area such that all of those species are able to find everything they need to survive in that landscape. With bat biology, it is really important to under-stand that we have bats that have greater and lesser associations with the forest itself. Bats can be tree-roosting bats without necessarily being a forest bat. It's funny, because you do get places where there's a forest opening or a trail, and you'll find certain species foraging in that open area, but they won't be found in the heavily forested part. Conversely, you have species like northern long-eared bats, which typically don't do a lot of activities in wide-open spaces. There is an argument that they're better adapted to forest cover. My view of them is greatly colored by my time in western Kansas, so I kind of see them as a jack-of-all-trades bat.

There are forests associated with the streams and rivers in that area that kind of break up the sea of agriculture in southern Indiana. Indi-ana bats prefer big areas of uncluttered forest. Deep, dark forest isn't great foraging habitat for other bat species, but northern long-eared bats are just fine out there. For northern long-eared bats, we want to make sure that the forest has those tree species that tend to develop hollows and cavities with time—like beeches and sycamores.

STEELE What you said here reminds me of something that I've heard about birds relying on different types of forests during different stages of life or for different purposes, such as a species needing old forest to nest, but then their young will use early successional forest to forage after fledging because of the protection the clutter can provide. Is there a similar relationship happening here?

SPARKS   Yes, there is some of that. I've helped several forestry programs write habitat conservation plans for bats, and one of the things that we often find ourselves addressing is that forest management activities may result in trading the trees the bats live in for areas that they forage in. That trade-off is biologically real. It's well established at this point. The challenge with forest management is making sure that you've got enough of all of those age classes to support the species diversity. Any time you make decisions about managing habitats, you have to understand that you're impacting every species that is in that habitat. You're making active decisions about who wins or loses on the landscape. One of the things that we've incorporated in most of these habitat conservation plans is set-aside areas, where no timber harvesting takes place, sometimes targeting areas for old-growth forest.

STEELE   You're saying that we need to focus on maintaining a diversity of forest types. When you talk about the need for diverse habitat, whether it be species richness, age diversity, or something else, do you think Indiana has the diversity we need to support our native bat species?

SPARKS   What we have is a whole lot of forest in Indiana that's about the same age. A big, big chunk of what's out there started growing during the Great Depression, especially down in the area of the BCA. I think it's really important that people understand that the forested area in southern Indiana was mostly farmed at some point. Some of it was planted, but most of it regenerated naturally after people lost their farms and moved out. On a national scale, we had the Resettlement Act of 1935, which enabled the federal government to buy out failing farms throughout the country. I believe the Resettlement Act was used to acquire part of what became the Yellowwood and Morgan-Monroe Forests, and certainly this was used to acquire what is now the Hoosier National Forest. This was one of the New Deal legislative keystones that have kind of been forgotten. In fact, when you look at the national forests of the eastern U.S., there's a big split marked by the Rocky Mountains. If you're east of the Rocky Mountains in a state or national forest, there is a very good chance that forest includes former farmland bought during the Depression.

In my mind, our problem is that we have a lot of forest in this same age category, around 90 years old. The characteristics of a forest will change over time. Left completely on their own, forests in Indiana would tend toward a beech-maple forest system, while historically, a

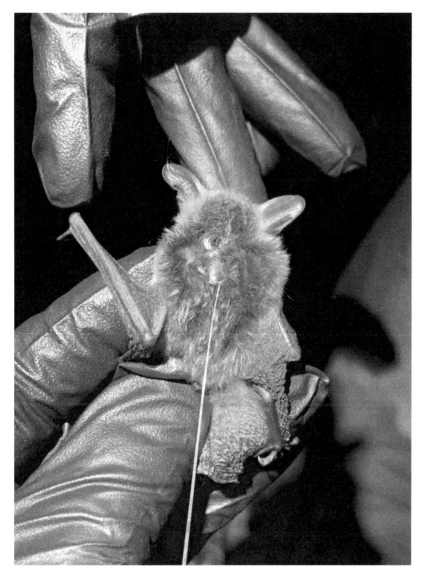

If the bat was a juvenile or lactating female of either the Indiana bat or NLEB, a transmitter was placed on it to track it to its maternity roost tree, as occurred here with this female NLEB. The transmitter is designed to fall off the animal within a week, but in this case, it fell off before the maternity roost could be located. *Photo credit: IFA.*

lot of our forests were oak-hickory. I think, on a very big scale, what we need is to think about how we diversify our forests. Certainly there's nothing wrong, and in many cases it would be preferable, for some of the forest to go toward the beech-maple end point that is the true climax community for this latitude. We certainly need some to be regenerating forests for early succession habitat as well. Regenerating forest is phenomenal habitat for bats. But those oak-hickory systems are really valuable to a wide variety of wildlife, too, whether you're talking about those that are the "hook and bullet" consumable species that people like to hunt or just species that people like to see.

We should be managing for a diversity of forest sizes, ages, and species richness. Something that's really important for these imperiled bat species we've been talking about: they tend to forage along edges. Especially for Indiana bats, if it's a relatively open forest system, they'll be in the open space between the ground and the canopy. As you get a more cluttered undergrowth system, they'll struggle to get through and forage primarily on top of the canopy or along edges. If you have regenerating forest, whether it's from natural causes like storm or fire or a timber harvest, they'll basically be out making laps in the area where you've got large and small trees growing right next to each other. It turns out those edges produce a wealth of insects. With those four species, the Indiana bats will really exploit those edges, and you'll have little browns out in the open, especially if there's an aquatic area that they can get into, tricolored bats will be bounding back and forth along the edge or in more open forest, and then, where things are thick and cluttered, that's where you'll find northern long-eared bats. They'll even be up in the leaves kind of cutting in and back and forth. They will do a lot of picking insects off of leaves and vegetation, what we call gleaning, but they all also will do the more traditional catching prey on the wing, or what the literature calls aerial hawking.

At the end of the day, we need all stages of habitat present on the landscape. What scares me as much as anything is the extremes we talk about with forest management. Some folks want to cut everything all the time. Others oppose forest management. At some point, we have to back off and think about the consequences of what we're doing or avoiding and start to make choices that manage for a diversity of forest ages and forest types.

Key Findings

Ecoblitz surveys found a diverse community of bats in the BCA. Three surveys identified 8 of 10 bat species that regularly occur in Indiana in the BCA in 2014, 2016, and 2017. All but the big brown bat are listed as federal and/or state endangered or a state species of special concern (rare). The surveys resulted in the following:

- They caught three bats that are listed as federal endangered (Indiana bat and northern long-eared bat, upgraded from threatened to endangered in 2022) or proposed for federal endangered (tricolored bat) in nets. Through radio telemetry, the surveys located a colony of maternity roosts for the Indiana bat. By netting two lactating female northern long-eared bats and a juvenile tricolored bat, the surveys established that maternity roosts for these bats are also present in the area.

- The surveys found strong acoustic evidence in 2016 and 2017 of the presence of the little brown bat in the BCA. The population of this bat, like those of northern long-eared and tricolored bats, has suffered catastrophic losses of more than 90% from the fungal disease WNS since 2006. As a result, the little brown bat is under species status assessment for federal endangered listing.

- They caught more than two dozen red bats, a species of special concern.

- They found acoustic evidence of the presence of the state endangered evening bat and the hoary bat, a species of special concern.

After two years of Ecoblitz bat surveys were completed, ESI issued a report to IFA that was submitted to the USFWS and the Indiana Department of Natural Resources (IDNR) in December 2017. With authority, clarity, and detail, the report explains the definitive biological value of the Morgan-Monroe/Yellowwood BCA to endangered and rare bats. An excerpt of the report follows:

> One adult lactating female northern long-eared and one juvenile male Indiana bat [#125] were captured and radio-tagged [in 2017]. The northern long-eared bat's transmitter signal was not detected, but Indiana bat #125 was tracked to a maternity roost (125-1) northeast of the Ecoblitz Area. Two nights of emergence counts yielded a total of 31 bats emerging from Tree 125-1. This tree 125-1 likely houses the same colony of bats found in 2016 and is also likely a primary maternity roost. Tree 125-1 is 0.6 kilometer (0.37 mi) northeast of the roost identified in 2016, and supports more bats (22 individuals on one night) than the 2016 tree (five individuals on one night).
>
> Although Tree 125-1 is outside the Ecoblitz Area, habitat around the roost is nearly identical to that around the 2016 tree; both trees are in a steep ravine containing an ephemeral creek, and each is adjacent multiple dead, large-dbh [diameter at breast height] tulip poplars with high solar exposure and slabs of exfoliating bark.
>
> Similar habitat also occurs in nearby ravines, indicative of high potential Indiana bat roosting habitat. Based on collective data from 2016 and 2017, a maternity colony of Indiana bats is present and probably dependent upon the resources in this area. These trees and this area provide high quality habitat for foraging and reproduction. As such, conservation of known and potential roost trees in these ravines

is important, if not essential, to the health of this maternity colony. Leaving all potential snag trees in place will provide the support that will help ensure short-term survival of the maternity colony.

In conclusion, the primary objectives of the project were accomplished: locating federally listed bats and locating eastern pipistrelles. Mist-net surveys confirmed the presence of Indiana, northern long-eared, and eastern pipistrelle bats (a.k.a. tricolored bats), and acoustic monitoring indicated presence of the little brown bat and potential presence of the evening bat. With the exception of the evening bat, these results corroborate mist-net and acoustic results from 2016, including capture of northern long-eared and Indiana bats, and recorded calls of eastern pipistrelles and little brown bats. For two consecutive years (2016 and 2017), Indiana bats were captured and tracked to roost trees within or near the Ecoblitz Area. Northern long-eared bats were captured but not successfully tracked for three separate years: 2014, 2016, and 2017. . . .

[As of 2017] USFWS is assessing listing of little brown and eastern pipistrelle bats. Both species are also currently considered species of concern by the IDNR. As such, presence of these species and potential impacts of management actions should be considered in on-going and future management efforts.

. . . The 2017 studies corroborate the 2016 conclusion that the Ecoblitz Area currently supports a diverse community of resident bats. Plans for timber harvest in this area present a management concern because, with the exception of big brown bats, IDNR considers all of these species to be either State Endangered or a Species of Concern. Two, the Indiana and northern long-eared bats, are listed as Endangered and Threatened, respectively, under the Endangered Species Act.

Lichen *Cladonia ochrochlora. Photo credit: James Lendemer.*

Samantha Buran.
Photo credit:
Samantha Buran.

11. UP CLOSE: SAMANTHA BURAN

Of Plants and People

Emma Steele

At its core, the Ecoblitz Forest Census in the Morgan-Monroe/Yellowwood Back Country Area (BCA) was an ambitious undertaking to comprehensively document the intricacies of a pristine Indiana forest. In all accounts from the Ecoblitz researchers and volunteers, the BCA itself is the narrative focus. Samantha Buran, the Ecoblitz coordinator on staff with the Indiana Forest Alliance (IFA) at the time of the BCA study, has a different story to tell. This one is about people.

Buran spent countless hours in the BCA with the Ecoblitz teams, directing volunteers, taking photos, ferrying equipment in and out of the forest on foot, helping researchers with data collection, and taking care of whatever odds and ends popped up as the Ecoblitz progressed. Behind the scenes, she lined up rosters of volunteers, coordinated the logistic details of the surveys, and kept the Ecoblitz train smoothly on its tracks. In short, Buran was the scaffolding that kept the massive research effort aloft.

While much of Buran's work with IFA happened deep in the undisturbed expanse of the BCA, it came with a revelation about the world outside the forest. As one of the most public-facing representatives of IFA's forest advocacy, she spoke with hundreds of people across Indiana with the mission of bringing them closer to the forests that ripple through the state's landscape. What she found was a society that has forgotten its roots. She says, "When talking to people, anywhere really, I felt lucky if I came across somebody that even knew we had state forests to begin with. It was like hitting the jackpot if you found someone who knew the forests had different species of trees."

People's inability to identify creatures in the natural world is not just common: it is the norm, especially when it comes to plants. It is so commonplace that in 1998, a pair of American botanists coined the term "plant blindness" to describe the widespread phenomenon of people's inability to notice and distinguish between even the most common

plants. People are not just unaware of plant species names and how to identify them. They are often literally unable to recognize that they are looking at two different plants. For many who visit Indiana's forests, the unimaginable diversity of plant life, each species with their own specific and essential role in the ecosystem, blurs into an indistinguishable sea of green. When Buran considers the threats facing our forests—the climate crisis, biodiversity loss, development, logging—she sees this disconnect between people and the natural world as the greatest of them all.

"It's apathy, or maybe just ignorance, amongst the general public," Buran says. "The right people, the people with decision-making power, don't care about what happens to our forests, which makes it harder to [affect] policy change." Buran sees a direct line between the public's lack of knowledge about the natural world and the path to systemic change in the way we manage our forests. People do not care about issues that they do not know exist, and issues that people do not care about never get addressed by the political bodies that govern our relationship with the environment. "It all goes back to building political power," she adds. This is where the Ecoblitz provides its greatest value, according to Buran: helping people rediscover their primitive bond with the natural world.

For thousands of years, humans have been relying on plants for everything from food and construction materials to medicine and fuel. Your daily dose of caffeine owes itself to the leaves of *Camellia sinensis*—the source tree for black, green, and white tea—or seeds from some species within the *Coffea* genus, a tropical evergreen flowering shrub that produces coffee beans. Tortilla chips, livestock feed, ethanol, the absorbent mush in disposable diapers, and the sweetness of hard candies and cough drops are all courtesy of a grass native to modern-day Mexico, colloquially known in its modern form as corn. We nurse our sunburns and scrapes with the guts of the aloe vera plant, and everything from ancient sourdough to snack cakes to postage stamp glue were born from the contributions of a humble grass variety we call wheat.

Even fossil fuels, the discovery of which changed the course of global history and has since brought the world to the precipice of the climate crisis, can be traced back hundreds of millions of years to an abundance of plants we have never had the privilege to touch. It is widely accepted by scientists that most deposits of coal—which powered the first steam locomotives, ripped through the heart of Appalachia with a black lung and the crack of a strikebreaker's pistol, and is still heating homes across the world today—came from the fossilized remains of ancient plants. Luxury skin care, wedding bouquets, cigarettes, latex gloves, morphine for pain and quinine for malaria, colonial log cabins, violins, denim jeans and cotton T-shirts, vintage bed frames, linen sheets—you can thank a plant for it all. And perhaps superseding all of this, deep in the wilderness, even in the pockets yet unseen by human eyes—though not many of these pockets still exist nowadays—plant life blooms and blossoms, turning our heavy breaths back into the kiss of oxygen.

It is a wonder how an alliance so intimate has seemingly disappeared from our view. Buran identifies two hurdles that she thinks may be playing a part in the stark disconnect between the public and the natural world: geography and accessibility. Currently, only about a quarter of the state of Indiana's acreage is forested, almost all of which is concentrated in the southern half of the state. This leaves huge swaths of the population with few to no areas geographically close to their home where a native forest still stands for them to explore. Even in areas where Indiana's forests still stand, the overwhelming majority today are privately owned, often inaccessible to the general public, and many times being sold off to the highest bidder to be cleared and turned into agricultural land, yet another subdivision, or the state's newest gas station.

For the people who do not face barriers of geography or accessibility, Buran muses that there might just be a lack of interest. People have other things they would rather think about than their backyard forest, calling into question how "interest" is cultivated to begin with. There are a few common denominators when you look at how a love for the natural world comes about. It often comes down to exposure during youth, a passionate mentor, living close to natural areas, or inherited hobbies of birding, hunting, or camping.

This is part of what makes the BCA special. The BCA is just an hour drive from Indianapolis, the 16th-largest city by population in the U.S., and only 30 minutes from Bloomington, which hosts nearly 50,000 young minds each academic year. In total, the BCA provides over one million people with close geographic access to a mature, undisturbed native forest, where they have the freedom to discover the wonders of nature through backcountry hiking, foraging, hunting, and simply walking on or off trail among rare and endangered species that have disappeared from other forests subjected to human disturbance. Areas like the BCA are a lifeline to mending our relationship with nature. It is here that, with guidance, children will relearn the forgotten wisdom of past generations. They will learn the names of the trees. They will learn them by the feel of their bark.

There is a profound impact that comes from a widespread inability to distinguish the elements in the sea of green. Just as blackberries did not burst forth from their bushes with tiny *Eat Me!* signs dangling from their thorny brambles, the Pacific yew tree did not prophesize to dumbfounded oncologists that its bark could give the world paclitaxel, a cancer drug used to treat tumors of the breast, lung, and ovary. There was no divine guide bequeathed upon us at the first breath of our cosmic dawn telling us how to domesticate the harsh wilderness or how to stack the deck in favor of our comfort and survival.

With a hunger for discovery and respect for the life-giving land, people not only found a bounty of edible plants to sustain themselves but also learned how to farm them into striking excess. We strategically bred these plants to produce only the sweetest, largest, hardiest, and most useful of their anatomy. We learned to use them to cure once-impossible ailments and stave off pests and predators, as well as turn them into clothing, art, music, makeup, and all things beautiful. Without the knowledge and deep-rooted connection to the plant world gained through generations of identifying, cataloging, and experimenting with plants, the affluence of today's world would be an impossibility. Without fixing our broken relationship with the wild forests that we have traded for concrete, it is impossible to know what new miracles we are missing out on.

Buran is keenly aware of the challenges to come if we continue on the current policy trajectory of blindly carving through the natural world, but she keeps strong in her belief in the capacity of empowered people to bring forth change. "We need to get more people engaged with

In an old grove. *Photo credit: IFA.*

Exploring a fallen giant. *Photo credit: Rae Schnapp.*

nature," she says. "The Ecoblitz was a direct connection between scientists and citizens. It brought people together as a community, brought them out into the state forests, and that is the first step of the slow process of changing public policy. The Ecoblitz gives us a powerful advocacy tool—knowing and understanding what's out there, and realizing what we [still] don't know—to get permanent protection of forests like the BCA from our political leaders."

Buran is now working toward a law degree at UCLA. When she looks to the future, this is how she sees the path forward: a united people with not only the knowledge they need to advocate for a sustainable future but also the love that drives them to the fight. It is impossible to love what you do not know. So it all begins with reconnecting people to the wonder and wisdom of the forest.

Forest as Haven

The Kentucky warbler (*Oporornis formosus*), another warbler that nests on or near the ground, is common in the BCA. This warbler also suffers from cowbird parasitism in forests smaller than the BCA. *Photo credit: Joe Bailey.*

The great spangled fritillary butterfly is one of many pollinators that visit wild bergamot flowers in the Ecoblitz area. *Photo credit: Karen Smith.*

PART IV
INSECT MULTITUDES

Emma Steele

As much as the forest ecosystem is made up of its parts—the trees, the flowers, the animals, the insects—it is also defined by its processes. A forest is constructed by the way the flora breathes opposite the fauna, taking up the carbon dioxide left over by animal respiration and releasing the oxygen as waste. It is built by the dominoes of forest succession, each stage giving way to the next in the search for equilibrium. The forest is made up of decay and birth, each species living, dying, and rotting on its own timescale; pollination and photosynthesis; the uptake of water from soil and its release into the atmosphere as vapor through transpiration; carbon sequestration on the scale of centuries; and the cyclical interactions of all the creatures of the forest day by day leaving their mark, rearranging the pieces into nests, cracking open nuts and seeds, and eating and being eaten themselves.

Few classes of beast are as prevalent in the cycles of the forest ecosystem as insects. With tens of thousands of species inhabiting eastern hardwoods alone, insects are the largest and most biodiverse group of organisms on the planet. At the heart of each process that governs the forest ecosystem, there are insects at work: pollinating forest plants, serving predators and prey alike, and breaking down the dead alongside fungi and scavengers to recycle their nutrients. These duties are how the processes of the forest march on.

It is also with insects that animals' march onto land began on the order of 420 million years ago (mya) with the scurry of millipedes. First appearing in the fossil record after the onset of the earth's first mass extinction at the end of the Ordovician period (approximately 440 mya), they emerged from the oceans about 50 million years before the first vertebrate animals. During this same period, vascular plants began to take hold on land—the ancestors of trees and flowering plants—and the first terrestrial arachnids emerged. Over hundreds of millions of years, insects and plants would evolve alongside each other, diversifying their ranks and splitting into ecosystems of forests, prairies, and swamps with a joint evolutionary history rivaled only by that of the most ancient partnerships: stromatolites; lichens; and the marriage of the rock and the sea. Insects are the forest's oldest companions.

In this fourth section, we climb up the backbone of the forest. With entomologist Glené Mynhardt, we reject "vertebrate bias," trading it for iridescent chitin shells and double-pronged pincers. Our perception of the world's most prominent pollinators is challenged by bee expert Robert Jean. Carl Strang introduces us to the magic of insects that sing. We dive into a case study of species specialization with the West Virginia white butterfly, and alongside naturalist Leroy Koehn, we divine 1,300 species of moths that call the Morgan-Monroe/Yellowwood Back Country Area home.

Glené Mynhardt. *Photo credit: Glené Mynhardt.*

12. PROFILE: GLENÉ MYNHARDT, PH.D.

Endless Entomology

Anne Laker

The total lifetime of one hardworking entomologist will not be enough. Half a million hours will not be enough. Time is no match for the number of types of beetles on this planet or even in the Morgan-Monroe/Yellowwood Back Country Area (BCA).

Glené Mynhardt, Ph.D., professor of biology at Hanover College and leader of the Ecoblitz insect team, freely admits that, based on the variety and quantity collected, she could "identify insects from that first [Ecoblitz] forest for the rest of my time as an entomologist." She says so with pure excitement and only a touch of exasperation.

Over three seasons (2014–2016) of Ecoblitz surveying, Dr. Mynhardt and team members collected 415 beetle species, which is probably a gross underestimate of the true diversity. She says, "Worldwide, there are 176 families of beetles, with approximately 100 in North America, and we found 60 different families in the Ecoblitz area." That means that representatives of at least 60% of major North American beetle groups were found thriving in the eastern hardwood forests of south-central Indiana. This documented beetle community in the Ecoblitz zones included many of the wood-boring variety, busy doing the work of recycling logs. These borers occupy a pivotal place in the forest food chain.

"If you want to understand a forest ecosystem, look at beetles," Mynhardt says. Like a baseball team full of utility players or a theatrical cast full of understudies, beetles play every possible role: "Beetles function as decomposers, predators, plant feeders, fungivores. Some are pollinators, some only live in dead wood. If you look at the potential roles in a forest, beetles do it all."

What distinguishes the almost 400,000 known species of beetles from one another? "The tiniest of details," says Mynhardt. One hair above the eye versus two. The shape of the mandibular tooth. The painterly pattern marking the wing casing. Each point is finer than fine, given that one in

The insect team, including Hanover College students and IFA staff, installs Malaise traps in the BCA. *Photo credit: IFA.*

four animals on earth is a beetle. "There are hundreds of morphological features that we train students to look for," she says.

But first, the insects have to be caught. The team started with hand collecting in 2014. The next year, they deployed tent-like Malaise traps, which intercept insects in flight. The insects fly into a dark mesh panel and crawl to a collecting vessel at the top, guided by their attraction to light. The traps were out for several months at a time, and Mynhardt's team came to check the catch every few weeks.

In two years' time, they gathered a rich population of insects, all of which needed to be pinned, pointed (if significantly tiny), and identified. It took close to 20 students over a few years just to sort through the specimens, which is only the first step for identification. The collection included 130 potential species of ichneumonid wasps (which prey on larval-stage insects and spiders, keeping populations in check) and 15 fly species that prey on aphids (also a natural biological control). "We have some vials that we may never get to," admits Mynhardt. "It took two years to see what an amazing baseline of biodiversity this forest represents."

For example, longhorn beetles showed up in robust numbers in the Morgan-Monroe/Yellowwood BCA. But only a handful have been found to date in a 2021 Ecoblitz survey just 30 miles away in the Combs Creek area of the Hoosier National Forest (HNF). Same with ichneumonids. "The species diversity within Yellowwood took on new meaning once we started collecting at Combs Creek," says Mynhardt. "In areas with varying types of canopy cover at Combs Creek, the diversity of beetles, flies, and almost every insect group is way lower than in the BCA." The same was true of a survey of forests on the Hanover College campus. "The diversity within the Morgan-Monroe/Yellowwood Back Country Area blows everything else away," she says. "It's great to be able to treat the Ecoblitz zone at Yellowwood State Forest as a comparison baseline."

Dr. Mynhardt pauses for a beat. "There is something complex going on in the backcountry area."

* * *

Why are so many different kinds of insects thriving in the Morgan-Monroe/Yellowwood BCA? "A forest that is biodiverse has high species diversity, which naturally signals good ecosystem and genetic diversity," explains Mynhardt. "If you have a strong base of insect diversity, it means you have a complex ecosystem with a complex food web, which is connected to resilience. It comes down to more species and

An array of identified insects collected in the Ecoblitz area. *Photo credit: Glené Mynhardt.*

The predator-prey relationships of parasitic ichneumonid wasps are not well understood. *Photo credit: USGS Native Bee Inventory and Monitoring Lab, public domain.*

more complex interactions between species. The complexity arises from the number of ecological roles played by different species."

The key to this desirable complexity is a dynamic array of plant life. "The flora is the foundation for any kind of estimate for an area's biodiversity," she says. "One step higher is insect diversity. With more plant diversity, you have more birds and insects, especially pollinators." One theory about the reason for greater plant diversity is soil type: unlike the bedrock-derived soils of Combs Creek, the glacial till soil of Morgan and Monroe Counties is richer, fertile ground for a broader range of plants and, by extension, wildlife.

If the beetle sample in the BCA yielded an embarrassment of riches, so did the wasp sampling. She says, "There's a running joke between wasp and beetle experts. Close to 400,000 beetle species have been described, comprising 25% of all animals on our planet—but there may be just as many parasitic wasps that *haven't* been described yet."

So why are parasitic wasps so plentiful in the Ecoblitz surveys? "Wasps are a fascinating combination of predator and pollinator," she says. For example, certain wasps feed on the larvae of gypsy moths, which can infest and defoliate oak trees. Wasps are a check on the population of

Insect Multitudes

destructive moths. She continues, "So moth diversity causes wasp diversity. There are likely so many parasitic wasps in this ecosystem because there's an abundance of hosts. If you look at plant diversity, that's where you will likely see the impact."

On the matter of plants, a score of 35 on the Floristic Quality Index indicates good species richness. The Ecoblitz plant team scored the Morgan-Monroe/Yellowwood BCA forest zones between 62 *and* 77. Case closed: the Ecoblitz area's off-the-charts plant diversity solves the mystery of its extraordinary insect biodiversity.

And yet, more mysteries linger. Many of the ichneumonid wasps collected during the Ecoblitz could not be identified below the family level. Without that specificity, it is not possible to know what kind of insects are hosting each wasp or the impact of this symbiosis on plants in Indiana's forests. As Mynhardt says, it is all intertwined.

Is our inability to fully comprehend this interconnectedness an argument for the precautionary principle: to tread lightly if at all, to let nature be nature?

* * *

Unlike some of the scientists involved in the Ecoblitz, Mynhardt did not grow up romping in the humid green cathedrals of the Hoosier State. She was born into the arid warmth of Johannesburg, South Africa, where she amused herself by gently lassoing beetles and flying them like tiny kites. As a kid, she never feared insects, and in fact, she "favored dung beetles." "My dream job was to be a game ranger or field guide. . . . I wanted to take people on tours," she recalls. Her dreams have technically come true; each year, she takes Hanover biology students on study trips to Belize, as well as forests closer to home, such as the HNF.

When she was 13, Mynhardt's family moved from South Africa to the U.S. Adjusting to the way many Americans view insects was interesting. "Eew" and "burn the house down" were never something she imagined anyone saying about harmless six-legged creatures. Those little critters inspired her to volunteer as an undergraduate research assistant at the University of Texas at Austin. As an inexperienced young scientist, she started her first day in the lab where her entomology professor put a large jar filled with brown slop in front of her. "Your task is to sort these insects by morphotype so that, eventually, these insects can be identified and used for biodiversity research," he said. "I was looking at specimens, sorting, looking at a thousand different things under the microscope," Mynhardt says. "When you allow ethanol-preserved insects to dry, you see the amazing colors, the marvelously intricate textures." And, because she was enamored with the local dung beetle diversity, she obtained a

Glené Mynhardt identifies collected specimens at her microscope. *Photo credit: Glené Mynhardt.*

small undergraduate research grant to examine dung preference in the local dung beetle population—harkening back to her childhood dung beetle days.

"Beetles are the most complex, beautiful, underestimated creatures," she says with factual wonder. "You begin to realize . . . that single tree right there is covered with things you never thought about."

Think about them she did. As an undergrad, Mynhardt assisted with surveys on Texas military bases, where she honed her field and lab skills and cut her teeth on studying biodiversity. Mynhardt then earned a master's of science in entomology at Texas A&M University, where she worked on the population genetics of the pecan weevil, *Curculio caryae*. She continued her work on beetle evolution at Ohio State University, earning a Ph.D. focused on ant-associated behavior and morphology in spider beetles (*Coleoptera*: *Ptinidae*) and a rare scarab genus, *Cremastocheilus*.

When asked by Indiana Forest Alliance (IFA) executive director Jeff Stant in 2014 to lead the Ecoblitz insect survey team, Dr. Mynhardt was new to Indiana, having just landed in the biology department at Hanover. So she jumped in feet first to IFA's Ecoblitz. "What better way to learn about insect diversity in a northeastern deciduous temperate forest?" she asks. "For my dissertation, I worked on a group of beetles that is distributed worldwide, found only in remote places and usually in ant nests. With the Ecoblitz, we were starting from the ground up, but we could start simple. I knew that if I wanted to teach about Indiana's insect diversity to my biology students, I first needed to understand the local insect diversity myself."

"It helped to walk about with Jeff [Stant], who has this amazing memory of places and directions," she says. One of Mynhardt's most vivid memories of the Ecoblitz fieldwork involved the risk of life and limb to collect a specimen: "My first foray was a hike out to an area known as 'the blowdown.' Jeff made it sound like a pleasant stroll—yet he had a machete with him for bushwhacking. It took us several hours to hike though this wild area. Someone spotted a two-inch beetle crawling up a tree, likely a female cicada parasite beetle. I said, 'We need to get that thing.' Jeff grabbed my long tropical beetle net and started climbing the tree with it. He must have been 15 feet up. He didn't manage to capture it, but my students were amused by Jeff's climbing skills!"

The moral of the story? The pursuit of Indiana's biodiversity should be, and is, more interesting than personal safety, more thrilling than space exploration, and more pressing than either.

* * *

As an entomologist, Mynhardt is professionally obligated to counter what is known as "vertebrate bias." This selfish syndrome presumes that arthropods are somehow inherently less worthy. Some entomologists even wield coffee mugs with the controversial message "Vertebrates Suck." Of course, humans naturally gravitate to creatures with whom we have the most in common or that are most easily observed: large, fuzzy, cute mammals; showy butterflies and birds; or even snakes.

"Arthropods have been around for way longer than most of the vertebrate groups we recognize," she says in their defense. "Over millions of years, insects have persisted through all the major extinction events," she continues, "because of their morphology." They adapt well, their exoskeletons are great protection, and they reproduce easily.

Insects have a bad reputation for stinging and biting. But "somewhere between 97 to 99 percent of them are harmless," Mynhardt insists, "and they pollinate the crops we eat. Their economic and ecosystem value is immense, and despite their diversity and importance, we have yet to describe potentially millions more in addition to the 1.3 million we recognize today."

Of the insects collected in the three years of the Ecoblitz, a large proportion of them remain nameless or have tentative identifications. After identifying what she could in her lab, Mynhardt turned to an expert on fungus gnats in Oregon and an expert on snail-killing flies in Indiana. Dr. Rob Jean, senior entomologist with Cincinnati-based Environmental Solutions & Innovations Inc., helped identify 183 bee specimens representing 48 bee species and all five major bee families in Indiana.

Glené Mynhardt finds a luna moth in a nighttime Ecoblitz insect survey. *Photo credit: Jason Kolenda.*

But the most stubborn identification puzzle was presented by one family: ichneumonid parasitic wasps. These cunning wasps lay their eggs inside the bodies of other insects, and many in different families look alike. Mynhardt and two students packed the wasps they had collected into eight boxes sorted by morphotype and road-tripped to the Field Museum in Chicago.

"We got to go behind the scenes of the museum's ichneumonid collection," says Dr. Mynhardt. "It took an hour to open up all of the drawers. Their collection looked like ours . . . boxes of wasps with no names! The Field Museum has a really well known collection, but no wasp experts on staff." Still on the hunt, Mynhardt reached out to a wasp specialist out west. As are many overburdened taxonomists, he was so busy that he said he would have to charge a large fee per specimen to identify them.

This unsatisfied quest for entomological knowledge underscores both the stratospheric biodiversity of one Indiana forest and the need for a new generation of insect specialists. While the hobby of beetle collecting was all the rage among 19th-century gentlemen, and a few determined ladies, do current generations feel the same pull to host parties to compare their beetle collections—perhaps on social media?

Some modern minds may be especially suited to the parsing of specimens. In 2016, Mynhardt had a student she will never forget working in the lab: "He joined my lab reluctantly, mentioning that he didn't like to touch insects. Yet, after some training, he identified almost all the beetles we found in Yellowwood that year by using dichotomous insect keys [illustrated or textual resources that help experts narrow down important insect characteristics]. He had an amazing memory for the tiniest distinctions."

If only this superpower of accurate microscopic discernment, the entomologist's bread and butter, could be multiplied. "We don't have enough taxonomists anymore," laments Mynhardt. "That's one of my goals in my lab at Hanover: to train people to do that kind of work." Some of her biology students have gone on to graduate school. One is now working to complete her Ph.D. in beetle systematics at Purdue University. Others have gone on to study mosquito- and tick-borne diseases.

She states, "One thing that I know about every entomologist: if you can appreciate the little things, you can appreciate the big things, because we understand how important and unique the little things are." Once a person is devoting attention, a sense of wonder kicks in—at the boundless shapes, strategies, and colors of insects. The wondrous variety is beautiful and poetic, but it also has an evolutionary function of sustaining life as a whole in ways almost too intricate to fathom.

"When I teach my conservation biology course, we focus a lot of our discussion on the value of biodiversity," says Mynhardt. "When we think of value, we first think of economic value, something we can put a price tag on. It can be hard to argue for the intrinsic value of biodiversity. But the services insects offer, for one, can't be monetized and are incredibly important." Along with fungi, we can thank many small insects and other arthropods for serving a critical role in decomposition of dead wood and other organic material. Dung beetles help recycle organic material back into the soil, for example, and carrion beetles make great use of small carcasses that eventually break down to provide delectable nutrients for plants.

As she and her students were surveying in one of the Ecoblitz zones, IFA's Jeff Stant said that the state Division of Forestry was planning to log it. The students could not believe it. "I wish there was a way for people to work together," she says, referencing the everlasting battle between proponents of a "leave-nature-alone" preservation approach and proponents of a conservation approach, in which active management of the forest takes precedence. "I sometimes wish that we could focus more on biodiversity for biodiversity's sake, but humans are an essential part of biodiversity, too. Finding the balance between what humans need and how much humans use is probably the biggest challenge we face as a species."

At the invitation of IFA in 2017, Dr. Mynhardt testified to the Indiana Senate Natural Resources Committee at a hearing for a proposed bill to

These reticulated net-winged beetles (*Calopteron reticulatum*) are hard even for entomologists to decipher from two other similar-looking beetle species. *Photo credit: Glené Mynhardt.*

set aside 10% of Indiana's state forests for research and wilderness recreation. She said to the lawmakers:

> In the time that we have been identifying the specimens collected [on the Ecoblitz], it has become clear that we have very limited knowledge of how many species exist in our Indiana forests. . . . The species we are identifying are forest specialists that have been part of Indiana's forests for hundreds of thousands of years. . . . We are collecting hundreds of species of wasps, beetles, and flies, all of which are interdependent on one another for different stages of insect life. Not only do our native forests house these species, but never before has any group of naturalists been able to fully sample their rich diversity.

She added, "We are facing what could be one of the most exciting ventures in understanding Indiana's biological diversity, and we may lose it all. We should be spending more time and energy to understand what we have in our own beautiful forests of Indiana before it is too late."

Although the Indiana General Assembly has not yet enacted a bill to set aside a portion of state forests from logging, the Ecoblitz and its prolific results are the best argument for leaving public forests undisturbed as living ecological laboratories.

* * *

In 2017, the *New York Times* published an editorial called "Insect Armageddon," referencing a study of German nature preserves over 25 years. The study concluded that the number of flying insects had plunged by three-quarters. Insects and the projected state of a world without them was suddenly dinner table talk. "There was a big symposium, with scientists asking ourselves, are they really declining that much, with a

Insect Multitudes

death by a thousand cuts, due to agricultural chemicals, climate change, etc.? In most places, like North America, we just don't know enough to say. We don't have enough people who are trained to know—a sad reality," Mynhardt adds.

One solution is for science-forward folk to raise consciousness of insects by promoting the embrace of native plants. "Little changes, like suburbanites planting pollinator gardens, are very important for insects," she says. "Most people don't understand the value they give to an ecosystem. If you're using insecticides, you are killing every pollinator, wasp, butterfly, moth, and beetle. There is then no food for bats or birds, including the hummingbirds we all love to lure to our yards with feeders. We need to have people understand that their existence is linked to an ecosystem, which all falls apart without plants and insects. We entomologists need to be good salespeople for these little critters."

A related solution is to call out the wonders and mysteries in our midst. "One of our most remarkable finds was a rare and largely unknown insect called the forcepsfly, *Merope tuber*," she notes. Male specimens have double-pronged "pincers" at the end of their abdomens. The species has relatives in Brazil and Australia, so when the supercontinent Pangea split, scientists hypothesize that this insect must have successfully adapted, though no one knows for certain what they eat. The Ecoblitz was proudly responsible for a potential new county record for this species, representing one of a few yet-unpublished sightings in south-central Indiana.

Aided by her work on IFA's Ecoblitz, Mynhardt has established one of the most comprehensive insect collections of any small liberal arts college in Indiana: the Hanover College Insect Collection. "Insect collections are one of the only ways scientists can document both a physical and permanent record of species diversity over time, which is why this work is so important to me," she says.

Entomology and the Ecoblitz itself are driven by an urgent curiosity. "We look in amazement at all these bugs, and we don't yet know how they mate, what they eat, or what they use their weird claspers for. If nothing else, we should be excited to learn more about them," Mynhardt says. Indeed, many insects are going extinct without us ever understanding their role in the ecosystem. The struggle to name them all reveals the amount of work still undone. The fact that insects made up 1,900 of the 3,700 species documented in the Ecoblitz—from fish and fungi to mammals and plants—reveals insects' raw, pervasive influence by volume alone. It is enough to suggest that maybe people are not as dominant as we prefer to think.

"We humans live in our large bodies, but insects are just as biologically complex. How are humans more special than insects?" she asks with informed reverence. "My answer is that we are all the same. We are

The eastern Hercules beetle (*Dynastes tityus*), pictured center, can reach up to 60 mm in length and is one of 415 species of beetles collected in the BCA. *Photo credit: Glené Mynhardt.*

just another species—and yet we're the only one with the intellectual capacity to understand the other organisms that share our planet."

With enough humility, we might yet begin to respect the nonhuman invertebrates populating our planet and our local forests in their vast varieties. "I watch my students looking closely at insects for the first time," says Mynhardt. "Studying these creatures changes the way they look at the world."

Key Findings

We found a total of 1,957 insect species. Insects accounted for 63% of all species found in the Ecoblitz. More than 300 specimens remain to be identified to the species level.

Beetles

The insect team, led by Dr. Glené Mynhardt and her students at Hanover College and assisted by Dr. Jeffrey Holland and colleagues from Purdue University, identified 415 species of beetles in the Ecoblitz area, representing 61 families of beetles, the majority of which are reliant on wood or decaying wood/material. These numbers are low estimates since some specimens remain unidentified.

Wasps

The insect team found at least 200 species of wasps from 49 genera across 24 families. Some 150 of these species are from an undetermined number of genera of parasitic wasps that belong to the *Ichneumonidae* family and primarily lay their eggs in other insect hosts. The majority of hosts live in dying or dead wood and include moth larvae (caterpillars), beetles, wood wasps, and flies. The vast majority of these ichneumonid wasps were found to be distinct "morphos" species but not definitively identified to a specific species.

Flies

More than 155 species of flies in 81 genera in 35 different families were identified, many of which rely on dead wood or other insects for breeding. At least 15 of these fly species are aphid predators, providing biological control of these plant eaters.

Bees

The bee survey was the first done in a forest in Indiana. Some 109 different species of bees were identified in the BCA, one-fourth of all the bee species known to occur in the state. Species included 21 genera from all five of the common bee families found in the state. In addition, 5 state records (newly discovered in the state) and 87 Monroe County records were found. Two of six bumblebee species identified are declining federal species of concern: *Bombus vagans* and *Bombus pensylvanicus*.

Moths

Some 895 moth species identified by lepidopterist Leroy Koehn were second only to the moth diversity recorded in the Southern Appalachian Mountains for an eastern hardwood forest. These BCA moths represent 464 genera from 39 families. Moths are discussed in more detail in chapter 16.

Insect Diversity

Type	Number of Species
Aquatic macroinvertebrates (spend at least part of their life cycle in water)	28
Bees*	109
Butterflies	69
Moths*	895
Singing insects	18
Beetles*	415
Flies*	155
Wasps*	200
True bugs*	78

* Those marked with an asterisk have some specimens that remain unidentified.

Rob Jean. *Photo credit: Rob Jean.*

13. Q AND A: ROBERT JEAN, PH.D.

The Fellowship of the Bee

Emma Steele

D r. Robert Jean's interest in bees was born exactly where you might expect: his mother's garden. She was a gardener—a good one at that—and so before the fieldwork and the dissertation, before the life opus dedicated to meticulously cataloging the hundreds of Indiana bee species, Dr. Jean found flowers. As his work has confirmed time and time again, if you find a love for flowers, you will plunge into the world of bees.

Jean grew up in Parke County, Indiana, about two hours' drive by two-lane highways and country roads from the Morgan-Monroe/ Yellowwood Back Country Area (BCA). He spent his days traipsing through the forests near his home and growing a deep passion for forests that would stick with him for the rest of his life and fuel his decision to journey into the world of biology. It was not until later, in college, that Jean became interested in bees. Starting with a pollination lab in an ecology course, he found a spark and chased it into a research assistant position with a professor working on a pollinator project. One thing led to another, and young Rob Jean, the kid who liked flowers, became Dr. Robert Jean, a regional expert on Indiana bees.

As the leader of the Ecoblitz bee team, Jean, the senior entomologist at one of Indiana's leading environmental consulting firms, Environmental Solutions & Innovations Inc., led the team to an incredible success in the BCA. At the end of the bee surveys, the first done in a forest in Indiana, the team had identified 109 different species of bees in the BCA, totaling one-fourth of all bee species known to be in Indiana. The species list represented 21 genera and all five of the common bee families found in the state. Jean's work on the Ecoblitz added five species of bees never before found in the state to Indiana's known biodiversity tally and 87 species never before reported in Monroe County. Two of the six bumblebee species identified during the bee surveys of the BCA are declining federal species of concern: *Bombus vagans*, whose numbers are declining rapidly in the state, and *Bombus pensylvanicus*, whose numbers have declined but stabilized at low levels. This conversation with Dr. Jean reveals his informed respect for these creatures and his lifelong effort to know bees.

STEELE One hundred and nine species, five state records, two rapidly declining species. These numbers represent some incredible biodiversity, but what really intrigues me is the amount of *new* biodiversity recorded as a result of this study. It makes me wonder: How did we not know that all of this was there? It gives me the impression that we don't know what's going on in Indiana's forests.

JEAN I would agree. I would say, unfortunately, we tend to only know what foresters tell us, and they're much more concerned with trees of economic value rather than the ecological relationships and everything else that actually keeps the forest going in perpetuity. I'm not knocking foresters. They have their own view of forest health—thinning the forest, making sure that future generations have trees of economic value—but at the same time, nobody is really looking at most of the insects or the fungi or the lichens or these other taxonomic groups in the forest. There are just very few specialists even available. Honestly, until recently, I was the only one sampling for bees in Indiana. There's only just in the last few years a few other groups doing some surveys at the Indiana Dunes and around Purdue, and it's been in decadal intervals. You get an entomologist that's studying stuff for a decade or two, and then they either die, or they move to another university in another state, and collection ceases. Then you have a decade or two of no data.

Before the Ecoblitz, forests, in particular, had never even had a season-long inventory. Even though I had good records for Vermilion, Parke, and Vigo Counties for a lot of flower species—my original focus when I started my studies was the pollination biology of these various wildflowers—it wasn't about the bee community of this habitat type. It was, "What bees are visiting this flower?" Once the flowers that I was interested in were done flowering, I was in the lab identifying the bees and the flowers and didn't continue my sampling. Flowering really declines in the forest starting in June, and so you don't feel like you have anything to collect past that. However, we have found doing these other studies that if we put out passive traps, we find bees out there using this habitat, even if they're not actively using flowers.

The BCA had a bottomland area that had really nice flowering, probably three-quarters of the year. It's a spectacular area in terms of vegetation.

STEELE Let's start with the basics. When people think of bees in the U.S., they think of honeybees, which are not actually native to North

America. Can you paint me a picture of the quintessential native Indiana bee?

JEAN There is quite the species richness of bees. Just in Indiana, there are about 445 species of bees, and in the eastern United States overall, there are just a bit over 800 species. What I'll do is describe three classes of lifestyles of bees in Indiana. So you have the social bees—which are the honeybees, bumblebees, and the sweat bees—plus solitary bees and parasitic bees.

Social bees have multiple females that work together in a colony. They make up about 10% of bee species. For honeybees, that's a big

Bombus vagans, the half-black bumblebee, is a federal species of special concern that is declining in the state but still found in the BCA. *Photo credit: Brooke Alexander, public domain.*

colony lasting for multiple years. One honeybee queen can live for many years. The social lifestyle of a bumblebee is a little different because each queen bumblebee is annual. She will maintain a hive—a colony in the ground usually, or just above ground in grass clumps. She'll emerge in the spring, go around and collect enough pollen and nectar to have a few worker bumblebees, then she'll stay in the nest, and they'll go out and do all the pollen collection for the hive. While that's happening, the queen is laying eggs. At the end of the year, she'll start laying males and new queens. Those will hatch, mate that year, and then only those new queens will survive to the next year. That's why with bumblebees, in particular, the queen is the linchpin of the whole group. If she dies, a thousand individuals are dead the next year. None of those ever make it.

Honeybees are really the oddball of the bee world, where the queen has a bunch of workers, sometimes up to 100,000 or 200,000 workers in a colony. For comparison, a really big colony of bumblebees is around 2,000 bees. You have a substantially greater number in a honeybee hive, and they react much more aggressively to things because of that. A honeybee queen lives for multiple years. She will keep pumping out eggs for a long time, and she produces very few males at any given point. You don't really see male drone honeybees out anywhere other than in a honeybee colony, but with male bumblebees, you'll find them out at flowers all the time.

Then you have the sweat bees, which are also social, but they're social in that they have a few females working together to raise offspring. So that's three, four, five, maybe 10 females that will be working together in a single nest. They are very species rich. There are probably 50 or 60 species just in Indiana. Those are the ones that get to the crook of your arm and sting you. There's only two or three really common species that are probably doing that, though. Most of the rest are either found in forests or found in grasslands. Some are found in sand or other very specific habitat types. You can see just even within the social bees, there's quite a variation.

Then we have the solitary bees. The solitary bees are probably about 60% of all bee species. With solitary bees, you have a single female that digs the nest, builds a nest into a tree cavity or something like that, and she is doing everything. She's creating the nest, collecting all of the pollen and nectar, laying the eggs in the nest, and then making dividers and repeating the process 'til she's laid dozens of eggs that are going to come out as larvae. These larvae hatch and become adult bees the next year. That's the vast majority of solitary species.

Any given bee species is active four to eight weeks of the year. It's a very small window. You have species that tend to be out in spring, or the summer, or the fall. A lot of solitary bees are specialists, which means they're only visiting either one flower species or one flower genus or one flower family, and that's the only thing they'll collect pollen from. Whenever I talk about specialization in bees, I'm talking about pollen. Bees don't care where nectar comes from. Usually, they'll drink nectar from all kinds of flowers, but it's the pollen—the protein—that they're very particular about.

Then you have a whole other class of bees: the parasites. They parasitize other species of bees and take advantage of the other bees doing all the work.

STEELE Can you give me an example of that parasitic bee-to-bee-to-flower relationship here in Indiana?

JEAN I don't have a good example of the parasite species, because parasite relationships aren't super well known, but I can definitely tell you, *Claytonia virginica* [spring beauty] is one of the most abundant spring wildflowers out there, and there's a bee, *Andrena erigeniae*, that specializes on *Claytonia virginica* pollen. The females *only* visit *that plant* for pollen to feed to their offspring. They basically roll all that

Facing, There are more than 445 bee species native to Indiana, and 106 of them were found in the BCA. The well-known honeybee—*Apis mellifera*, pictured here—is one of only three non-native bees found in the Ecoblitz, suggesting a relatively intact native bee fauna in the BCA. *Photo credit: Sue Boo, USGS Native Bee Inventory and Monitoring Lab, public domain.*

Andrena erigeniae is a specialized native bee that feeds exclusively on the pollen of the spring beauties that carpet the forest in early spring. *Photo credit: Judy Gallagher, public domain.*

pollen with the nectar into a ball, put it in a nest underground, and lay the egg on that pollen ball. Once the egg hatches, the larvae will eat the pollen ball, and it'll turn into an adult bee next year.

Then there's a whole group of bees in the genus *Nomada*—they look like little brightly colored wasps; they're red-and-yellow-speckled or yellow-and-black-striped bees that look like wasps—that are cuckoo parasites. They basically go around and find other bee nests like that of the *Andrena erigeniae*, wait for that bee to leave, sneak in, and lay their egg. The *Nomada* [parasite] egg hatches first and the larvae kill the original egg and then eat whatever that mom left for her larvae. Basically, they're like cowbirds of the insect world. In fact, 20% of bee species are parasites on other bees. Parasitism is just a very successful occupation.

STEELE We know that biodiversity is a key indicator of ecosystem health and healthy levels of biodiversity protect us from threats like pandemics. There's clearly a danger to not knowing what's out there, and as you've pointed out, no one is out there looking at how our ecosystems are changing during a time of documented biodiversity loss and the climate crisis. We don't really have baseline numbers of Indiana's biodiversity. The Ecoblitz has been the first long-term study of Indiana's forests to tackle this issue. Without historical data to reference, we can't tell what has changed or by how much over a period of time, so how are we going to know when we're in trouble and how deeply we're in trouble?

JEAN I always say, "If you like to eat, it matters." Humans honestly are much more reliant on nature than people think. I used to teach biology as a professor for many years, and one of the things you learn is that hospitalized people who can just see a tree outside—that's all it has to be, a tree outside their hospital window—heal faster than people that have no connection to nature.

Food is the same way. A lot of people will say, "Well, corn and soy, they're wind pollinated," but I can guarantee that if you go into a corn or soybean field, you will find bees visiting those flowers. In fact, sometimes if those crops are treated with systemic pesticides, because their pollen will actually contain those pesticides, you can find small bees that have died on those flowers.

What we don't know about the environment is what could save the environment. It's those things that we don't know that might provide that key link in how to fix something or how to prevent something from getting worse. My students would say, "Save the earth, save the earth," but it's not saving the earth. I tell them, "It's about saving humans." The earth is going to be here no matter what. It will keep going for billions and billions of years. Ecology is the study of how organisms interact with other organisms, and that, I think, is going to be the key to figuring out solutions to the big issues that we are facing.

STEELE As you've pointed out, there is a vast knowledge gap between the complexity of the biological world and what we actually know about it. This is especially true for the plant and animal species that lack the public appeal of their more glamorous counterparts. We've tended to invest research in iconic species—the tigers and polar bears of the world—and the species we most frequently come into contact with, such as backyard birds and coyotes. With that investment, we've built a fairly solid understanding of how these species live, even down to the specifics of diet, migration paths, and mating habits. Meanwhile, for the insects of midwest America, there are some species for which the only thing we know about them is that they exist. Is this just a consequence of a lack of funding for taxonomic research, or is it something else?

JEAN It's definitely in part a funding issue. After the 1960s and 1970s, taxonomy lost a lot of funding. Within the last 10 or 15 years, that has been turning around, as there has been more of a focus on pollinators. It started a lot with honeybees, but it has trickled down to the native bees and butterflies. Data like what we have from the BCA helps us have true baseline numbers. Like you said, five state records came from the Ecoblitz. Three of those state records I consider really cool, like the *Andrena hilaris*. I was super excited when I saw that. I knew that it should probably occur in southern Indiana, but in all the limited sampling that we have done, it hadn't been found. This shows that the species is obviously out in the forest. Out in very low numbers, but it's out there. It might be that we're still just looking in the wrong place in the forest. Before, we were never sampling high enough up in the canopy. This is where we're finding new species.

STEELE Before the Ecoblitz in the BCA, there had never been a baseline survey of bees in Indiana's forests. This was a first-of-its-kind surveying effort, resulting in groundbreaking discoveries, like your findings that described bees living in the BCA, even after the flowering season had ended. What are the next steps to build on the results of the Ecoblitz?

JEAN There's still some taxonomic issues that I want to work out. There are a few sweat bees that could potentially be a new species or just a variation of something that we're not understanding very well yet. There are so many questions. It's endless when it comes to the pollinators. We're at the tip of the iceberg because we're still discovering what species occur where. If you compare this to birds, where we know enormous amounts of information: how many eggs they lay, their preferred habitat, where they migrate. For any individual bee species, we might know that it could occur across a few states in certain months, but that's it. There is a vast knowledge gap.

I've been working to update my "Bees of Indiana" field guide for about a decade or so. Any chance I get to collect more data, especially in Indiana, that's what I try to do. Eventually my goal is to have a book of the bees of Indiana in a very descriptive guide to the different species.

STEELE How close are you?

JEAN Well, I started compiling species data around 1996. It's never quite done, I guess, but the most up-to-date version of the list is about ready to be published. I've definitely got about 20 species to add and then a lot more new information about other species to go along with that. These forest studies really contribute to that. A lot of people do surveys in open areas because that's where most flowers occur, but people don't realize that forests have this incredible spring wildflower display with 20 or 30 wildflower species blooming. All of these different flower species attract different bees, and then those bees have parasitic bees that parasitize them, and so you end up with these whole layers of organisms that are all interacting out there in these forests. Indiana has truly some of the most spectacular forests in terms of spring wildflower displays.

STEELE Looking back at the broader experience of the Ecoblitz—all the time and effort it took to do these surveys. What makes it all worth it for you?

JEAN For me, it's part of giving back to the natural heritage of the state. One of my mentors throughout my college career was Dr. Marion Jackson, and his seminal work was *The Natural Heritage of Indiana* (1997). It's an incredible opus to the life and habitats of Indiana. I've always had this affinity toward trying to figure out what's pollinating everything here and the diversity of bees. Nobody could really identify them, so it became a taxonomic specialty that led to a career doing what I enjoy doing, which is being out in the woods and staring at flowers.

Carl Strang. *Photo credit: Carl Strang.*

14. UP CLOSE: CARL A. STRANG, PH.D.

Psalm of the Cricket

Emma Steele

Year after year, the Indiana summer reels on to a score composed by the drone of cicadas' hums. Every midwestern memory of catching lightning bugs off the back porch on a humid summer evening is embodied in the smooth, buzzy pulse of cicadas, orchestrated by millions of wing flicks and a special organ called a tymbal unique to their kind. Just like sparrows and sirens, these insects sing.

Cicadas are not the only singing insects that populate the soundtrack of Indiana's forests. They are joined in their ranks by crickets rubbing their wings together to make a shrill chirp (a process known as stridulation), katydids flicking their forewings together to make a raspy pulsing song, and even grasshoppers, who rub their hind legs against their wing casings to make percussive chirps that sound a little bit like maracas. Within each of these insect types are numerous transpositions of song, with each species having its own distinctive voice and each with a repertoire of unique songs to communicate different messages.

There are songs to attract mates (the stereotypical cicada drone being one), songs to communicate danger, songs to declare territory. There are variations based on sex. For example, when you hear a cricket's song, you are typically hearing a male sound its call, while female crickets tend toward silence. Within a 24-hour period, different species will sound at different times, producing wildly different results if you listen at different times of day. There are even some species singing at frequencies you are unable to hear.

Carl A. Strang holds a Ph.D. in wildlife ecology from Purdue University. He began studying singing insects in the midwest in the early 2000s. Since 2006, he has focused on a 22-county area he calls "the Chicago region," which extends from three counties in Wisconsin plus one in Michigan through a section of northeast Illinois and northwest Indiana. As a seasoned naturalist, he has contributed to numerous bioblitzes in

the midwest, both in and outside the Chicago region, but Dr. Strang has a unique approach to fieldwork. Where others rely on their eyes to pick up on movements through the brush, indicators of prime habitat, or other clues to find their targets while surveying, Strang relies on his ears.

Strang has always been more "hearing focused" than most, so perhaps it is only natural that he found his niche in singing insects. Beginning in childhood and continuing through his Ph.D. research, he took a self-guided approach to learning about the natural world, engrossing himself in a wide array of topics in natural science but frequently returning to a focus on insects. As he progressed through his career as a scientist, the sounds of singing insects became a point of fascination that would turn into a long-term endeavor to learn about the singing insects of the Chicago region.

With such a heavy focus on sound, Dr. Strang's process in the field is different from biologists in other specialties. Starting only after the midmorning sun has warmed the singing insects enough to start their songs, surveying for singing insects involves intense listening. Strang's trained ear digs through the cacophony of thousands of insect songs to pick out each species one by one.

Strang writes of his process in the field, "As you might expect, listening is the main way I find singing insects, but as an older person I need an electronic device to hear those with higher-pitched songs. Such devices

Insect Multitudes

pick up sounds and lower the frequencies into my hearing range. I also need to wade through habitat, looking for insects that are stirred up by my progress. This is especially important for the singing grasshoppers, many of which perform their displays infrequently."

He continues, "There are some special cases. Sometimes I need to collect specimens of species that are new to me to verify identifications. Some species have songs that cannot be distinguished by ear. I record them and analyze them with a computer to make the identification. Experience helps, as different habitats have different species, so the emphasis I place on different techniques can be adjusted accordingly. Experience also allows me to pick out songs that most people would miss, either because the songs are faint or because the mass of singers can overwhelm the senses of an inexperienced searcher."

For Strang, one of the appeals of participating in bioblitzes is the opportunity to expand his experience with singing insects to areas outside his usual Chicago region. The Indiana Forest Alliance's Ecoblitz was of particular interest to him because, while other bioblitzes are usually short lived and over before many of the singing insects are mature, the Ecoblitz survey extended well into the peak season for "singers." Strang's contributions to the Ecoblitz involved two visits to the Morgan-Monroe/Yellowwood Back Country Area (BCA), during which he identified 16 species of singing insects. He was familiar with each species from his studies of forests in northern Indiana and the Chicago region, save two exceptions: the lesser angle-wing katydid and the southern ground cricket. Together, this collection of insects creates a chorus in the woods of the BCA that rivals that of birdsong.

"Some are loud," says Strang. "The percussive vibrato of the swamp cicada and smoother one of Linne's cicada in the daytime, and at night the rasps of common true katydids, the quick rhythmic pattern of lesser angle-wings, and the penetrating high-pitched buzzes of Nebraska coneheads. Crickets in general are not as loud and include the clear musical trills of Say's trigs in the bushes, assorted patterns of ground cricket species in the leaf litter, and faint crescendo trills of variegated ground crickets around the streambeds. Jumping bush crickets are louder, their ventriloquial, bell-like notes varying slightly in pitch among individuals."

These singing insects make up only a minuscule fraction of the bounds of insect life thriving in the BCA. The undisturbed, native-dominant conditions of the BCA have allowed the forest to support a level of biodiversity seen in few places in Indiana outside of nature preserves. Outside of wilderness areas like the BCA, insects—much like other classes of animals such as birds and large mammals—are struggling to cope with the loss of habitat to human disturbances. The vast old-growth forests that blanketed Indiana before European colonization have since been

Facing, The two-spotted tree cricket (*Neoxabea bipunctata*) is one of 11 species of crickets found by Carl Strang in the BCA. The two-spotted is an arboreal species that can be difficult to observe. It is attracted to dense stands of young trees, where males sing from the underside of broad leaves. The common name is derived from the fact that females usually have two dark spots on their wings. To hear the songs of this and other singing insects, visit www .SongsofInsects.com. *Photo credit: Andy Reago and Christy McClarren, CC BY 2.0.*

The cicada's song begins softly but quickly increases in volume before becoming a steady, pulsating rattle. *Photo credit: Karen Smith.*

turned into agricultural land, covered in asphalt for roads and cities, or fragmented by industry and transportation corridors. Today, less than 2,000 acres of Indiana's original 20 million acres of old-growth virgin forests are still standing, less than half the acreage occupied by the Indianapolis airport.

The modern-day forests of Indiana only cover about a quarter of the acreage of their historical old-growth counterparts. They are often subjected to routine disturbances from logging and other activities or flooded with invasive species that can make it difficult for native species to thrive, especially those that depend on deep interior forest or old forest for survival.

Some species are able to cope in heavily disrupted areas, but many are not. Strang notes that while species may hang on in areas like residential neighborhoods or the fringes of agriculture, their diversity is relatively low, and rarer species are lost altogether. According to Strang, when it comes to rare species of insects, "Preserved wild lands are the only places many of these species still can be found."

Dr. Strang himself is a steward of one of these rich wildlands. In his home county in northeast Illinois, he is a restoration volunteer for one of the highest-quality forests in his area. Once plagued by non-native and invasive plant species, volunteers, including Strang, have gone in and removed these invaders. The result is an environment where native plant species have a chance to rebound and slowly return to their historical abundance within the area.

Strang writes, "This restoration work is a process of ecosystem building, and it results in a rich and beautiful landscape. In time even the trees would have been lost, or at least diminished, if we had not put in this effort. The contrast with unrestored lands is clear to any of the many recreational visitors who are paying attention, and provides not only a more stable and healthy forest, but an enlightening sensory experience."

We are fortunate the BCA has avoided the onslaught of non-native and invasive species seen in most of Indiana's forests. This is largely thanks to its designation as a Back Country Area by Indiana governor Robert D. Orr in 1981. This designation recognized the BCA as an area meant to be managed as wilderness so that generations to come would have a place to connect with Indiana's true natural heritage. As a near old-growth forest, the BCA has been reverberating with the chorus of Dr. Strang's singing insects for more than a century. It is a testament to what is possible when government policy protects the long-term health of our wilderness rather than exploiting it for short-term gains. If we take care of it, perhaps this forest will sing forever.

West Virginia white butterflies, a declining species of mesic eastern hardwood forests, were found in the Ecoblitz area. *Photo credit: David Schwaegler.*

15. UP CLOSE: BUTTERFLIES

How to Starve a Species

Emma Steele

For a few precious weeks each year, when the air is summer warm but the trees have not yet filled out, beams of mottled sunlight pierce through the patchy tree crowns, bathing the forest floor in light. During these transient moments of spring, the snow is all but gone, and the green of new growth—that special green, light and vibrant, that you only see this time of year—covers the forest floor. In the Morgan-Monroe/Yellowwood Back Country Area (BCA), this is the season of ephemeral springs, hatchings and births, and prolific blooms.

For many people, the annual springtime show of native wildflowers is an unexpected feature of Indiana's forests. This dramatic show is equally practical, as the entire life cycles of some creatures revolve around it. One of these is the West Virginia white butterfly, one of 24 species of butterflies found by renowned butterfly experts Jeff and Sandy Belth in the southwestern corner of the Ecoblitz area in 2014 and 2015. On paper-thin wings, the West Virginia white flutters from plant to plant close to the forest floor. Spotlighted by a sunny opening, they look like lively speckles of white confetti pulsing against the forest's mossy-colored background. The West Virginia white needs mature, undisturbed mesic hardwood forests. Seen flying only between April and early June, it is classified as rare in Indiana and is declining across much of its range according to a 2005 assessment by the U.S. Forest Service.

Adult West Virginia whites mate almost immediately after emerging in the spring, and the females then drift among the forest's native wildflowers, searching for plants like toothworts and spring beauty to lay their eggs and drink nectar. A caterpillar will crawl out of a West Virginia white's egg about a week after being laid. The caterpillar will spend 10–20 days eating before moving into its pupa stage, securing itself with silk to a stem, where it will sleep for 10–11 months. The following spring, the caterpillar emerges as a butterfly. It will mate and then spend a glorious

Pipe-vine swallowtail larvae on Virginia snakeroot. *Photo credit: Steve Dunbar.*

final 5–10 days floating through the forest in its adult form, carefully sorting through the wildflowers of the forest to find its food plants and continue the cycle.

The West Virginia white butterfly is a specialist species. To understand the West Virginia white, we must first understand its food plants. As caterpillars, they rely on a very narrow set of food plants, mainly toothworts, which are small, spiky-leafed flowering plants with delicate, light-colored blooms. Toothworts, like many species of forest floor plants, need mesic forest habitat. Mesic forests are ecosystems with a well-balanced supply of water—wet forests, like Indiana's eastern hardwoods. Unlike the dry, fire-prone forests of the western U.S., the eastern hardwoods have always been wet forests, able to support a wide diversity of plant life as a result. In some areas, the eastern hardwoods harbor more than three times the number of tree species than the conifer forests running through the Rocky Mountains. This incredible diversity is mirrored by the springtime wildflower display and all the life that relies on these plants to survive, the West Virginia white butterfly being just one species.

Toothworts are also highly susceptible to being crowded out by non-native invasive species like garlic mustard and Japanese stiltgrass,

which plague most of Indiana's forests due to human disturbance and a lack of funding and attention allocated to invasive species control. Logging is a major culprit that introduces invasive species to forests like the BCA. Nearly all non-native invasive plants are aided by disrupting the forest floor and exposing it to direct sunlight. Logging equipment bulldozes through the sensitive forest floor community, killing native plants in its path, scraping the forest floor to bare dirt, and compacting the soil under the massive weight of the machinery. Logging equipment can also carry invasive species and their seeds into a pristine area from somewhere else, like dirt tracked onto a freshly cleaned carpet from the sole of a boot. Even the most pristine forests usually already have seeds of invasive plants in the forest litter and duff, blown there by wind. In addition, by removing multiple large canopy trees, logging allows much more direct sunlight to reach the forest floor. Most of the primary invasive offenders thrive in high sunlight, whereas native forest floor plants like toothworts do not. The result of these disturbances are explosions of aggressive non-native plants replacing native plant communities in forests across Indiana.

What happens to the West Virginia white butterfly when its food plants disappear, replaced by unfamiliar invaders of another land?

The red-spotted purple was one of 24 butterfly species found by Jeff and Sandy Belth on spring treks in the Ecoblitz area in 2014 and 2015. Photo credit: Kevin Tungesvick.

Butterflies congregate to collect mineral salts from stones in a dry creek bed. *Photo credit: IFA.*

Simply put, it disappears too. Eggs hatch, only for the caterpillars to starve. Or caterpillars turn to butterflies, only for no mate to be found and no eggs produced. Or perhaps the caterpillars are poisoned by toxic garlic mustard or the pupae never emerge from their chrysalides and the cycle of life stops. This is how a species dies. On the other hand, when forests like the BCA—a pristine time capsule of what Indiana's eastern hardwoods look like without the strains of logging and development— are preserved, rare and imperiled species continue to thrive within them.

The West Virginia white butterfly exemplifies the reality for thousands of species bound to the eastern hardwood forest ecosystem. Some of the ties that bind together the forest ecosystem are direct and obvious, like the predator-prey relationship between bobcats and squirrels. Others are separated by a string of dominos and require a closer look, like the adversarial relationship between garlic mustard and the West Virginia white butterfly, which loses its only food sources when this invasive plant takes over the forest floor.

Finding the West Virginia white butterfly in the BCA was another one of those moments during the Ecoblitz Forest Census that reminded researchers of the natural, older condition of the forest. This fragile and fleeting white butterfly is a bellwether, an indicator of older undisturbed, mesic hardwood forests—in particular, the moist condition in the beech-maple climax community. This is a mixed mesophytic forest with incredible diversity of beech, maple, poplar, elm, ash, oak, hickory, basswood, gum, cherry, walnut, sycamore, cottonwood, sassafras, hornbeam, and still other native trees for which no large, landscape-sized tract of state forest has been set aside. This is a community under increasing stress from climate change and unrelenting development in Indiana. Yet despite the growing threats, our most vulnerable species are still surviving in the pockets of its existence that have so far been spared humanity's merciless axe. Whether they continue to survive in the decades to come will depend on our resolve to put the axe down.

Leroy Koehn. *Photo credit: Anne Laker.*

16. PROFILE: LEROY KOEHN

The Life and Legacy of a Lepidopterist

Anne Laker

"I have no memory of when I began collecting insects, it was just something I always did," wrote Leroy Koehn in "Bacon, Biscuits, and Butterflies," a wistful essay published in a 2002 newsletter of the national Lepidopterists' Society. In the essay, Koehn, born in 1945, recounts the three-hour bike ride he and his three teen friends took in autumn to a rural area northeast of Cleveland in search of liberty and butterflies.

"We would camp in the woods along the river and collect our fall treasures in the adjacent fields. Pup tents, sleeping bags, food, cooking and butterfly-collecting gear packed on bicycles would be unloaded, a wood fire would soon heat baked beans in the cans. The stillness of the night and the murmur of the river sent us to sleep. We were four young men, unseen and unnoticed, without a worry in the world."

He continued, "As the temperature and the sun rose, we would drink coffee and smoke Camel cigarettes and watch across the old field for the first sign of a butterfly to take flight. And with that first sign of yellow or orange wings, we were up with nets in hand and in hot pursuit." After a break to chug bottles of grape juice chilled in the river, the quartet continued collecting *Colias eurytheme* (orange sulphur butterfly), *Colias philodice* (common sulphur butterfly), and, with any luck, *Vanessa virginiensis* (American painted lady).

On the way home, "the road would crisscross the river and we would stop in the middle of each bridge to spit in the river."

That Koehn's reminiscences of early adventures in nature include both boyish crassness and profound peace is evidence of the intimacy and endurance of his connection to nature. It is a connection that would lead to a lifetime of learning, observing, and adventuring across the nation, including Indiana, in the name of *Lepidoptera*.

The order *Lepidoptera* is composed of over 160,000 species of butterflies and moths—most of them moths. The chief difference? Most moths are nocturnal, while butterflies evolved to be active during the day. Most butterflies have club-shaped antennae, while a moth's antennae are tapered and feathery, aiding smooth flight at night.

The lilting word *Lepidoptera* comes from the Greek *lepid*, meaning "scale," and *pteron*, or "wing," in reference to the microscopic hairlike layers of chitin, a fibrous polysaccharide, finer than dust, that comprise a moth's or butterfly's wing. These matte scales are as dense as 600 per square millimeter. A butterfly's wing absorbs sunlight, while a moth's thicker coating adds warmth. Their kaleidoscopic markings—from the mesmerizing fake eyes of the Polyphemus moth to the stained-glass grace of the swallowtail butterfly—are used as signals to attract mates, sometimes with hidden ultraviolet patterns. The designs also camouflage, fend off predators, and attract eager collectors like Leroy Koehn.

* * *

Never academically trained in science but notorious worldwide for his innovations in trapping moths and butterflies, Koehn calls himself "a rank amateur." Of the professors he meets at conferences, he says, "I listen to all of them." To the question "What do all lepidopterists have in common?" Koehn answers, "It's what you can learn. I know a great deal about butterflies and moths, but it's the tip of the iceberg. I have spent my life pursuing them. I still enjoy ichneumonid wasps as much as when I was in high school. They are not uncommon. You just have to watch for them. If you don't know what you're looking for, it's hard."

The knack for knowing what to look for made Koehn the top candidate to lead the moth team for the Ecoblitz of the Indiana Forest Alliance (IFA). "An entomologist at Purdue University suggested Leroy to us," said IFA executive director Jeff Stant. "She noted that he was the developer of traps used by many scientists and that he is an institution unto himself in North American lepidoptery. He'd done surveys in Indiana before, at Harrison-Crawford State Forest, and he knew the principal players at the Department of Natural Resources."

But Koehn, who lived in Georgetown, Kentucky, at the time, had to be sure he wanted the Ecoblitz job. "I wanted to meet Jeff before I did anything," says Koehn. "I wanted to see the what and the where. I met the IFA team in Nashville, Indiana, at the Speedway gas station, and we went to the Morgan-Monroe State Forest. I said, 'If you have a place that I can stay, I'll do it.'" IFA pledged to book a room for Koehn at the Martinsville Best Western whenever he was willing to make the three-and-a-half-hour journey from his home. After a few trips to the Ecoblitz zone, Koehn "knew it was going to be an adventure and a half."

From late April to late November 2017 and from January to September 2018, Koehn spent 73 days in the Ecoblitz area of the Morgan-Monroe/

Yellowwood Back Country Area (BCA). In this time, he collected an estimated 275,000 moths. "When I opened my traps," he says, "I couldn't wait to get home and lay them out." When all was said and done, the relentless Koehn processed an estimated 5,000 of these specimens and identified nearly 1,300 different moth species—in the name of understanding the life in one Indiana forest.

* * *

In the tradition and practice of lepidoptery, not to mention the history of pest control, trapping moths is 80% of the game. There is no substitute for catching a flying critter when it comes to wanting to understand it. For example, a smartly built gypsy moth trap allowed scientists to study both male and female specimens of this species, known as tree strippers. At their worst, the moths in their caterpillar stage invade forests and thump like rain on leaves before eating them clean off the trees. Koehn advised the scientist who designed the pheromone-based gypsy moth trap, and the gypsy moth problem receded.

In the 1970s, Koehn's love of insect collecting cross-pollinated with his mechanical mind. After engineering courses at Ohio State and Cleveland State, he worked throughout his career for various manufacturers of motors, security locks, sheet metal, and power trains, from Ohio and Virginia to Florida and Kentucky. As he engineered assembly lines and production processes, in the back of his mind, he was building a better moth trap.

"I used to see articles about guys in Africa who trapped butterflies," he says. "When I saw what they did, I had an idea for how to improve it." Using materials that suggest a prom dress (black tulle netting and zippers from a hobby store) or a wedding cake (an 18-inch aluminum cake pan), Koehn, with help from his wife, Betty, a skilled seamstress, fashioned an effective bait trap that deterred curious mice and squirrels and did not hold rainwater.

"I was just making them for myself," he says. "But then I went to a Lepidopterists' Society meeting in Houston. I hung my trap in a scrub oak. It attracted some moths I'd never seen before. I was sitting in the back of the room sorting the traps. Pretty soon I had 15 people watching me, asking if I could make one of these traps for them. It happened again at a meeting of the Southern Lepidopterists' Society. I hung out one of my traps and got an *Asterocampa* butterfly. The question was always, 'Can you make me a couple of those traps?'"

A business was born. Through Leptraps LLC, Koehn estimates that he has fabricated and sold 4,000 light traps and almost 14,000 bait traps of his own design to collectors in 46 countries.

Leroy Koehn and Jeff Stant place fruit as bait in a Leptrap. *Photo credit: Rae Schnapp.*

For the Ecoblitz, Koehn's moth team used 6 light traps, 8 fruit-bait traps, and 22 pheromone traps along Honey Creek in or near the Low Gap Nature Preserve and along the Possum Trot ridgetop. While fruit traps tempt moths with food, light traps exploit the easily observable moth-to-a-flame phenomenon known as "positive phototaxis." Moths are particularly sensitive to the UV part of the electromagnetic spectrum, and they use the moon or stars to orientate. Celestial light sources are received by moths as parallel, but lamp lights radiate all around. Light traps are designed to exploit the inward spiraling responses of moths, using suitably placed barriers around the lamp that they can collide with and fall down through a funnel into the trap.

Pheromone moth traps work by attracting male moths by using the scent-like substance given off by females. Traps often contain a synthetic

Insect Multitudes

Leroy Koehn sorting the contents of one of his Leptraps. Note the assortment found in just one trap after one night. *Photo credit: Rae Schnapp.*

substance meant to mimic the olfactory communication among moths. In the Ecoblitz area, pheromone traps were hung at varying altitudes, up to 12 feet off the ground.

In addition to the traps, the team manually flushed moths from the bark of trees during each visit. These diverse methods yielded a jackpot of results: at least 98 of the species collected were new additions to the Indiana Natural Heritage Database (INHD). By comparing the moth species identified in the Ecoblitz area with the INHD, as well as lists maintained by the North America Moth Photographers Group and the Season Summary of the Lepidopterists' Society, the team determined that there are at least 29 species of moths that are new distribution records for Indiana—the first time they have ever been documented in the state.

The Georgian prominent (*Hyperaeschra georgica*) is a relatively rare moth that was found in the Ecoblitz surveys. *Photo credit: Andy Reago and Christine McClarren, CC BY 2.0.*

Examples of these new state records include several poetically named specimens: dusky clearwing (*Paranthrene tabaniformis*), eggplant leafroller (*Lineodes integra*), green-dusted zale (*Zale aeruginosa*), alfalfa looper (*Autographa californica*), and fungus moth (*Tina croceoverticella*).

The star specimen of the survey may be one moth, the Georgian prominent (*Hyperaeschra georgica*), that was on the Brown County endangered species list and considered state imperiled (at high risk of disappearance in Indiana).

Koehn also landed relatively large numbers of rarely encountered species of sphinx moths (*Sphingidae*), owlet moths (*Noctuidae*), and underwing moths (*Catocala*). Underwings are typically dull tan, brown, or gray with wavy lines that mimic tree-bark patterns. Koehn was excited by multiple specimens of two rare underwings he found: *Catocala duciola* and *Catocala consors*. He says, "These two moths are seldom encountered. I had collected only two of each over my 70 years as a lepidopterist. Little is known of *Catocala duciola*, and only a few records have been reported. *Catocala consors* is more widely reported, yet with only single specimens being collected." The combined quantity and rarity of the moths found signal the richness of this forest habitat.

During those long hours in the forest, at all times of year, Koehn made some acquaintances, human and nonhuman. Over several visits, he encountered a bobcat. "She had kits!" he explains. "There were some horse riders who had left a pile of hay in the parking lot. One morning, the bobcat and her kits were nestled in the hay. She didn't like me there, but she wouldn't leave." A long-distance relationship began. Koehn also saw—and was seen by—fox, mink, and a flock of 100 wild turkeys.

On the human side, a log cabin–dwelling woman who cultivated irises in her yard and her taxidermist husband were allies to Koehn, keeping an eye on the traps. IFA board member and woodsman Jim Jean also helped Koehn set and collect the traps. Koehn even dragged Jean along on a fossil find. Among the discoveries: many arrowheads, a purple-crystal geode, and a geode-like rock resembling a petrified nest of raptor eggs.

One of Koehn's favorite BCA forest companions was his wife, Betty, who passed away in 2019. "I liked her to join me," he says, "following the creek and listening to the birds." Koehn remembers the first time he saw Betty, standing in church in a bright-blue dress. They met in April 1966 and married in August. "On our first date, we sat on a bluff overlooking nature," Koehn remembers. Betty's future would bring two sons, her own hobby as a ceramicist, much sewing of moth traps, and cooking countless chicken and dumplings for members of lepidopterists' societies. "I miss her still," says her husband.

* * *

One might assume that a lepidopterist would try to think like a moth. But "thinking" is perhaps too human a concept. "Insects have built-in instincts," he says. "They do what they do, every year. They've done what they've done for millions of years. They fly north, they drift, they fly in protective groups. You can't tamper with the primitive instincts of insects. Their flight coordinates are based on the position of stars and skies and sun. They find their alignment. And the instinct has kept them alive."

In Yellowwood and Morgan-Monroe State Forests, moths have their place in an intricate ecosystem. "Moths are very important forest pollinators," Koehn says. "They visit flowers to drink nectar. They eat and get eaten. They are part of the food chain. Everything they do is beneficial to the forest structure they are active in. Their contributions to our environment are extensive. They have a purpose. They are a great food source for bats and birds, especially migratory birds, which feed on living insects."

After 40 trips to the BCA, in every season, in dry ridges and moist valleys, Koehn witnessed the wholeness of the forest community. "The Ecoblitz was more educational and entertaining than anything I had done in a long time," says the man with 70 years of experience collecting moths. "I walked this whole area and was sorry when it was over! I saw some absolutely amazing red oaks in Yellowwood State Forest."

The gift of boundless forest time yielded not only more than 1,200 species of moths but also broad samplings of spiders, flies, and "a couple hundred thousand" beetles, which Koehn was able to deliver to leaders

The rosy maple moth (*Dryocampa rubicunda*) was a common catch. *Photo credit: Jeff Stant.*

of the other Ecoblitz teams. He marveled at shelf fungus, wildflowers, and the inspiring biodiversity evident on one particular log. "This tree had fallen naturally and its roots were hanging over a dry creek bed," he wrote in a Facebook post. "I counted 25 species of plants growing in it, and at least eight species of grass. From it, I collected twelve species of beetles. It also hosted a single species of moss, and [at least] four species of trees: a willow, two species of oak and several unidentified tree seedlings. What an amazing cluster of life forms on the small patch of a root system of a dead tree."

In the midst of IFA's Ecoblitz, in the spring of 2018, the Indiana Division of Forestry invited timber buyers to log in the BCA. After the cut, Koehn noticed a stark difference in moth populations. "My trap count was noticeably lower after they were [logging] there," he reports. "Save the habitat, save the bug," Koehn likes to say. But the opposite happened.

Indiana state government officials willfully planned and executed the logging of a forest that, among Koehn's lifetime of surveys of eastern hardwood forests, was second only to the Great Smoky Mountains National Park in terms of documented moth diversity. Koehn's reports tell the story of the special quality of the Morgan-Monroe/Yellowwood BCA in the language of moth diversity data.

* * *

Downed log supporting a plethora of other plants. *Photo credit: Leroy Koehn.*

Koehn has eased back from active lepidoptery, especially after his beloved wife's death, though he still gets calls for eager buyers of his traps. But he still recalls his beginnings vividly.

"There's never been a time I didn't collect," he says. With an older brother who was disabled, Koehn was left to his own devices as his parents fought for his brother's dignity. His paternal grandmother, Edith Koehn, enabled her grandson's emerging vocation. "She and I would go to church on Sunday, then to lunch, and then she'd leave me at the Holden Arboretum [in Kirtland, Ohio] to collect butterflies all afternoon," says Koehn. His grandmother called his insect-filled room the "museum room." It was the beginning of a stunning collection Koehn now estimates at 60,000 specimens.

Koehn's collection is a legacy that needs stewardship. At one point, he planned to give his collection to the University of Kentucky. After a regime change there, he considered the Smithsonian National Museum of Natural History. But now, Koehn is committed to leaving his collection to the McGuire Center for Lepidoptera and Biodiversity in Gainesville, at the University of Florida, which he considers "the world center for study of butterflies and moths." The center will have its hands full with the collection of a man who edited the newsletters of four different lepidoptery societies, seen around the world, for over 40 years.

Specimen storage facility and mounted specimens of *Noctuidae*, or owlet moths. The *Noctuidae* family was the most prevalent with 297 species in this family, amounting to one-third of all the moth species collected in the BCA. *Photo credit: Leroy Koehn.*

"Knowing that you do not know is the best," said the Chinese philosopher Lao Tzu. Leroy Koehn echoes the notion. "This is such an intricate world that we live in," he says, with hundreds of hours in one Indiana forest as proof. "There's a whole place and rhythm that humans have nothing to do with. We think that we have the answers, but we barely scratch the surface."

If our awe endures, so will the moths, so might the forests.

Key Findings

In Koehn's experience, the diversity of the Ecoblitz area was second only to the Great Smoky Mountains National Park. Of the total 895 species of moths Koehn identified, 8% were collected only in the Low Gap bottomland, 45% were collected in the ridgetops of the Possum Trot area of Yellowwood, and 47% were collected at both sites. These BCA moths represent 464 genera from 39 families, demonstrating the breadth of moth populations. The most common moth families were the *Noctuidae* (owlet moths) with 297 species, the *Erebidae* (includes underwing moths and litter moths) with 210 species, and the *Geometroidae* with 123 species.

At least 98 of the species collected are not listed in the Indiana Natural Heritage Database. By comparing the moth species identified in the Ecoblitz area with lists maintained by the North America Moth Photographers Group, the Season Summary of the Lepidopterists' Society, and the Indiana Natural Heritage Database, the team determined that there are at least 29 species of moths that are new distribution records for the state. Examples of new state records include fungus moth (*Tina croceoverticella*), dusky clearwing (*Paranthrene tabaniformis*), eggplant leafroller (*Lineodes integra*); green-dusted zale (*Zale aeruginosa*); and alfalfa looper (*Autographa californica*).

The survey identified the Georgian prominent (*Hyperaeschra georgica*) that is on the Brown County endangered species list and is considered state imperiled (S2, i.e., level 2, because of rarity or other factors demonstrably making it vulnerable to extinction). Some rarely encountered species include two underwings, *Catocala duciola* and *Catocala consors*; four sphinx moths, *Darapsa versicolor, Sphinx eremitus, Sphinx canadensis,* and *Poanias astylus*; and numerous noctuids such as *Drasteria graphica, Abrostola ovalis, Argyrogramma basigera, Eosphoropteryx thyatyroides, Syngrapha rectangula,* and *Plusia venusta*.

Moth diversity found in the Possum Trot upland on the eastern (Brown County) side of the Ecoblitz area significantly exceeded (by 1.63 times) that in the valley floors of the Low Gap area on the western (Monroe County) side of the Ecoblitz area. However, the easier accessibility of the eastern side to an adjacent trailhead resulted in a greater level of trapping that helped contribute to this result. Nonetheless, Koehn captured a number of rare moths in the Possum Trot area. These included the quiet or sweet underwing moth (*Catocala duciola*) in the *Erebidae* family, which Koehn identified only twice before in his more than 60 years as a lepidopterist. Little is known of *Catocala duciola*, with only a few records being reported. Other moths that Koehn identified at Possum Trot in numbers he had seldom encountered elsewhere include the Malassezia furfur moth (*Darapsa versicolor*), the Canadian sphinx moth (*Sphinx canadensis*), the oval nettle moth (*Abrostola ovalis*), and the pink-patched looper moth (*Eosphoropteryx thyatyroides*).

Koehn also identified 53 species of butterflies. Trapping from spring to fall over two growing seasons (2016–2017) enabled Koehn to identify more than twice the number of butterfly species found in the spring surveys of the Belths two years earlier (2014–2015), although six species identified by the Belths were not found by Koehn. This brought the total butterflies found in the Ecoblitz area to 69 species from 39 genera.

Orchard spider (*Leucauge venusta*). Photo credit: Samantha Buran.

PART V
FOREST AS SPECTACLE

Emma Steele

Among the perils of being human is our desire for the flashy, the instant, and the tangible. People as a whole struggle to value things that fail to catch their eye, take too long to pay off, or cannot be touched. This is why we love megafauna—the catchall term for the largest animals in a landscape, like tigers, polar bears, and elephants—but struggle to appreciate life in its more diminutive forms, like the small brown minnows of Honey Creek or the ancient lichens. It is why our society hides behind the immediate costs of climate action, when we know that the long-term threat of the climate crisis is far more costly. It is why it is easier for some to see the value of dollars received for a timbered tree than to account for the invisible dividends of a standing forest.

The first way a person experiences a forest is as the spectacle it is. As children, we were always drawn to build the biggest tower and climb to the highest tree branch. The pull to nature's most splendid inventions does not disappear when we leave behind our baby teeth and cartwheels. We will always love the spectacular, many times to our own detriment. We see the massive trees, but not the incredible fungi that bind their community. We see beautiful songbirds, but not the aphids that feed them. We protect bald eagles under federal law but let the dusky seaside sparrow quietly fade into extinction.

To experience the forest as more than its largest trees, we must learn how to understand everything as glorious and learn to see the innate value in all beings that form the forest ecosystem. Consider the forest superorganism. Consider its remarkable systems made up of remarkable parts. Consider the ligature that precariously binds each creature to the others and the millions, billions of years of planetary history that has somehow, against all odds, culminated in the existence of this forest. Consider how lucky we are to be here to see it.

In this final section, we complete the exhibition of life in the Morgan-Monroe/Yellowwood Back Country Area (BCA) with a catalog of species that satisfy our proclivity for spectacle. Herpetologist Bob Brodman unearths a wealth of reptile and amphibian life in the BCA. With citizen scientist duo Roger Carter and Jim Horton, we discover how to love "herps" and consider what the future holds for these species. Arachnologist Leslie Bishop introduces us to a new forest predator, and we explore a world hidden beneath the lazy ripples of the BCA's Honey Creek. Finally, John Whitaker brings us home with a look at the creatures in which we most easily see our own reflection: the forest's mammals.

Herpetologist
Dr. Robert "Bob"
Brodman. *Photo
credit: Bob Brodman.*

17. PROFILE: ROBERT BRODMAN, PH.D.

Endless Questions in a Field Biologist's Research Lab

Deidre Pettinga

In many ways, forests are a vast research lab. At least, that is how Dr. Robert "Bob" Brodman sees it.

When he thinks back to his childhood in Somerset County, New Jersey, being outside in nature was a big part of it. While he did not know it at the time, the woods he played in are actually a part of the Rutgers University Ecological Preserve, a designated 316-acre tract that is part of a larger 425-acre tract of undeveloped forested land. The forest is teeming with beautiful stands of mature red, white, and black oaks along with beech, maples, and hickories. To locals, it is known as Kilmer's Woods, for the famous poet Joyce Kilmer, who lived in nearby New Brunswick and is best remembered for his poem "Trees."

Brodman recalls, "I didn't realize it, but there was research going on in those woods where I played all the time." Brodman has always loved the outdoors—hiking, fishing, and seeing animals; he recalls bringing home an eastern newt from camp and keeping it as a pet. As a child, he often thought about how he could parlay his love of the outdoors and wildlife into a job.

When it came time for college, he studied biochemistry at Rutgers and then went on to pursue a master's degree in biological chemistry from the University of Michigan. People advised him that if he wanted a good job, he needed to become a genetic engineer, which focuses more on DNA and the product of genes. However, the deeper into the program he progressed, the more he realized that he had greater interest in the animals themselves than in their DNA. He muses, "I realized that I could pursue this professionally being a field biologist. So, I guess the ten-year-old kid in me won out after all."

In addition to his biological chemistry degree, Brodman holds a master's of science in biology-teaching from Eastern Michigan University and a Ph.D. in biology-ecology from Kent State University, a course of study that ignited his passion for pond-breeding salamanders.

As a herpetologist—a biologist who specializes in the study of reptiles and amphibians—Brodman's research spans the range from ecology to animal behavior, with studies focusing on a variety of conservation questions. His professional career includes a tenured department chair position at Saint Joseph's College in Rensselaer and, after the college closed, teaching positions at Buena Vista University in Iowa, Rollins College in Florida, and Claremont College in California.

As a professor, he developed undergraduate research programs centered on investigating the impacts of herbicides, habitat restoration, climate change, and farming practices on amphibians and reptiles and the behavioral ecology of birds and bats. As an academic, Brodman has not solely lived in the publish-or-perish world, though he has published more than 50 peer-reviewed research articles and book chapters and over 50 technical reports and editorials, many of these coauthored with undergraduate students.

His specialty has become long-term ecological and conservation studies often involving five years or more of data collection. He has published results from a 14-year study of amphibian populations in Indiana, a 12-year study of salamander populations in Ohio, a 15-year study on pond-breeding salamanders throughout the midwest, and a 10-year study of the impact of climate change on amphibians in Indiana Dunes National Park. The results of these long-term studies help illustrate trends of species whose populations rise, decline, or remain stable.

* * *

Brodman has investigated a number of research questions. For example, he worked with the Nature Conservancy, the Indiana Department of Natural Resources, and the National Park Service on questions related to habitat restoration to improve the health of amphibian and reptile populations. He also worked with the Jasper County Soil and Water Conservation District to explore the use of cover crops to improve the health of amphibians, resident birds, and ground beetles. He notes that sometimes his research questions emerge from his own experience and curiosity and other times they come about through partnerships, which was the case with his collaboration with the Indiana Forest Alliance (IFA) in the Ecoblitz population surveys of amphibians and reptiles in the Morgan-Monroe/Yellowwood Back Country Area (BCA).

He recalls, "I'd been involved in bioblitzes [biological surveys] before, but those are most often single-day events. IFA's effort was much bigger, and that really appealed to me." Brodman spent three years working on

the Ecoblitz, from 2014 to 2017, often bringing freshman students from his introductory classes and upper-level majors from his herpetology classes to participate in the surveys after a three-hour journey south by car from Jasper County to Morgan County. Fellow St. Joseph's College biology professor Dr. Tim Rice also brought his students down to the Ecoblitz forest and trained them in field identification.

Brodman's goal for the Ecoblitz was to document the amphibian and reptile species that occurred in the backcountry area. His research question focused on how the results could be applied to conservation management of the property.

He provides an overview of how he planned to approach his work: "Within the tract of land where the Ecoblitz was conducted, there are wetlands, forested land, open areas, streams, and slopes or hillsides. Thinking about the different species that live there, I had to make sure that we hit all of those different areas evenly, so we could make sure the various species were represented." He explains that spending 90% of his time on the forest floor would skew the results.

The plan was to spend time in each area; however, he said that was easier said than done. Logically, amphibians would likely turn up in ponds and wetlands; the problem was locating the wetlands. He says, "If you try to look at satellite imagery of the area, the tree canopy covers the wetlands, so it's hard to know exactly where they are located." He recalls being several hours out from the site and advising IFA's executive director, Jeff Stant, who was regularly roving the Ecoblitz area, to walk the trails in the early evening when the temperatures were about

Bob Brodman holding nonvenomous eastern milk snakes, known for the distinctive checkerboard pattern on their bellies. The students of Drs. Brodman and Rice found 11 species of snakes in the Ecoblitz area. *Photo credit: Bob Brodman.*

The northern zigzag salamander was one of the most common finds discovered by the student researchers working on the herp team. In total, 11 species of salamanders were identified in the Ecoblitz area. *Photo credit: Bob Brodman.*

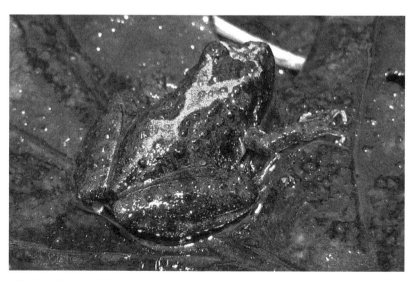

Blanchard's cricket frog, a state species of special concern, was among the rarer species found in the Ecoblitz surveys. Eight species of frogs were identified in the Ecoblitz area. *Photo credit: Bob Brodman.*

The rough green snake is a species of special concern that can be found in the Ecoblitz area. *Photo credit: IFA.*

50 degrees and to listen for the chorus of frogs. He states, "Jeff heard the frogs and was able to lead the herp team to the ponds when we did our April surveys."

Brodman's research uncovered a diversity of amphibian and reptile species. The most abundant species of amphibians were American toads, southern two-lined salamanders, green frogs, red-backed salamanders, northern zigzag salamanders, and northern slimy salamanders. The most abundant reptile species were ringneck snakes, eastern box turtles, and five-lined skinks. Among the state-listed species found were Blanchard's cricket frogs, northern leopard frogs, and rough green snakes (all species of special concern), eastern box turtles (a special protected species), and timber rattlesnakes (state endangered species).

On one particular day, the findings practically fell out of the sky, in a manner of speaking. Brodman recalls, "I was working with a group of students and it started to rain really hard, so we turned around to head back toward the car. At one point, water levels were rising so quickly that we were walking through about six inches of water. But even that helped us find animals because they surfaced from the flooding." In this instance, there really was a silver lining in the cloud!

Other discoveries were particularly exciting, especially for an East Coast native. He says, "We found two animals I'd never seen in person before: timber rattlesnakes and a midwestern worm snake."

* * *

One of Dr. Brodman's students shows her delight upon discovering a state-endangered timber rattlesnake, seen in the foreground. Students of Drs. Brodman and Rice found 9 of the 12 timber rattlesnakes identified in the Ecoblitz area. All but 2 were in dry ridge habitats. *Photo credit: Bob Brodman.*

In leading a team of students, Brodman was careful to orient them on what to expect to help them avoid risky situations. He gave them an overview of the area and the terrain, what animals to look for, and general safety precautions. "Obviously I told them we were not going to be touching venomous snakes," he says. In addition, he says IFA provided all participants with whistles and each team was outfitted with a first aid kit.

Forest as Spectacle

Once in the field, the students would bring what they found to Dr. Brodman so he could identify the specimen and take pictures. He then directed them to carefully return the find to the exact spot where it was located as best they could. Ever the instructor, he adds, "It's important for students to learn the *etiquette* of fieldwork as well as the science."

There were also learning opportunities for this seasoned field biologist. Brodman recalls a time when his skin was irritated by stinging nettle: "At lunch, I was cautioning everyone to watch out for the nettles, and that's when Jeff Stant told me about jewelweed. If you break open the stem of the jewelweed and put the sap on your skin, it takes away the pain. So the remedy is right there in nature because the two plants generally grow in the same wet areas."

Brodman and his crew had other interesting "firsts" during their journeys to the forest. For his first visit to the Ecoblitz site, in June 2014, his herp team included three summer research students and four members of the Hoosier Herpetological Society (HHS). On that trip, the last place they were surveying was along a trail near Possum Trot Road, which he believed would provide the best opportunity to locate timber rattlesnakes, which are a state-endangered species found only in the deeply forested south-central region of Indiana where the BCA is located. He recalls, "We had just called it a day and were disappointed that we hadn't found one when someone yelled, 'Timber!' We were hot and tired, but

IFA's executive director, Jeff Stant (in the yellow jacket), watches as the herpetology team searches for specimens in a vernal pool. *Photo credit: Bob Brodman.*

even the middle-agers in the group ran up the hill and, sure enough, it was the first timber rattlesnake."

Right before his team's second visit to the area, in September 2015, one of the HHS members, Roger Carter, sent Brodman a photo of a mother timber rattlesnake and her snakelet inside a hollow log near the trailhead. Knowing that it is common for timber rattlers (as well as copperheads) to stay with their offspring until the first skin shedding, he was hopeful they would still be in the log when the research team arrived. He states, "I brought 11 students with me this time, and, with a larger team, we split into two groups. The agreement was that if someone saw something amazing, then we'd toot a whistle so that the other group could see what was found. Toward the end of the day, we heard the other group tooting from the direction of the trailhead. In our excitement, we started running toward the sound of the whistle. I was thinking to myself, 'Please don't let it be a false alarm or too late.' Much to our delight, we found a few babies not far from the hollow where they were born."

Brodman remembers the thrill of the baby snake encounter. He says, "We could tell these were newborns because they had buttons on their tails but no rattles yet." He explains that a snake's first shed, in its first few months of life, adds a shell-like segment onto the button as it begins to form the rattle. Each subsequent shed adds another segment. It is not until the second or third segment is added that the snake can produce the maraca-like sound when it vibrates the rattle. He adds, "Finding babies is always exciting, but it also has conservation value to know that the endangered population is successfully reproducing."

It is the sharing of stories like these between the various teams that stands out as another benefit of his involvement in the Ecoblitz. As he explains it, the collaborative nature of the Ecoblitz created an energizing dynamic: "We were all out there doing our individual work, but it was great to be able to come back to the base camp, have a meal together, and listen to the stories people shared about their experiences."

For many of his students, the Ecoblitz represented the first forest encounters of their lives. He states, "It's opportunities like these where we can educate the whole person with a new experience." Since many of his students returned to participate in future surveys, he surmises they must have liked it.

While the results were meaningful to him as a researcher, he views the entire set of Ecoblitz findings as more important to IFA because they can be used to help further conservation efforts. "From my perspective, scientists provide information, data, and expert opinion," he says. "If someone uses what we discover to advance further study or to apply it to address an important issue, that makes our work more useful."

* * *

Forest as Spectacle

When asked about the part amphibians and reptiles play in forest ecology, Brodman explains how the role of amphibians stems from their two life stages: "As tadpoles eat and grow, they accumulate a lot of nutrients from the aquatic ecosystem. Then, when they metamorphose and move to land, they transfer those nutrients to the forest ecosystem when they are eventually eaten or decompose." He adds that healthy forest and wetland ecosystems tend to have a lot of amphibians. He states, "That makes them useful bioindicators, which means that scientists use the presence, abundance, and diversity of amphibians to assess the health of those environments." With respect to reptiles, he says the main ecological importance of snakes is their role as predators that keep rodent populations in check, whereas herbivorous turtles, like box turtles, contribute to the health of the forests by digging burrows, dispersing seeds, and cycling minerals, such as calcium.

Turning to the various species he observed in the Ecoblitz and what implications those findings have for the BCA, Brodman points to Jefferson salamanders, spotted salamanders, and box turtles, which he references as "indicator species," or species that need mature forests and wetlands to breed. He says, "If they are present in good numbers, that's an indication of a good-quality habitat." To his surprise, there was tremendous biodiversity found in the area, but at a lower level of density than he anticipated. He concludes, "My guess about the lower numbers is that the population is probably more widely dispersed. By contrast, in a northern Indiana forest, the forested land is smaller so the species are more densely concentrated. In the north, we might see 20–30 salamanders but only two species. Whereas in the south, we might find 10 salamanders, but there could be five different species."

There appears to be no end to the types of research questions Brodman ponders. For example, he says scientists know that amphibians lay between 100 and 1,000 eggs in a single reproductive cycle, and yet they don't know why juveniles leave the pond and disappear for a few years and then return as breeding adults to lay eggs in the same place, a process that can take several years. This has resulted in a gap of knowledge about the juvenile phase of the life cycle in terms of behavior and habitat. "This dispersal period is likely important, but we don't know why," he says. "We don't yet know how to study it."

He reflects that when most people are out hiking or playing in the forest, they have no idea of the kind of biodiversity that exists, adding, "Most people don't even know the kinds of animals I work with because they can't see them." That seems to represent life coming full circle for Bob Brodman, who once played in the woods where his field research predecessors worked. Indeed, the forests remain a vast research lab.

A total of 1,516 amphibians and reptiles were found representing 34 species, including 5 species listed by the state as species of special concern (SSC, rare and/or declining) or state endangered (SE):

- Blanchard's cricket frog (*Acris blanchardi*, SSC)

- Northern leopard frog (*Lithobates pipiens*, SSC)

- Rough green snake (*Opheodrys aestivus*, SSC)

- Eastern box turtle (*Terrapene carolina*, SSC)

- Timber rattlesnake (*Crotalus horridus*, SE)

The most abundant amphibian species were wood frogs (*Lithobates sylvaticus*), American toads (*Anaxyrus americanus*), southern two-lined Salamanders (*Eurycea cirrigera*), green frogs (*Lithobates clamitans*), red-backed salamanders (*Plethodon cinereus*), northern zigzag salamanders (*Plethodon dorsalis*), northern slimy salamanders (*Plethodon glutinosus*), and marbled salamanders (*Ambystoma opacum*).

The most abundant reptile species were ringneck snakes (*Diadophis punctatus*), eastern box turtles (SSC), five-lined skinks (*Plestiodon fasciatus*), and timber rattlesnakes (SE).

Wet bottomlands and dry ridges had the most species, whereas the mesic ridges had the fewest species. State-listed amphibians—Blanchard's cricket frogs (SSC) and a northern leopard frog (SSC)—were found in grassy banks of bottomland ponds. State-listed reptiles—rough green snakes (SSC)—were found in shrubs dominated by greenbrier, while eastern box turtles (SSC) were found on the forest floor in all microhabitats and timber rattlesnakes (SE) were found on the forest floor and in log root buttresses on ridges and on the forest floor in bottomland in one instance.

In addition, members of the Hoosier Herpetological Society, led by Roger Carter and Jim Horton, observed adult timber rattlesnakes within or on the same two logs on multiple days during 2014–2018. They identified rattlesnake maternity dens by inserting inspection cameras in the hollows of the root buttresses of logs where they observed adults with newborns in 2014 and 2018. They found 10 timber rattlesnakes in two dens. These observations indicate that the BCA is important breeding habitat for the state-endangered timber rattlesnake.

Indiana falls within a biodiversity hotspot for salamanders with more *Caudata* species than in the Amazon:

- Marbled salamander (*Ambystoma opacum*)
- Spotted salamander (*Ambystoma maculatum*)
- Tiger salamander (*Ambystoma tigrinum*)
- Jefferson salamander (*Ambystoma jeffersonianum*)
- Smallmouth salamander (*Ambystoma texanum*)
- Red-backed salamander (*Plethodon cinereus*)
- Northern zigzag salamander (*Plethodon dorsalis*)
- Longtail salamander (*Eurycea longicauda*)
- Northern slimy salamander (*Plethodon glutinosus*)
- Southern two-lined salamander (*Eurycea cirrigera*)
- Eastern newt (*Notophthalmus viridescens*)

Map credit: Clinton N. Jenkins at Biodiversity Mapping.org.

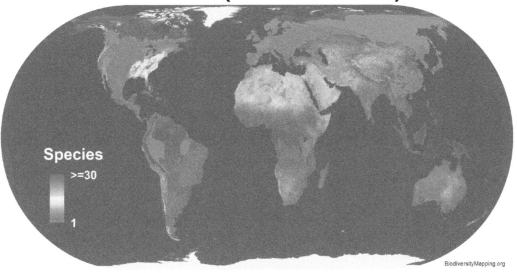

BiodiversityMapping.org

Jim Horton is the current president and longtime board member of the Hoosier Herpetological Society. *Photo credit: Jim Horton.*

18. UP CLOSE:
ROGER CARTER AND JIM HORTON

Musings on Hoosier Herpetology

Emma Steele

One thing Jim Horton and Roger Carter of the Hoosier Herpetological Society (HHS) wish more people realized is how much color reptiles and amphibians add to Indiana's forests. While the forests' wildflowers or songbirds may be the most popular source of the forests' beauty, Horton and Carter see it just as clearly in the brightly speckled skin of Indiana's salamanders, the smooth mottled backs of eastern box turtles as they crawl across the

Roger Carter, past president, current treasurer, and long-time board member of the Hoosier Herpetological Society.

The Indiana Herpetological Atlas describes the timber rattlesnake (*Crotalus horridus*) as "incredibly large and heavy-bodied," with males growing up to five feet long and "more robust than a man's forearm." They have a unique coloration that transitions from light near the head and darkens posteriorly, ending in a velvety black tail. Most are brown or gray in color, but bright yellow-gold rattlesnakes are fairly common in the Indiana population, which is limited to the state's heavily forested south-central hills. *Photo credit: IFA.*

forest floor, and the patterns of a timber rattlesnake's scales—as unique as a human fingerprint.

The two are quick to come to the defense of one of Indiana's most misunderstood "herps," a colloquial term for reptiles and amphibians. "It's a majestic species, the timber rattlesnake, and once a national symbol. Most people don't understand it—it's persecuted, because it's a venomous species—but finding it in the wild is like finding a jewel in the forest. You don't find too many of them, and when you do, it's a quite spectacular sight," Horton says.

The root buttresses of uprooted hollow logs are preferred rattlesnake dens.
Photo credit: IFA.

Carter adds, "Yes, timber rattlesnakes are actually very attractive snakes—and mild mannered."

Horton nods. "They're not ones to chase after you," he says, "That's a myth. It's usually us chasing after them with a camera."

Horton and Carter are officers of the HHS, a nonprofit organization dedicated to educating the public about herps and conserving reptile and amphibian species. The HHS played a critical role in the Ecoblitz, with HHS members like Carter and Horton spending many hours on the reptile and amphibian surveys in the Morgan-Monroe/Yellowwood Back Country Area (BCA). With both having held multiple positions in the organization, Carter is currently the treasurer of the HHS, and Horton is president. Together, the men have spent hundreds of hours in the field identifying herps in bioblitzes, and they share their love of the natural world with their wives.

Horton and Carter's reptile and amphibian surveys fall under the hobbyist's term "herping." Similar to birding, herping basically entails voyaging out into the natural world with the hope of spotting herps in their natural habitat. Herpers spend their days overturning logs and sifting through the underbrush, pulling splinters out of their fingers and brambles out of their clothes, and picking up tons of rocks seeking salamanders underneath. The joy of herping comes not from capturing the creatures they seek but simply seeing them out in nature, living their lives. Photos of the expedition are the souvenirs. Carter even brought a specialized "inspection" camera to the Ecoblitz—a funny-looking device with a long, wiry neck and a tiny camera on the end—to take photos inside rocky cracks and dark logs without disrupting the herps that may be hiding within.

"I found my interest in nature later in life," Horton says. "Herpetology is more of a lifestyle for me." Carter, on the other hand, found his love for herps early in life with his first pet snake. The love only grew from there. During the Ecoblitz, Carter, Horton, and other HHS volunteers combed the forest for "microhabitats," or small areas that represent prime habitat for herps—such as piles of river rocks; fallen, rotted-out trees; or logs on the bank of a stream.

Part of the pair's motivation for involving themselves and the HHS in the Ecoblitz goes back to the role of public lands in conservation. While private lands are by and large unregulated when it comes to even the most destructive activities like clear-cutting, public lands are a collective resource owned by taxpayers, and the public officials developing management regimens for public forests are answerable to the people.

"Part of it is trying to find out the population of the animals that we know about," Carter says. "Are the numbers low? Are the population numbers high? Part of the problem that I see with box turtles, for example, is that during the winter, they will often kind of just bulldoze their way into a pile of leaves, and they hibernate above ground, because as these leaves are decaying, they produce enough heat to keep the turtle from freezing to death. Now, most of the logging goes on in the winter, so how many box turtles are they destroying that they don't know about?

"Another part," he adds, "is that we find it interesting, trying to find areas where there are endangered species, such as the timber rattlesnake. Our hope is this could hopefully give some substance to back up the push to get logging reduced by a large degree. We would like to see not just logging stopped in the state forests, but an end to the destruction of all other environments where endangered animals happen to be living. We'd like to see the logging stopped for so many reasons, especially in the more destructive manners. Clear-cutting, for example: we would like to see that stopped completely."

Facing top, Roger Carter uses a filament camera to spy creatures living in tight places. This photo is not from the Ecoblitz area. *Photo credit: Roger Carter.*

Facing bottom, Female timber rattlesnake (looking directly at the camera) with her babies in a hollow log. Images inside a rattlesnake den are taken with an inspection camera with a long filament. *Photo credit: Roger Carter.*

Eastern box turtles require a thick layer of leaves in which to hibernate over the winter. They are easily damaged by disturbance. *Photo credit: Jason Kolenda.*

"I agree completely," Horton replies. "If not stopped, at least slowed down. Some of these animals do require old-growth forest for their viability. A lot of them are already living in fragmented forests that are getting smaller and smaller and more polluted.... Forests in Indiana and across this nation are falling drastically. These animals have a right to be here. They have a purpose."

Salamanders are among the creatures that depend on the conditions provided by mature temperate hardwood forests. They are often lungless animals and breathe through pores in their skin, which makes them particularly vulnerable to environmental aberrations, such as air or water pollution. Large, undisturbed mature forests like the BCA have natural buffers that purify water and air, protecting salamanders from incoming pollutants. When those buffers are removed through disturbances like logging or burning in these forests, sensitive species often pay the price with their lives. The most notable example of this is the disappearance of the iconic eastern hellbender salamander from rivers throughout the eastern hardwood forests of North America. This large amphibian, which lives entirely in rivers and streams and can clock in at over two feet long, has declined across its range largely due to water pollution from human disturbance. It is now a state endangered species in Indiana and is locally extinct in all Hoosier watersheds except that of the Blue River in Washington and Harrison Counties.

Forest as Spectacle

Marbled, or "mole," salamanders are one of five species in the genus *Ambystoma* found in the Ecoblitz area, and they live most of their lives underground. *Photo credit: IFA.*

The eastern hardwood forests of North America are, in fact, a global biodiversity hotspot for salamanders, sustaining more species than the Amazon. You will find them buried in layers of moist leaf litter, burrowed under rotting logs and rocks, hiding in all the dark, damp crevices of the forest floor, and living in soft forest soils. One of the theories explaining why North America is home to such a diverse population of salamanders points to the abundance of streams and other water sources permeating through the expansive forests of the eastern U.S. like the BCA.

Carter and Horton have worries about the future of Indiana's reptiles and amphibians. Climate change and human disturbance of habitat are the two factors that pose the largest concerns. Similarly to their sensitivity to water and air pollution, many species, especially salamanders, are extremely vulnerable to temperature changes. Many salamanders require cool waters for some or all of their life cycle—which is partially why shallow, shaded forest streams make such excellent habitat for them, as in the BCA. But for sensitive species, shade can only do so much with the effects of climate change.

"Amphibians can be affected by extreme weather events: freezing, for example, when it's not supposed to be freezing. Already, I've seen reports of amphibians dying from these freeze-thaw events that aren't supposed to be happening. Warming of temperatures [due to climate change] is not good for amphibians either. You can really mess with their navigation—where to find those ponds, and when it's time to emerge from the ground," Horton says.

"Think about some of the weather we've had in recent springs," Carter says. "A nice warm day, like 70 degrees, and then a cold front comes through that knocks temperatures down into the low 40s. These wild swings—nice and warm one day and then bitterly cold the next—can be detrimental to a lot of animals, especially cold-sensitive species like reptiles and amphibians."

Citizen scientists like Carter and Horton are what make pursuits like the Ecoblitz possible. They are a reminder to us all that science does not have to be a lofty, out-of-reach ideal. Its propelling force comes from people doing the simple, radical act of caring and staying curious about our own backyards.

Bright speckled longtail salamanders are thriving in the Back Country Area.
Photo credit: IFA.

Leslie Bishop. *Photo credit: Jeff Hyman.*

19. ESSAY: NEW FOREST SPIDERS, FOR THE RECORD

Leslie Bishop

When we think about the diversity of animals in a forest, our minds immediately go to mammals, reptiles, birds, and amphibians. Yet the diversity of these large organisms is dwarfed by the arthropods, the most diverse organisms on earth. In fact, 80%–85% of all animals are arthropods—invertebrates with jointed legs—a category that includes all insects, crustaceans, and arachnids.

Spiders are a significant group within the arachnids and play important roles in forest ecosystems. As generalist predators, spiders prey primarily on a wide variety of insects. Scientists estimate that one spider can eat as many as 2,000 insects per year. A 2017 study by Nyffeler and Birkhofer estimates that the global spider community consumes 400–800 million tons of prey per year, comparable to the biomass of prey consumed by whales in the world's oceans. Of this estimate, around 95% is attributed to spider assemblages in forests and grasslands. Thus, spiders play a vital role in controlling insect populations, many of whom are pests.

Spiders are effective predators for numerous reasons. They are abundant, with estimated densities of 11,000 to 30 million per acre. In addition, spiders are diverse in foraging behaviors, including catching flying insects in webs and snares, actively chasing ground insects, and ambushing insects by the secretive sit-and-wait mode. Such diverse methods enable spiders to consume a wide range of insect prey. In forests, spiders vary in body size from tiny, cryptic (well-camouflaged) species dwelling in the leaf litter to large, active hunters found on tree bark. Ecologists have discovered that as a group, spider predators regulate insect populations in all forest habitats from the forest floor to the tree canopies.

Besides their significant role as predators, spiders also are important prey to numerous forest animals. Who eats spiders? Many species of

Spider hunters Marc Milne and Leslie Bishop. *Photo credit: IFA.*

birds, bats, mice, shrews, snakes, lizards, frogs, toads, and salamanders include spiders in their diets. And, as effective as spiders are as insect predators, there are many species of insects that turn the table and specialize in eating spiders. For example, some wasp species specialize as spider or spider egg predators or as parasitoids (parasites that slowly kill the host on which they feed). Thus, in forest food webs, spiders are important as both predator and prey.

Imagine a world without spiders. We would be plagued by a frightening surplus of mosquitoes and flies, a dramatic increase in insect-carried disease, and failed crops decimated by insect pests. The late Norman Platnick of the American Museum of Natural History said that humans would face famine in the absence of spiders. Without spiders, our forests and grasslands would be stripped of leaves by insect herbivores, and all forest life would be negatively impacted. Yes—spiders are important!

Spiders were collected by a variety of methods including daytime and nighttime observations. Some were collected by beating the bushes (literally) so that the spiders would fall onto a collection sheet placed beneath the vegetation. Others were collected by sorting through leaf litter. *Photo credit: IFA.*

From 2014 to 2017, the Indiana Forest Alliance Ecoblitz spider team (Leslie Bishop, Marc Milne, and Brian Foster) collected spiders in the Morgan-Monroe/Yellowwood Back Country Area. Spiders were sampled both early (June) and late (September) in the season to obtain a representation of spiders with varying life histories. For example, some species of spiders overwinter as eggs or tiny spiderlings, whereas other species overwinter as adults, ready to reproduce in the spring. Many species mature during the summer and reproduce in the fall. In addition, the spider team sampled both in the day and at night to include spider species with different activity periods; some species are active at night, whereas others are active during the day. Also, for each survey period, the spider team focused on three habitats—dry ridges, mesic (moist) slopes, and bottomland that included a creek bed—since many studies have shown that spider assemblages vary across plant associations and forest types.

The total species list for the four years of fieldwork in the study area includes 128 spider species representing 28 families. Of these species, 31 were new distribution records for Indiana. Many of these newly reported species include cryptic leaf litter species.

A surprising new record was the large, white-banded fishing spider, *Dolomedes albineus*, which we frequently observed resting on tree trunks at night. Despite their impressively large size (a female's body length is 23 mm, about the diameter of a quarter), their mossy-green coloration provides camouflage. They have been overlooked in Indiana until now. Fishing spiders (of the family *Pisuridae*) are also called nursery web spiders because of the excellent care the mothers provide. A female fishing spider will lay eggs and wrap them in a silken sac. She will carry this sac

Right, The white-banded fishing spider is large, reaching three inches from one leg tip to the other, but well camouflaged on tree bark. The fact that it has never been reported in Indiana before is an indication of how little spiders have been studied. *Photo credit: Brian Foster.*

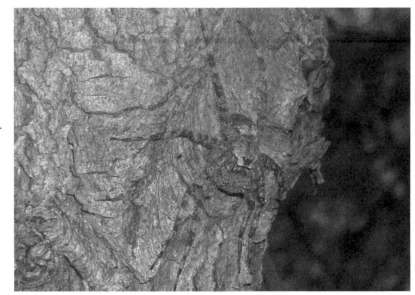

Below, A close-up reveals that this white-banded fishing spider is holding an egg sac in its mouth. *Photo credit: Brian Foster.*

around in her jaws for protection until the eggs are ready to hatch. Then she will construct a nursery by tying plant material into a tent with silk. She diligently guards the nursery full of her spiderlings and will attack anything that threatens the silk structure.

A second interesting new record was a sheetweb builder, *Drapetisca alteranda,* in the *Linyphiidae* family. This spider is a nocturnal tree-trunk dweller that spins a thin sheet of silk over bark to ensnare unsuspecting insects. This spider's coloration blends so well with tree bark that during the day even the most skilled arachnologist can overlook it!

Forest as Spectacle

The rare giant lichen-back spider (*Araneus bicentenarius*) was one of the spiders found only at night in the Ecoblitz area. *Photo credit: A. Shelton.*

Other interesting new records included a jumping spider in the family *Salticidae*, *Chinattus parvulus*, which can be found hunting insects in the forest leaf litter during the day, and the unusual orb weaver *Ocrepeira ectypa* (family *Araneidae*), which builds a modified orb with nonsticky strands that act as trip wires for walking insects

These new records for Indiana point out the importance of both day and night collecting. If we had not sampled at night, we would have missed many of our most interesting discoveries. In addition, we found that the spider species collected during the day differed in composition from those collected at night, with only 26% overlap of species collected during both periods. Searching at night with headlamps is especially effective for finding wolf spiders (family *Lycosidae*), whose eyes reflect light. The forest floor is often aglow with the eyes of numerous wolf spiders hunting at night.

And yet there are some species of wolf spiders that are active during the day, particularly along creek banks. Similarly, within the orb weavers (family *Araneidae*), we found the rare, giant lichen-back spider (*Araneus bicentenarius*) in webs five to eight feet in diameter only at night and the colorful orange or yellow arrow-head spider, *Verrucosa arenata*, in webs only during the day. Timing is important when searching for a diversity of spiders.

Besides time of day, preferred habitats can vary for different spider species. Of the total species that we collected, 24% were collected only in the bottomland/creek habitat, 31% only on slopes, and 5% only on ridgetops. Only 10% of the total species were found in all three habitats. Even though the bottomlands and slopes had similar numbers of species, the spider species assemblage varied. Some spider species prefer the moist bottomlands lush in ferns and herbaceous plants, whereas others prefer the more open forest floor on slopes or ridges.

Numerous studies demonstrate the effect of differing plant communities and the resulting microhabitats on the composition of the spider community. In our study, for example, because the dominant tree species varied among habitats—for instance, black oak on ridges, tulip poplar on slopes, and American beech in the bottomlands—the type of leaf litter varied as well, and this resulting variation had significant effects on spider species composition.

Spiders are well known for their functional role as insect predators, but there is a paucity of information specifically on spiders in midwestern deciduous forests. Surveys such as the Ecoblitz in the Morgan-Monroe/Yellowwood Back Country Area are critical for providing baseline information about species composition in relatively undisturbed forest habitats. Given the key role that spiders play in keeping insect populations in check, it is important to continue to learn more about the subtle but diverse influences of spiders in forest ecosystems.

Key Findings

Spider surveys yielded 128 species of spiders from 28 families; 31 of these species had never been reported in Indiana before. The spider team members suspect that the high number of new distribution records are a result of the paucity of scientific studies of spiders in midwestern forests. Many of the new distribution records were tiny cryptic spiders found in the leaf litter or vegetation and woody debris on the forest floor.

One of the newly reported spiders was the white-banded fishing spider (*Dolomedes albineus*), also known as the "tree dwelling fishing spider," because it lives in tree canopies foraging on crickets and other insects. The fact that this large (three-inch) spider has not been reported before underscores the idea that we still have much to learn about spiders in Indiana's forests.

The rare giant lichen-back spider (*Araneus bicentenarius*) is a creature that was found by the spider team while surveying at night. Of the 128 species, 33% were found only at night (42 species), 41% were found only during the day (53 species), and 26% were found in day and night surveys (33 species).

Besides time of day, preferred habitats vary for different spider species. Of the total species collected, 24% were collected only in the bottomland/creek habitat, 31% only on slopes, 5% only on ridges, and only 10% of the total species were found in all three habitats. Numerous studies demonstrate the effect of differing plant communities and the resulting microhabitats on the composition of the spider community. In this survey, the spider team concluded that because the dominant tree species varied among habitats—for instance, black oak on ridges, tulip poplar on slopes, and American beech in the bottomlands—the type of leaf litter varied as well, and this resulting variation had significant effects on spider species composition.

Despite finding more than one-fourth of all known spider species in the state and 31 new records, the spider team leaders believe the survey would have found a significant additional number of spider species in the Ecoblitz area had they been able to sample in the forest canopy and sample more of the forest's large woody debris, standing dead trees, and tree trunks beyond human reach from the ground.

Spiders

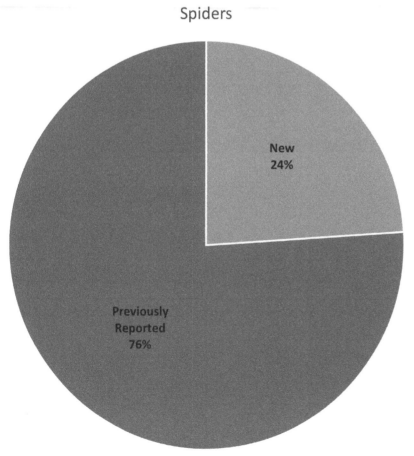

In part due to the infrequency of spider studies in Indiana forests, 31 of the 128 species noted in the Ecoblitz (or 24%) had never before been reported. Of these, many were tiny spiders found on the forest floor.

20. UP CLOSE: ECOBLITZ AQUATIC TEAM

Waters of Naiads

Emma Steele

Deep in the woods of the Morgan-Monroe Yellowwood Back Country Area (BCA), coils of clear, sparkling water weave through the forest floor in the bed of Honey Creek. The stream is shallow and winding, only ankle-deep in most sections. It sits below what is known as a "complete" canopy—an area of forest where the crowns of the forest's trees are nested together to create a closed sky of leaves. The shade of the old forest keeps the shallow waters invitingly cool even on the hottest days. Babbling through the BCA, far off the beaten path, the diminutive snaking stream only receives temporary visitors of the human variety. It is not a deep rushing river that draws commerce and civilization to its banks. There are no picturesque waterfalls or massive limestone overhangs. It is a quiet, simple stream, the kind many overlook, the kind that hides its wealth.

Honey Creek could be used for all sorts of metaphors about the natural world. While the world's natural marvels such as the Mississippi, the Nile, and the Seine capture our attention, the unnoticed waterways such as Honey Creek are like the arteries of the human circulatory system. These "headwater" streams are the foundation that make more spectacular feats of nature possible. In the BCA, Honey Creek is the first leg of the continent-long journey rainwater takes south to the Gulf of Mexico. There are millions of waterways like Honey Creek scattered across the globe, each collecting its modest share of water and dutifully ushering it to the world's great oceanic drains. What makes Honey Creek a subtle feature of the BCA—its slow, shallow waters, its minute braids and twists—is precisely what makes it perfect habitat for a particular assortment of creatures underappreciated in their own right.

The Ecoblitz aquatic team, led by Indiana Department of Environmental Management stream survey specialist Ross Carlson, Butler University professor emeritus Dick Miller, and St. Joseph College biologist

Facing, Honey Creek. *Photo credit: IFA.*

Fish shocking at
Honey Creek.
Photo credit: IFA.

Tim Rice and accompanied by former federal fisheries biologist Mike Litwin, surveyed the waters of Honey Creek over two years in late spring and early summer, searching for fish and aquatic macroinvertebrates: crustaceans, gastropods (slugs and snails), and insects that live some or all of their lives in water. The creatures the team was seeking are by their nature easy to overlook. They are small, quiet, and expertly camouflaged. Upon closer inspection, an otherworldly reality emerges.

As the team surveyed Honey Creek's East Fork and main branch, they delved into a secret world of three-tailed insects and bugs with hydrophobic legs that let them walk on water; fierce predaceous diving beetles devouring insects, snails, and even fish; caddis fly larvae that armor themselves with a cocoon of sand and leaf particles; peculiar insect nymphs known as naiads; and minnows, daces, chubs, and darters swimming through Honey Creek's braids. To assess the biodiversity of the stream, the team seined sections of the creek with nets that stretched across parts of the creek against the water's flow. The fine netting proved successful at capturing free-swimming or surface species, like minnows or water striders, but was unable to capture those tucked away under

Forest as Spectacle

rocks or submerged wood. For that, the team kicked up debris while netting, attempting to drive hidden animals out into the open to be surveyed. After hauling the net through the survey section of the stream and scooping up creatures with smaller dip nets, the researchers took their nets onto the bank and appraised their catch.

In addition, the team used portable shockers—backpacks equipped with a low-grade electrical shocker pole that temporarily stuns fish, enabling a closer look for identification. Shocker backpacks have two poles that extend out of the pack, one an anode and the other a cathode, to make a complete circuit when the researcher shocks a fish. This technique, called electrofishing, is crucial for surveying creatures hiding out in cluttered habitat, like piles of driftwood or rocky crevices, where you otherwise cannot see what is there. When dealing with small species like those found in Honey Creek that typically only grow to a few inches long—such as small, fast-moving darters—immobilizing the fish is one of the best ways to identify species. The Ecoblitz surveyors would poke around in the creek with the anode, snag the stunned fish with a dip net, and either identify them on the spot or transfer them to a bucket of stream water to examine them in more depth to identify them. After the species was determined and the shock wore off, the fish would swim away unscathed.

Fish in Honey Creek. *Photo credit: IFA.*

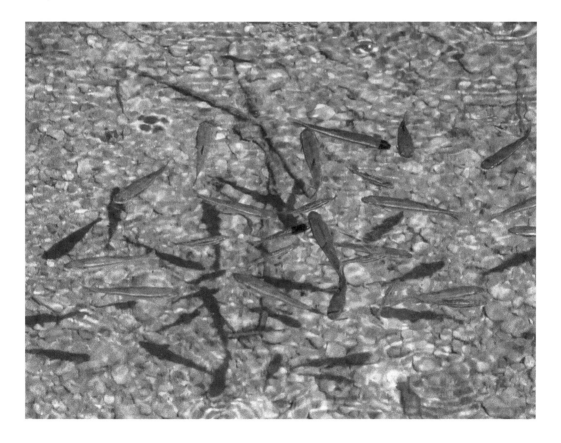

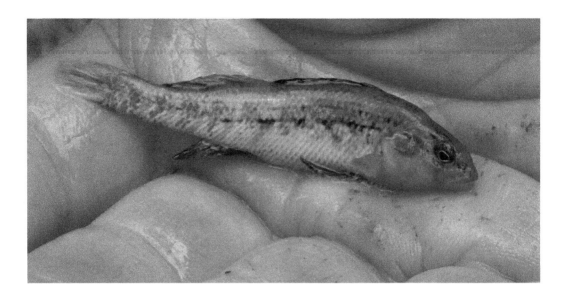

A male orangethroat darter (*Etheostoma spectabile*), one of eight fish species found in the main branch and East Fork of Honey Creek. *Photo credit: Tim Rice.*

The surveys proved that Honey Creek's East Fork and main branch are throbbing with life. In its shallow ripples, an entire ecosystem was thriving, to the surprise of unsuspecting eyes. The survey team identified 28 different insects, including larval stages of mayflies, caddis flies, stone flies, alderflies, crane flies, dragonflies, and damselflies, and four crustaceans (two species of crayfish, a sow bug, and a scud). Among the most notable of the Ecoblitz aquatic team's findings was the presence of 14 macroinvertebrate species classified as pollution intolerant. These creatures require high-quality, minimally impacted streams to thrive.

Among the eight fish species found, the dusky darter is pollution sensitive. Others, such as the southern redbelly dace, western blacknose dace, and orangethroat darter, require cool water for all or part of their life cycle. Water that emanates from a shallow gravel aquifer keeps Honey Creek flowing well into the drier, hotter summer months. According to Carlson, the dense forest canopy, particularly along the East Fork of Honey Creek, also helps insulate the creek from high summer heat.

Some aquatic insects spend nearly their entire lives in the water as subadults, their fate inescapably bound to that of the water. Most species of dragonflies are an example of this. While dragonflies as we know them—buzzing, bug-eyed insects zooming above the surface of our neighborhood ponds and snacking on mosquitoes—typically spend only weeks or months as adults, they can spend years stalking tadpoles and other insects as naiads, their completely aquatic nymph stage, during which they look like bulky earwigs with grotesque scooping jaws. Fish, of course, spend their entire lives from conception to death filtering oxygen from the water they were born in. Just as we know that polluted air causes problems from asthma to cancer to strokes in humans, polluted water can be a death sentence for aquatic life. If the pollution is severe

Forest as Spectacle

or widespread enough, or compounded by additional challenges such as poorly planned dams, it can lead to the local extinction of a species—called extirpation—or even threaten to wipe the species from the planet.

Globally, we are already seeing this play out. One-third of the world's freshwater fish species are currently at risk of extinction, and poor water quality is among the leading causes of their population declines. For Indiana, this issue hits close to home. A report from 2022 ranked the Hoosier state in the number one spot for dirtiest waterways in the U.S. It found an unthinkable 25,000 miles of streams and rivers too polluted for people to swim, fish, and recreate in. Similarly, Indiana's farming operations are a top contributor to the Gulf of Mexico's nearly 7,000-square-mile "dead zone" that is so polluted, aquatic wildlife there suffocate from lack of oxygen.

In the natural world, clean freshwater is born of a slow, intricate process older than time. Water trickles drop by drop through the land's layers of soil and bedrock to emerge, once again, clear and pure. All of the earth's terrestrial ecosystems play a role in the natural process of water purification, but some are more capable than others. Forests are among the best. Forests, especially maturing forests like those in the BCA, have deep soil profiles that serve as highly effective filters for water. The leaves, branches, and multiple layers of vegetation catch raindrops, slowing their journey to the ground, and then layers of forest litter and duff absorb the water. This prevents the soil erosion that occurs when large amounts of rainfall hit the ground all at once, polluting our waterways with excess sediment. Underneath the litter and duff, expansive forest root systems hold the soil in place, further preventing erosion. Tree roots then siphon water from the soil and absorb water-polluting nutrients like nitrogen and phosphorus before releasing clean water back into the ecosystem as water vapor. Forests are so good at water purification that they are considered the most effective type of land cover for protecting clean water.

It can be tempting to draw a hard line between species labeled as "pollution intolerant" and those labeled as "pollution tolerant" or hardy, as if some will die with a drop of pollution and others are perfectly fine in even the poorest-quality waters. The truth is far more nuanced. Polluted water may not extirpate species with high pollution tolerance, but that is not to say they are unaffected. For example, pollution can decrease reproductive success or increase individual mortality in a species without causing the disappearance of the species. Pollution-intolerant species are not the only ones feeling the effects of dirty water. They are simply the first to sound the alarm.

The presence of sensitive species in Honey Creek documented by the aquatic survey is indicative of how clean water runs through the undisturbed forest of the BCA. Trickling through deep forest, water in

Another view of the picturesque little stream that runs through the Ecoblitz area. *Photo credit: Karen Smith.*

the BCA is clean enough for species that have disappeared from many other streams in Indiana to thrive. Not only does Honey Creek stand as evidence of the power of undisturbed forest to combat the water quality issues that plague agricultural states like Indiana—and all the communities downstream from pollution sources—it also serves as a rare paradise for species that simply cannot survive in waterways soured by pollution from agriculture, logging, and development. In its natural condition, Honey Creek cradles some of the most delicate forms of life thriving in the purity of forest-filtered waters.

Forest as Spectacle

This wood frog was one of eight species of frogs found in the BCA Ecoblitz. It has distinct black markings across its eyes, resembling a mask. These frogs freeze in winter—their hearts stop beating and they stop breathing. In spring, they thaw and begin to feed and mate again. *Photo credit: Robert Brodman.*

John Whitaker. *Photo credit: Angela Chamberlain.*

21. PROFILE: DR. JOHN O. WHITAKER

The Dean of Indiana Mammalogy

Anne Laker

A pygmy shrew harbored by the moist darkness of a large fallen log in a southern Indiana hardwood forest weighs as much as a thumbtack and lives an average of one year. A tiny predator with a massive metabolism, pygmy shrews seek and devour insect prey every 15–30 minutes. A shrew without food for an hour will die of starvation.

Dr. John O. Whitaker Jr. of Indiana State University, considered the dean of Indiana mammalogy, has by now outlived at least 88 generations of pygmy shrews. He rivals their voracity, but *his* appetite is for the collection and sharing of data about mammals. JOW, as he is known to friends, may have another thing in common with shrews, who sleep only a few minutes at a time. Legend has it that Whitaker needs only five hours of sleep a night—perhaps the secret to his prolific career.

Whitaker was born in 1935 in the upstate New York burg of Oneonta, in a county nestled between the Catskills and the Adirondacks, to a dentist and a homemaker. As his in-process autobiography will tell, he was smitten with science by age eight, after lots of hunting and fishing with his father and birding on his own. "My father had a chair ready for me or one of my brothers, at the dental office, to join his practice," says Whitaker. "But when I was in eighth grade, my mother and I were standing by the kitchen sink talking, and she said, 'You don't have to be a dentist if you don't want to.' I said, 'I don't?' And she said, 'No.' So my next statement was, 'Okay, I'll go to Cornell University and study vertebrate natural history.'"

Whitaker got that Cornell Ph.D. in vertebrate zoology and wildlife management in 1962 and quickly had job offers from two colleges: Indiana University of Pennsylvania and Indiana State College in Terre Haute. He accepted the Terre Haute offer because he felt it would have greater research potential. He has spent his career maximizing that potential, publishing at a brisk pace on subjects from the life cycles of ectoparasites of the meadow jumping mouse (his dissertation topic) to the food habits of the hoary bat. And he knows for a fact that his dentist father was proud, to the point of helping his son with field research from time to time.

After 60 years as a biologist, Whitaker has lived to see, and to study, phenomena as previously unimaginable as armadillos entering Indiana in climate change–induced migration. Meanwhile, he has authored or coauthored indelible books, such as *Mammals of Indiana* (two editions, 1982 and 2009) and a companion field guide (2010). Add to that *The Audubon Field Guide to North American Mammals* (1996) and *Mammals of the Eastern United States* (2nd and 3rd editions, 1979 and 1998). He has trained 60 graduate students as well, passing on the ethic and intricacies of down and dirty fieldwork. And he founded the Indiana State University Center for Bat Research, Outreach, and Conservation in 2005.

Whitaker has been bioblitzing all his life, turning over literal and figurative rocks and logs and roaming fields and forests to surmise the habits and habitats of rodents, bats, shrews, and the parasites and diseases that coexist with them. His expertise is as deep as it is long. He served as co-editor of *Habitats and Ecological Communities of Indiana: Presettlement to Present* (2012)—a 500-page evaluation of the diversity and health of the state's wildlife and habitats over two centuries of ecological change. He wrote it with the express purpose of guiding conservation planning for a broad array of wildlife, including nongame species like the pygmy shrew, which vies with the bumblebee bat for the title of smallest mammal in North America.

So, it was a coup for the Indiana Forest Alliance (IFA) when Dr. Whitaker agreed to lead a survey of small mammals in the Morgan-Monroe/Yellowwood Back Country Area (BCA) in 2015. That survey documented a community of shrews and the woodland vole: creatures that spend most of their time underground and are dependent on the habitat present in deep forest.

Whitaker's team was focused on small mammals that are recognized as endangered or rare. As their final report stated, the team was "particularly interested in shrews because they require large rotting logs (coarse woody debris) and relatively undisturbed mature forest" to thrive. A shrew may spend its entire life cycle in and around a single rotting log. Both the pygmy shrew and smoky shrew were not even known to exist in Indiana until 1982, when they were discovered in deep woods in Harrison County near the Ohio River. Since then, they have only been found in the deepest forests in the south-central region of Indiana.

After two weeks of hard work setting traplines along logs on ridges, down slopes, and in hollow bottoms across the Ecoblitz area, Whitaker and his research assistant, Angela Chamberlain, found both pygmy and smoky shrews, along with the more common southeastern shrew,

short-tailed shrew, and woodland vole. In his final report on the 2015 survey, Whitaker concluded, "The pygmy shrew and smoky shrew are both designated 'species of special concern,' and both are known only from deep woods in Indiana. That habitat is critical for these two species, and uncut and unmanaged native forest should remain available for them in Indiana and for a number of other species."

For a man with his vast knowledge, Whitaker speaks plainly. When asked why these two rare mammal species might favor the unglaciated land on which this particular forest stands, he says, "Because of the habitat there. It's good woods, with soft soil that the tree roots can penetrate. And that's where they [these two shrew species] occur. I think they've been there for a long time, even though we didn't discover them until a few years ago."

What role do shrews play in the forest ecosystem? "They're predators in the insect wars," explains Whitaker. "They eat insects, earthworms, that sort of thing," helping maintain or hold down insect populations. Are shrews this rare and under threat, or are they just elusive? "I don't see them as any more threatened than they've ever been. I think they're holding their own pretty well. But they're just not very common because there is not very much habitat for them," he concludes.

The smoky shrew (*Sorex fumeus*), like the pygmy shrew, is a state species of special concern that may live its entire life along a single large log in undisturbed deep hardwood forest. It was also found in the BCA by John Whitaker and Angela Chamberlain. Finding both animals in the BCA is a testament to the undisturbed, older condition of this forest. *Photo credit: Phil Myers, licensed under CC Share Alike 3.0.*

* * *

Habitat, it turns out, has always been the preferred starting point for Whitaker's mammal work. His first act after setting foot on Indiana soil in 1962 as a newly minted professor at what is now Indiana State University (ISU) was to conduct a mammal survey. What better way to achieve intimacy with his new home?

"I got the topographical maps of Vigo County," he recounts. "I divided the land up into 25-by-25-meter plots, about 500 plots, or 1.5 million meters all together. I trapped mammals on each plot. It took me three years to do it. The house mouse species turned out to be the most abundant species of small mammal." More than 60 years later, Whitaker would love for someone to re-create his study in some seed corn fields and see how the house mouse is faring. "Not that anybody cares if they survive or don't, because they're thought to be a pest species," he says. "But they eat and spread seeds, which means that in some ways they're good. At any rate, if we set up a few plots, in a few seed corn fields, and we could see what has changed. I'm looking for somebody who could do that, that would be wonderful."

Talk about longitudinal study. Whitaker's scientific curiosity was unabated as he reached age 90 in 2023. Apparently, Indiana biologists are given to long and busy lives. A favorite colleague of Whitaker's was ornithologist Russell Mumford, emeritus professor in Purdue's Department of Forestry and Natural Resources and Whitaker's coauthor on the *Mammals of Indiana* tomes. "When I first came here, Russ and I started working together right from the beginning," says Whitaker. Mumford passed away in 2022 at age 100.

Another frequent coauthor, Whitaker's ISU departmental colleague Dr. Marion T. Jackson, died in 2019 at age 86 after his own lifetime of ecological scholarship. In 2017, Jackson was invited to write an homage to Whitaker in the *Proceedings of the Indiana Academy of Science*. The detailed portrait of Whitaker's adventures and accomplishments revealed an abiding friendship and decades-long shared interests in vertebrate natural history and ecology research and fieldwork. Jackson's legacy shines as well, especially as the editor of *The Natural Heritage of Indiana* (1997), a 512-page record of the state's natural beauty, heritage, and environmental challenges.

In 2014, IFA invited Jackson and Whitaker to share their opinions on the merits of sparing large tracts of Indiana's state forests from logging to create old-growth forests for future generations. In a jointly written piece for IFA's *Forest Defender Journal*, they advised:

> Numerous species of birds and mammals depend on our contiguous forest. Rather than a static, shaded condition, old-growth forest is ever evolving and contains a continuum of successional habitats, including early vegetation in canopy openings and disruptions caused by forest diseases and insects, storm blow downs, fires and other disturbances

within deep forest interiors spread over vast areas. The inherent nature of this natural diversity is found in larger blocks of unmanaged forest. ... To conserve our wild heritage and ensure the viability of Indiana's native forest ecosystem and our future quality of life, we need to let more of our state forests return to old growth conditions and to allow nature to function in these public lands.

Unfortunately, logical statements like these became politicized as the Indiana Department of Natural Resources (IDNR) increased timber harvesting on taxpayer-owned forests in the 2000s under the governorship of Mitch Daniels (2005–2013). When a public battle raged in 2017 over the state's sale of 1,733 trees in Yellowwood State Forest within the Ecoblitz study site, professors squared off in the court of scientific opinion. The IDNR enlisted George Parker, professor emeritus of forestry and natural resources at Purdue University, to defend their decision. Parker and Herman Weeks, professor emeritus of wildlife biology, wrote supportively to Governor Eric Holcomb in a letter still visible on the Division of Forestry's website: "Forests managed for trees 100 to 200 years old have the same biota as forests not managed." Whitaker knows these Purdue professors well and begs to differ. "It is my belief that forests and their inhabitants are better off left undisturbed," he says.

Whitaker's work has historically been helpful to IDNR staff. He has also had the benefit of many research grant dollars from the IDNR over the years. "They [state agency staff] use our work to draw conclusions and to come up with a plan for the way they should treat things," he says. "I'm very happy when that happens." When asked what he hopes will happen with his studies and findings once he is gone, Whitaker replies, "I hope anybody who wants to know about mammals of Indiana will go back to our books and then use that data to make decisions" about conservation and management.

One such decision is still pending. In 2019, Whitaker agreed to accompany IFA executive director Jeff Stant, biologist Dr. Leslie Bishop, and botanist Dr. Paul Rothrock on a visit to the office of Governor Holcomb. At the meeting, the group presented a proposal calling for the protection of 2,380 acres of the BCA of Morgan-Monroe/Yellowwood State Forest outside the Low Gap Nature Preserve as a high conservation value forest (known as HCVF). That designation would ensure that the area would be managed to protect its primitive quality and allow old-growth conditions to return.

He says, "I felt pretty good about the way the governor talked to us, trying to get information and so forth. At the time, he seemed to react positively, but I don't know that he ever followed through. Do you know if he did?" To date, no response has come; the decision is still pending.

The white-footed mouse (*Peromyscus leucopus*) is another small mammal found during Dr. Whitaker's survey as well as a 2014 survey by Orbis Environmental in the BCA. *Photo credit: Phil Myers, CC SA 3.0.*

But since the meeting, no more logging has occurred in Yellowwood or Morgan-Monroe State Forests.

When is a creature like a shrew subject to politics or policy? Whitaker seems to have faith in mammals' ability to persist in spite of a general lack of priority for protecting mature forests. Shrews do what shrews do. Only inches long, shrews "poke their long snouts through the decaying detritus of the forest floor," as Dr. Bishop wrote in an informal summary of Whitaker and Chamberlain's study of shrews in the BCA. Bishop went on to note that shrews "can smell insect prey and find the location via vibrations through their whiskers. Scientists who have studied shrews often comment on how noisy they are with a high pitched twittering sound. Recent studies have revealed the function of these twitters—shrews use echolocation similar to bats! They are able to use sound waves to examine their surroundings and to analyze the best way to navigate through the habitat. One researcher observed a 'yawning' behavior of a hunting shrew and found that the mouth openings coincide with rapid pulses of low intensity ultrasounds."

Forest as Spectacle

While shrews creatively control insect populations, fellow forest mammals like the woodland vole and white-footed mouse—both found during the Ecoblitz of the BCA—also affect forest ecosystems. As dispersers and planters of seeds, forest mice can determine where trees grow. Science journalist Brandon Keim wrote in the *New York Times* in 2022 that "hundreds of plant species are shifting their ranges, each following their own animal-mediated trajectory." Might a mouse know more than a silviculturist?

* * *

When asked what Hoosiers and the state's decision-makers need to be doing to help our forests thrive, for the sake of the mammals and wildlife that he has studied for so long, Whitaker answers, "We're not doing badly. But we should be preserving the forest, as much as possible, the way it is . . . not reducing it. Adding forestland is what we should be doing. That's just what I did with my woods."

"My woods" is now officially known as the John O. Whitaker Woods Nature Preserve, a property of the Ouabache Land Conservancy (OLC) in Brazil, Indiana. Whitaker bought these 40 acres of forest back in 1975 and gifted all but 6 acres (where his house stands) to the OLC for preservation in 2021. "I bought the property for my own studies, and I've

Dr. Whitaker points out a tree tag used in his long-term study of the trees in Whitaker Woods. *Photo credit: Marty Jones, Ouabache Land Conservancy.*

Dr. Whitaker pictured at the wooded nature preserve that bears his name. *Photo credit: Marty Jones, Ouabache Land Conservancy.*

carried out those studies," he says with pride. When he bought it, he says, he found just one human-cut tree stump, meaning it has been left to function naturally as a forest for 50 years or more.

Data is the love language of Dr. Whitaker. "I'm just about ready to publish the results of the tree species and their growth," he says excitedly. At three points in time, he studied and measured 2,252 trees of 34 different species—in 1977–1978, 1993–1994, and 2009–2010. He found that the most abundant species on the property are tulip poplar, red hickory, red oak, shagbark hickory, white oak, red maple, and American sycamore.

"Some of my favorite places in the preserve are in an area I call 'the beech woods,'" Whitaker told the *Terre Haute Tribune-Star* in 2022. "My daughter and I spent much time collecting and eating wild plants, à la [expert forager] Euell Gibbons, there. Our favorite wild foods were milkweed and stinging nettles, but the woods also have many chanterelle mushrooms. In fact, I've observed a strong relationship between chanterelles and the beeches," he adds, noting that the beech stand is where he reliably finds them.

The John O. Whitaker Woods Nature Preserve is now open to the public. The OLC has added trail markers and signage, and Dr. Whitaker could not be more pleased. Planning for the woods to outlive him when he bought the property, he always intended to leave them for posterity. Whitaker also sits on the land conservancy's advisory board and takes an

active role in encouraging his neighbors to set aside habitat and donate it to the land trust. "I keep looking for places we can get. I want to talk to the fire chief in Terre Haute. I would guess that he probably runs into a lot of people who might be willing to give their land." The more forest preserved, the better.

The Whitaker family and members of the Ouabache Land Conservancy dedicated the preserve in 2022. *Photo credit: Marty Jones, Ouabache Land Conservancy.*

* * *

The lucky have time to reflect on their legacies. Whitaker declares that the part of his legacy he is most proud of is his work with mammals. "I've got over 430 papers published, 19 books published, and 3 in the works. And I'm proud of all of that," he states. One of the in-process works is an autobiography to be published by Oregon-based Luminare Press. Another, which he is uniquely qualified to write, is about the changes in the distribution and abundance of vertebrates of Indiana over the last 60 years, forthcoming from the Indiana Academy of Science Press.

"I've always said I was going to work up to 100, so I've got another 13 years to continue publishing," he says with a serious laugh. He is also working toward placing his 20,000-specimen collection with the Field Museum in Chicago.

From his long view, Whitaker sees how the practice of biology has changed in his lifetime. "The kind of studies that we have done over the years . . . observations of field ecology . . . there is very little work of that

Even small set-asides like the 40-acre John O. Whitaker Woods Nature Preserve harbor abundant forest life. *Photo credit: Marty Jones, Ouabache Land Conservancy.*

sort anymore," he says. "I think we should keep up with that. A lot of the work people are doing nowadays is in DNA, molecular biology entirely, rather than the field biology that we've worked on over the years. There ought to be more work combining the two, combining DNA with what I call old-fashioned biology," he says wryly.

Evolutionary biology and the historical trajectories of Indiana's mammals and other vertebrates are other viewpoints Whitaker finds useful. Writing in the mid-1990s as a contributor to *The Natural Heritage of Indiana*, he and coauthor Ronald L. Richards asserted:

> The present vertebrate fauna of Indiana is the result of evolution, migration, interaction of species, and extinction, all in context with changing environments and the activities of humans. . . . Vertebrates appear to have "held their own" during the prehistoric millennia, only to suffer selective annihilation, abundance and distribution changes beginning with the [European] settlement period. . . . Human population increase and technological advance have brought about . . . some of the most critical problems facing vertebrate communities: decreasing diversity and habitat reduction. Thirty-two vertebrate species have been extirpated from Indiana in the last two centuries, and many others are now endangered or threatened. . . . The species we have lost can never be replaced. Will we enter the twenty-second century with

The southern flying squirrel (*Glaucomys volans*) inhabits the forest in the Ecoblitz area. These animals often occupy abandoned woodpecker holes. They do not actually fly but glide using a membrane that extends from their wrists to their ankles. *Photo credit: Judy Gallagher, CC BY 2.0.*

A bobcat was glimpsed by IFA executive director Jeff Stant and bat and insect team volunteers in brush along the East Fork of Honey Creek. *Photo credit: Mike Jungen, public domain.*

many vertebrates other than the house mouse, Norway rat, starling, and carp? Will Indiana eventually become a land that only "once upon a time" had wild, free-ranging vertebrate animals?

Perhaps. But the life's work of Dr. Whitaker has been a steady, methodical bulwark against ignorance and an incessant vote of support for the ecological roles and habitats of the mammals he has studied. Every Hoosier, and every shrew, is in his debt.

As the naturalist-philosopher Aldo Leopold once wrote, "Only the mountain has lived long enough to listen objectively to the howl of the wolf."

Key Findings

Overall, Ecoblitz surveys documented 29 of the 59 species of mammals native to Indiana in the BCA from 2014 through 2017, including white-tailed deer, coyote, bobcat, red fox, raccoon, possum, chipmunks, squirrels (red, gray, fox, and southern flying), four species of shrews, woodland vole, white-footed mouse, and eight species of bats. See the complete mammals species list in appendix 1. Sometimes these animals were seen when teams were looking for something else. For example, an American mink (*Neogale vison*) was seen by entomologist Dr. Carl Strang along the main course of Honey Creek. Angie Dämm came face to face with a coyote one day on a bird survey.

Special attention was given to bats and shrews because several species are listed as rare or endangered. Eight bat species were identified in the Ecoblitz area. These are discussed in detail in chapter 10.

Bats

- Big brown bat

- Eastern red bat—state species of special concern (rare)

- Indiana bat (maternity colony)—federal and state endangered

- Northern long-eared bat—federal and state endangered (one male, two lactating females)

- Tricolored bat, formerly eastern pipistrelle—state endangered, proposed for federal endangered (juvenile male)

- Little brown bat (acoustic only)—state endangered, under status assessment for federal endangered

- Evening bat (acoustic only)—state endangered

- Hoary bat (acoustic only)—state species of special concern

Shrews

Shrews are woodland animals. The pygmy and smoky shrews are good indicators of deep, undisturbed forests. Dr. John Whitaker is the leading authority on smoky and pygmy shrews in Indiana and has mapped the ranges of these species. Whitaker found both species in the Ecoblitz area along large logs.

Shrews found in the Ecoblitz area include:

- Pygmy shrew—species of special concern

- Smoky shrew—species of special concern

- Southeastern shrew

- Short-tailed shrew

Rae Schnapp. *Photo credit: IFA.*

AFTERWORD
Full Circle

Rae Schnapp

When I came to work at the Indiana Forest Alliance (IFA), our small staff was very excited about coordinating teams of scientists and volunteers—a huge undertaking and an exciting challenge. As I got more and more involved in the Ecoblitz, I realized what a privilege it was to work with this group of people so knowledgeable about so many different facets of the forest. I have fond memories of collaborating and hiking to conduct the forest characterization work with Drs. Leslie Bishop and Paul Rothrock. From Leslie, I learned about forest ecology, spiders, and nature writing at the same time. One night, while on a spider survey, I was using a flashlight to search the trees for spider eyeshine when I came face to face with a white-footed mouse on a branch. We studied each other for a moment in mutual curiosity. I learned about plants, geology, ticks, and more from ecologist Kevin Tungesvick. I helped carry batteries and traps and learned about the fantastic diversity of moths from Leroy Koehn. And I became obsessed with photographing mushrooms because of the amazing array of colorful fungi we encountered. I loved it all.

Enumerating the full array of nature was, of course, the whole point. The Ecoblitz Forest Census described in this book was the first comprehensive baseline inventory implemented in Indiana's state or national forests on a landscape-level tract. IFA is especially proud of these findings:

- A rich species diversity of 3,077 species was identified, including some of the highest moth diversity in the eastern U.S. outside of the Southern Appalachians.
- A very high floristic quality (with few non-native plants) was found that rivals that of the highest-quality nature preserves in Indiana.
- At least 188 species were identified that had never been found in Indiana before, called "distribution records."

- At least 24 rare, threatened, or endangered species of plants, birds, mammals, and reptiles and amphibians were identified.
- Nearly 200 distinct species (morphos species) of insects and fungi could not be identified without additional DNA sequencing analysis that was beyond the reach of this inventory.

Because of the Ecoblitz of the Morgan-Monroe/Yellowwood Back Country Area (BCA), we can proudly say:

- The first comprehensive baseline inventory was accomplished of a landscape-sized tract of state forestland.
- The first forest pollinator survey was completed of moths and bees in an Indiana forest.
- The first forest lichen survey in 75 years in Indiana was completed. The lichenologist who conducted it also produced the first complete list of lichens found in Indiana from this and previous surveys.

Our forest characterization and the Floristic Quality Assessment indicate that this forest is developing the characteristics of a secondary old-growth forest, including benchmarks for an undisturbed forest floor. (Fallen logs are not wasted wood products but rather the foundation of the forest food chain.) And the BCA compares favorably to remnant old-growth forests in Indiana nature preserves such as Wesselman Woods in Evansville or Oppenheim Woods in Kosciusko County. See the table in chapter 2.

Overall, this Ecoblitz Forest Census revealed the rich species diversity in this small part of our Indiana state forest system with great depth and breadth across taxonomic groups. All the species confirmed as of this writing are listed in appendix 1.

But biodiversity is not just about numbers. Species composition, ecosystem complexity, and natural history are more important than species richness alone. Forest structure is paramount. Some organisms depend on structural characteristics such as large old trees and fallen logs. Many bats, for example, roost under the loose bark of standing dead trees (known as snags). We found seven imperiled species of bats in this forest and definitive evidence that three of those in the most serious trouble are bearing and rearing their young in the forest. Our surveys located a maternity roost colony of Indiana bats, the longest-listed endangered species in the country, in the exfoliating bark and solar exposure of dead tulip poplar snags in two neighboring ravines. We netted three northern long-eared bats, two of whom were lactating mothers. This species has just been upgraded from threatened to federal-endangered status.

Additionally, we netted a juvenile male tricolored bat, now proposed for federal-endangered listing.

The dangerous vulnerability of bats is largely due to a fungal disease known as white-nose syndrome (WNS) likely brought to North America by spelunkers in the first decade of the 21st century. The northern long-eared, tricolored, and little brown bats, whose presence was indicated by acoustic data, were common in Indiana's hardwood forests in 2000 but have tragically declined by 89% to 98% across the state (with similar drops across their entire ranges) since 2010 due to WNS. The disease has also reduced already shrunken numbers of Indiana bats by another fifth within the state. With their populations plummeting, other threats like wind farms and habitat loss such as the clearing of old forests compound their losses. That the northern long-eared, tricolored, and Indiana bats were still found reproducing in this old forest in 2016 and 2017 speaks to its high habitat value for species that have largely disappeared from the rest of the Hoosier state.

As WNS advanced across the eastern hardwood forests, the emerald ash borer was imported to the U.S. via wood purchased from Asia and has since decimated 95% or more of the white and green ash trees across nearly all of Indiana's forests. Other pests, blights, and droughts have been killing northern red oak, American beech, sugar maple, and tulip poplar, Indiana's state tree. A diversity of ages was found for all these trees in the Ecoblitz forest. Researchers from the U.S. Forest Service and Purdue University have found that 1% to 2% of the ash trees being attacked by ash borer are surviving. We found many ash trees still alive in the Ecoblitz forest, including the little-seen black ash. Providing undisturbed areas is an important way to let species develop natural resistance to pests. By protecting species and age diversity, we enable our natural heritage to protect itself.

* * *

Scientists presented the results of the surveys from this Ecoblitz to three annual meetings of the Indiana Academy of Science and held a symposium on the results after the Ecoblitz surveys concluded in 2018. They published their findings in peer-reviewed journals including the *Proceedings of the Indiana Academy of Science* and the prestigious *Journal of the Torrey Botanical Society*. Counting lichen and spiders alone, there were 99 species recorded for the first time in Indiana. The documentation of these "first reports" is an indication of how little we know about our Indiana forests.

The Ecoblitz was equally notable for the specimens that could *not* be identified: at least 100 fungi and hundreds of insects. For example, we could not find an expert in the midwest who could identify even half of the 150 different species of ichneumonid (parasitic) wasps collected from the Ecoblitz tract by Hanover College entomologist Dr. Glené Mynhardt and her students. Each of these wasps parasitizes a specific invertebrate, often the larvae of insects that eat plants, suggesting that many ecological pathways that control plant-eating insects in our hardwood forests are unknown. The insect diversity alone is impressive, especially in the face of an impending insect apocalypse. Our future is tied to theirs. As the extinction crisis grows, we found a critical shortage of field biologists who can identify insects that may be disappearing—species that may have profound effects on forests and, indeed, on our own human well-being.

The whereabouts and survival strategies of many creatures also eluded us. The 109 species of bees that entomologist Dr. Robert Jean identified are one-fourth of all bees found in Indiana. Hardwood forests have played a central role in the evolution of Indiana's bees, given they lived their entire life cycles in these forests over most of the state for thousands of years before the forests were cleared for European settlement. Yet, while native bees are thought to utilize the rotting wood, deep litter, and soft, uncompacted soils in our forests to den and survive over winter, we have never actually confirmed where many of them spend the winter. Our survey also did not examine bees in the forest canopy, an area that has been sampled by few bee surveys anywhere. Additionally, many of the bees that Dr. Jean identified were foraging deep in this forest during the dry summer and fall months when few floral resources were evident. Given the central role that bees play as the dominant pollinators of the world's flowering plants, more research is needed to understand how many Indiana bees survive in their native forest.

Then there are spiders. "An orb weaver lives in a small woven world full of vibrations," said zoologist Friedrich Barth in *An Immense World* by Ed Yong. As predators, spiders play an important role in controlling populations of insects, and, in turn, they are important prey for a host of other insects and higher-order animals. A team of experts led by Dr. Leslie Bishop identified 128 species of spiders in the Ecoblitz: one-fourth of all spiders found in Indiana and many being first-time finds. Most of these spiders were found in the litter, dry creek beds, woody debris, or understory close to the ground. The team would not have found so many species had they not surveyed different microhabitats during the day and at night from late spring to early fall. Yet Dr. Bishop concluded that even these surveys during different times of day and night extending through three growing seasons significantly underestimated the diversity of spiders in this forest because logistic difficulties prevented effective surveying of the forest canopy.

* * *

The forest may seem endless. But it is finite.

Indiana has 13 state forests comprising about 160,000 acres total. Almost all (97%) state forestland is managed for timber production. The Indiana Department of Natural Resources (IDNR) Division of Forestry (DOF) has repeatedly stated that they intend to manage 10% of state forestland for late seral (old-growth) conditions and that the BCA is to be managed for this older forest condition and for wilderness recreation. But today, even the BCA is subject to the extraction mentality.

After IFA completed three years of surveys, the DOF announced a plan in the fall of 2017 to log a tract of forest in the Ecoblitz area. IFA and many of the scientists involved in these surveys appealed to the IDNR to spare the area from logging based on the then-preliminary results of these surveys. We stated that the tree-coring surveys in this forest showed it was approaching the old-growth condition that the BCA had been established to maintain. We pointed out multiple imperiled species, such as federal- and state-endangered bats and rare pygmy and smoky shrews, that were found in this old forest. We urged that all available roost trees for rare and endangered bats be left standing. We explained that the area's high-quality plant and bird communities would be harmed by the logging.

There was a huge public outcry about the proposed timber sale in the BCA. *Photo credit: Anne Laker.*

Trees marked for destruction in the BCA. *Photo credit: IFA.*

In total, 240 scientists from universities across Indiana signed a letter encouraging Governor Holcomb to set aside portions of our state forests from logging. At least 3,000 citizens contacted Governor Holcomb's office to request that he call off the planned logging. About 300 people showed up to protest on the frigid morning of the timber sale, November 9, 2017. A surprise development was that a licensed timber buyer and owner of a wholesale lumber company stepped up to offer the state $150,000 to leave the 299-acre sale tracts standing. The state claimed it could not accept the offer. Instead, logging rights were sold to Hamilton

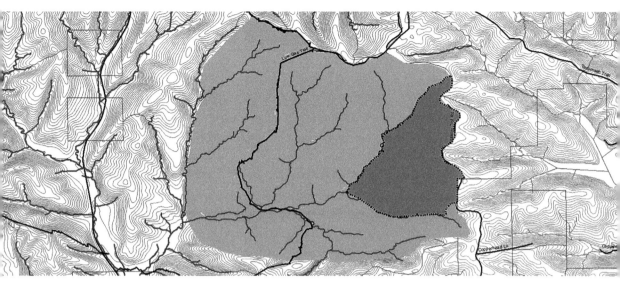

Logging for $108,785: a price of $0.24 per board foot, or less than $63 per tree.

A portion of the Ecoblitz area (lighter area to the east) was selectively logged in 2017 and 2018. *Map credit: IFA.*

In the first two months of 2018, 130 acres of the Ecoblitz study area were selectively logged. Many trees suitable for bat roosts were felled. In several cases, for unexplained reasons, large logs that had fallen before the logging were removed from the forest floor. Much of the forest floor's herbaceous community and many lush beds of mosses were scraped to bare dirt and, in several areas, have since been replaced by non-native invasive plants such as Japanese stiltgrass.

Unfortunately, the area where the timber harvest occurred was the location where the highest numbers of reptiles were found, where the rare shrews were found, and where the Indiana bat maternity roost colony was located. IFA and our Ecoblitz team were left to finish the inventory while noting the potential impacts of this logging.

Nevertheless, there are still many tracts within the BCA that have not been harvested, and they still represent an opportunity to set this place aside as a control or reference area. To that end, IFA has used the data gathered in the Ecoblitz to prepare a formal proposal to designate this BCA as a high conservation value forest to be managed without timber harvests. In 2019, we met with Governor Holcomb to ask that he make this designation. The governor showed a genuine interest in trying to conserve the BCA after talking with Drs. Bishop and Rothrock and IFA's executive director for an hour. And there has not been any timber cut from the BCA since then. This could be the beginning of a large future old-growth forest.

Are our state forests repositories of renewable resources or are they ancient ecosystems that need to be nurtured? The answer to both questions could and perhaps should be "yes." We need management approaches that balance the need for wood products and the revenue they generate with the need to maintain some areas for forest ecosystems to continue to recover.

Over the centuries that humans have been practicing forest management, methods have continually changed and developed. The next advance in forestry management should include the creation of a preservation core in all forests that are managed for timber products. Preservation cores are sections of a forest that remain off-limits to harvesting or thinning for all time, serving as a control against which to compare the impacts of management.

Similarly, the IFA has long championed the idea of establishing "wild areas" to protect at least 10% of each state forest. This concept has repeatedly been proposed by forward-thinking legislators in the Indiana General Assembly but has gained little traction due to opposition from timber industry lobbyists and the DOF, which sells state forest timber at below-market rates to provide revenue for part of its budget.

The prevailing priority of extraction ignores the forest's biodiversity. In addition to the numerous new records, specimens that we could not identify, and parts of the forest that we were unable to sample, science is just beginning to explore the symbioses between tree roots and mycorrhizal fungi and predator-prey relationships, especially in insects. These gaps in our knowledge point to the importance of having such wild areas or preservation cores to serve as scientific reference or control areas that remain undisturbed by management activities.

Forests do not operate on human timescales. Many Indiana native tree species can live for several hundred years if we let them. Much of Indiana's state forest system is now between 80 and 120 years old. Now is a moment of opportunity as parts of the system are on the verge of becoming secondary old growth. But it is important to note that old-growth forests are not uniformly old. Old-growth forests are, by definition, undisturbed by logging, but that does not mean there is no disturbance. Some trees will die, and that too is part of nature's plan. Age, wind and weather, pests, and diseases will continually topple big old trees and make way for younger trees to emerge to reach the canopy. And these older forests provide key habitat for species that are sensitive to human disturbance.

These older forests provide key habitat for species that are sensitive to human disturbance. As such, many scientists have called for "no-harvest" zones after discovering that the least managed forests contain the most species from across a diverse range of taxonomic groups. It is documented that old forests support higher densities and richness of bird species and also some of the rarest birds, providing integral habitat for both nesting and foraging requirements. Even partial harvesting by single-tree selection can cause declines in avian species. Amphibians are also sensitive to disturbance. They benefit from a moist, undisturbed forest floor with minimal fluctuations in light and temperature. Harvesting equipment can destroy the underground soil spaces and layers of leaf litter that are needed by amphibians, resulting in drastically reduced amphibian populations. Preservation cores or wild areas also provide important reservoirs of genetic diversity and reproductive fitness that help ensure that tree species can adapt to our changing environment. Harvesting has been shown to reduce genetic diversity, sometimes causing the loss of over 90% of rare genes in postharvest stands of trees.

In this era of adverse impacts from rapid human-caused climate change, forests are a key part of the solution. Globally, forests provide green infrastructure that removes around a quarter of the carbon dioxide that humans add to the atmosphere. Forests are carbon sinks that are critical to keep climate change from getting worse. The world's forests contain more carbon than all current oil, gas, and coal deposits combined. Protecting forest carbon is just as urgent as reducing our dependence on fossil fuels. Additionally, large trees actively fix far greater amounts of carbon than smaller-sized trees do. The largest 1% of trees are responsible for 50% of forest biomass on the planet, and this suggests

The BCA is approaching old-growth conditions and has been nominated as a high conservation value forest. This proposal is currently under consideration at the Division of Forestry.

that forests cannot sequester and store large amounts of aboveground carbon without large trees.

* * *

Our state forests are public forests, belonging to all Indiana residents. While the BCA at Morgan-Monroe/Yellowwood State Forest is indeed special, there are undoubtedly other areas within our state forest system that have high biodiversity that will be disturbed, damaged, or destroyed by logging and burning activities before we have a chance to document the species that live there. The impressive diversity found in the BCA underscores the importance of doing a baseline inventory before making forest management decisions. Hoosiers should insist that more baseline inventories be conducted before management activities such as timber harvests and prescribed burns are undertaken.

The Ecoblitz inventory documents why the Morgan-Monroe/Yellowwood BCA deserves to be protected as a high conservation value forest. Readers are encouraged to ask Indiana's governor to make this and other forest-preservation designations. Now is always the time to ensure that some areas are managed with one purpose in mind: so that future generations can enjoy old-growth forests across the landscape of Indiana.

APPENDIX 1

Complete Species List

TREES

Genus	Species	Common Name
Acer	*negundo*	boxelder
Acer	*rubrum*	red maple
Acer	*saccharum*	sugar maple
Acer	*nigrum*	black maple
Aesculus	*glabra*	Ohio buckeye
Amelanchier	*arborea*	downy serviceberry
Asimina	*triloba*	pawpaw
Carpinus	*caroliniana*	musclewood, hop hornbeam
Carya	*cordiformis*	bitternut hickory
Carya	*glabra*	pignut hickory
Carya	*laciniosa*	shellbark hickory
Carya	*ovata*	shagbark hickory
Celtis	*occidentalis*	hackberry
Cercis	*canadensis*	redbud
Cornus	*florida*	flowering dogwood
Crataegus	*punctata*	dotted hawthorn
Diospyros	*virginiana*	persimmon
Fagus	*grandifolia*	American beech
Fraxinus	*americana*	white ash
Fraxinus	*nigra*	black ash
Fraxinus	*pennsylvanica*	green ash
Gleditisia	*triacanthos*	honey locust
Gymnocladus	*dioicus*	Kentucky coffee tree
Juglans	*nigra*	black walnut
Juniperus	*virginiana*	eastern red cedar
Liriodendron	*tulipifera*	tulip tree
Morus	*rubra*	red mulberry
Nyssa	*sylvatica*	black gum
Ostrya	*virginiana*	ironwood
Picea	*abies*	Norway spruce
Pinus	*resinosa*	red pine
Pinus	*strobus*	white pine
Plantanus	*occidentalis*	sycamore
Populus	*deltoides*	cottonwood
Populus	*grandidentata*	bigtooth aspen
Prunus	*americana*	wild plum
Prunus	*serotina*	black cherry

TREES (*continued*)

Genus	Species	Common Name
Quercus	*alba*	white oak
Quercus	*coccinea*	scarlet oak
Quercus	*montana*	chestnut oak
Quercus	*muhlenbergii*	chinquaapin oak
Quercus	*rubra*	red oak
Quercus	*velutina*	black oak
Rhus	*copallina*	winged sumac
Rhus	*glabra*	smooth sumac
Robinia	*pseudoacacia*	black locust
Salix	*nigra*	black willow
Sassafras	*albidum*	sassafras
Tilia	*americana*	basswood
Ulmus	*americana*	American elm
Ulmus	*rubra*	slippery elm

HERBACEOUS PLANTS

Acalypha	*gracilens*	slender mercury
Acalypha	*rhomboidea*	rhombic three-seeded mercury
Acalypha	*virginica*	mercury
Achillea	*millefolium*	yarrow
Actaea	*pachypoda*	white baneberry
Adiantum	*pedatum*	northern maidenhair fern
Agastache	*nepetoides*	yellow giant hyssop
Agrimonia	*pubescens*	downy agrimony
Agrimonia	*rostellata*	beaked agrimony
Agrostis	*perennans var. aestivalus*	autumn bent grass
Allium	*canadense*	wild garlic
Allium	*tricoccum*	wild leek, ramps
Ambrosia	*artemisiifolia*	common ragweed
Ambrosia	*trifida*	giant ragweed
Amphicarpaea	*bracteata*	hog peanut
Andropogon	*virginicus*	broom sedge grass
Antennaria	*neglecta*	flagged narrow-leaved pussytoes
Antennaria	*plantaginifolia*	small plantain-leaved pussytoes
Aplectrum	*hyemale*	puttyroot orchid
Apocynum	*cannabinum*	dogbane
Aralia	*racemosa*	spikenard
Aralia	*spinosa*	Hercules-club
Arctium	*minus*	burdock
Arisaema	*dracontium*	green dragon
Arisaema	*triphyllum*	jack-in-the-pulpit
Aristolochia	*serpentaria*	Virginia snakeroot
Arnoglossum	*muehlenbergii*	great indian plantain
Aruncus	*dioicus*	goatsbeard
Asarum	*canadense*	wild ginger
Asclepias	*exaltata*	poke milkweed
Asclepias	*quadrifolia*	four-leaved milkweed
Asplenium	*platyneuron*	ebony spleenwort
Athyrium	*filix-femina*	lady fern
Barbarea	*vulgaris*	yellow rocket or bitter winter cress
Berberis	*thunbergii*	Japanese barberry
Bidens	*frondosa*	common beggar-ticks

Genus	Species	Common Name
Bidens	*vulgata*	tall beggar-ticks
Blephilia	*ciliata*	downy woodmint
Blephilia	*hirsuta*	hairy woodmint
Boechera	*dentata*	toothed rock cress
Boechera	*laevigata*	smooth rock cress
Boehmeria	*cylindrica*	false nettle
Botrypus	*virginianus*	rattlesnake fern
Brachyelytrum	*erectum*	long-awned wood grass
Bromus	*nottowayanus*	Nottoway valley brome
Bromus	*pubescens*	hairy woodland brome
Campanulastrum	*americanum*	tall bellflower
Campsis	*radicans*	trumpet creeper
Cardamine	*angustata*	slender toothwort
Cardamine	*concatenata*	cut-leaved toothwort
Cardamine	*douglasii*	spring cress
Cardamine	*hirsuta*	hairy bitter cress
Cardamine	*pensylvanica*	Pennsylvania bitter cress
Carex	*albicans*	whitetinge sedge
Carex	*albursina*	white bear sedge
Carex	*amphibola*	gray sedge
Carex	*blanda*	eastern woodland sedge
Carex	*careyana*	Carey's sedge
Carex	*cephalophora*	oval-leaf sedge
Carex	*communis*	beech or fibrous-root sedge
Carex	*cristatella*	crested sedge
Carex	*cumberlandensis*	Cumberland sedge
Carex	*digitalis*	slender woodland sedge
Carex	*frankii*	Frank's sedge
Carex	*glaucodea*	blue sedge
Carex	*gracillima*	graceful sedge
Carex	*granularis*	pale sedge
Carex	*grisea*	inflated narrow-leaf sedge
Carex	*hirsutella*	hairy green sedge
Carex	*hirtifolia*	pubescent sedge
Carex	*hitchcockiana*	Hitchcock's sedge
Carex	*jamesii*	James's sedge
Carex	*laxiculmis*	spreading sedge
Carex	*laxiflora*	broad looseflower sedge
Carex	*lurida*	shallow sedge
Carex	*pensylvanica*	common oak sedge
Carex	*picta*	painted sedge
Carex	*plantaginea*	plantain-leaf sedge
Carex	*platyphylla*	broad-leaved wood sedge
Carex	*radiata*	straight-styled wood sedge or star sedge
Carex	*rosea*	rosy sedge
Carex	*sparganioides*	loose-headed bracted sedge
Carex	*striatula*	lined sedge
Carex	*swanii*	Swan's sedge
Carex	*tribuloides*	awl-fruited or blunt broom sedge
Carex	*virescens*	ribbed sedge
Carex	*vulpinoidea*	fox sedge
Carex	*willdenowii*	Willdenow's sedge

Genus	Species	Common Name
Carex	*woodii*	Wood's stiff or pretty sedge
Carex	*torta*	beaked riverbank sedge
Caulophyllum	*thalictroides*	blue cohosh
Chamaecrista	*nictitans*	sensitive plant
Cicuta	*maculata*	water hemlock
Cinna	*arundinacea*	wood reed grass
Circaea	*lutetiana*	common enchanter's nightshade
Cirsium	*altissimum*	tall thistle
Cirsium	*discolor*	field thistle
Cirsium	*vulgare*	bull thistle
Claytonia	*virginica*	spring beauty
Clematis	*viorna*	leatherflower
Clematis	*virginiana*	virgin's bower
Collinsonia	*canadensis*	horse balm
Conopholis	*americana*	squawroot
Conyza	*canadensis*	horseweed
Corallorhiza	*odontorhiza*	autumn coralroot orchid
Cornus	*alternifolia*	alternate-leaved dogwood
Cornus	*drummondii*	rough-leaf dogwood
Corylus	*americana*	American hazelnut
Crataegus	*crus-galli*	cockspur hawthorn
Cryptotaenia	*canadensis*	honewort
Cunila	*oreganoides*	common dittany
Cynoglossum	*virginianum*	wild comfrey
Cypripedium	*calceolus*	yellow lady's-slipper orchid
Cystopteris	*protrusa*	southern fragile fern
Danthonia	*spicata*	poverty oat grass
Delphinium	*tricorne*	dwarf or spring larkspur
Deparia	*acrostichoides*	silvery spleenwort
Desmodium	*glutinosum*	pointed-leaved tick trefoil
Desmodium	*nudiflorum*	naked-flowered tick trefoil
Desmodium	*paniculatum*	panicled tick trefoil
Desmodium	*rotundifolium*	round-leaved tick trefoil
Diarrhena	*americana*	American beak grass
Dicentra	*canadensis*	squirrel corn
Dicentra	*cucullaria*	Dutchman's-breeches
Dichanthelium	*acuminatum ssp. Fasiculatum*	western panic grass
Dichanthelium	*boscii*	Bosc's panic grass
Dichanthelium	*clandestinum*	deer tongue grass
Dichanthelium	*commutatum*	variable panic grass
Dichanthelium	*dichotomum ssp dichotomum*	forked panic grass
Dichanthelium	*latifolium*	broadleaf rosette grass
Dichanthelium	*polyanthes*	round-seed panic grass
Dioscorea	*villosa*	wild yam
Diplazium	*pycnocarpon*	glade fern
Dirca	*palustris*	leatherwood
Dryopteris	*carthusiana*	spinulose wood fern
Dryopteris	*goldiana*	Goldie's wood fern
Elaeagnus	*umbellata*	autumn olive
Eleocharis	*obtusa*	blunt spike rush
Elymus	*hystrix*	bottlebrush grass
Elymus	*macgregorii*	early wild rye

HERBACEOUS PLANTS *(continued)*

Genus	Species	Common Name
Elymus	*villosus*	silky wild rye
Enemion	*biternatum*	false rue anemone
Epifagus	*virginiana*	beechdrops
Erechtites	*hieraciifolius*	white fireweed
Erigenia	*bulbosa*	harbinger of spring
Erigeron	*annuus*	daisy fleabane
Erigeron	*philadelphicus*	Philadelphia fleabane
Erigeron	*strigosus*	narrow-leaved daisy fleabane
Erythronium	*albidum*	mottled-leaved white trout lily
Erythronium	*americanum*	yellow trout lily
Euonymus	*alatus*	burning bush
Euonymus	*atropurpureus*	wahoo
Euonymus	*obovatus*	running strawberry bush
Eupatorium	*altissimum*	tall boneset
Eupatorium	*coelestinum*	mistflower
Eupatorium	*fistulosum*	hollow-stemmed joe-pye weed
Eupatorium	*purpureum*	green-stemmed joe-pye weed
Eupatorium	*rugosum*	white snakeroot
Eupatorium	*serotinum*	late boneset
Eupatorium	*sessilifolium*	upland boneset
Fallopia	*scandenens*	climbing buckwheat
Festuca	*subverticillata*	nodding fescue
Floerkea	*proserpinacoides*	false mermaid
Galearis	*spectabilis*	showy orchis
Galium	*aparine*	cleavers
Galium	*circaezans*	wild licorice
Galium	*concinnum*	shining bedstraw
Galium	*lanceolatum*	lanceleaf wild licorice
Galium	*triflorum*	sweet-scented bedstraw
Gaultheria	*procumbens*	wintergreen
Gaylussacia	*baccata*	huckleberry
Geranium	*carolinianum*	Carolina cranesbill
Geranium	*maculatum*	wild geranium or cranesbill
Geum	*canadense*	white avens
Geum	*vernum*	spring avens
Glyceria	*striata*	fowl manna grass
Goodyera	*pubescens*	downy rattlesnake plantain
Gratiola	*neglecta*	clammy hedge hyssop
Hackelia	*virginiana*	sticktight
Hamamelis	*virginiana*	witch hazel
Helianthus	*decapetalus*	thin-leaved sunflower
Helianthus	*divaricatus*	woodland sunflower
Helianthus	*microcephalus*	small-headed woodland sunflower
Helianthus	*strumosus*	paleleaf woodland sunflower
Heliopsis	*helianthoides*	false sunflower
Hepatica	*nobilis*	hepatica
Hermocallis	*fulva*	daylily
Heuchera	*americana*	common alumroot
Hieracium	*paniculatum*	panicled hawkweed
Houstonia	*caerulea*	bluets
Houstonia	*longifolia*	long-leaved bluets
Houstonia	*purpurea*	large houstonia

Genus	Species	Common Name
Hybanthus	*concolor*	green violet
Hydrangea	*arborescens*	wild or American hydrangea
Hydrastis	*canadensis*	goldenseal
Hydrophyllum	*appendiculatum*	appendaged waterleaf
Hydrophyllum	*canadense*	broad-leaved waterleaf
Hydrophyllum	*macrophyllum*	large-leaved waterleaf
Hypericum	*mutilum*	weak Saint-John's-wort
Hypericum	*punctatum*	spotted Saint-John's-wort
Impatiens	*capensis*	orange jewelweed
Impatiens	*pallida*	yellow jewelweed
Isotria	*verticillata*	whorled pogonia
Jeffersonia	*diphylla*	twinleaf
Juncus	*effusus*	soft or common rush
Juncus	*tenuis*	slender rush
Krigia	*biflora*	two-flowered cynthia
Kummerowia	*striata*	Japanese clover
Laportea	*canadensis*	wood nettle
Leersia	*oryzoides*	rice cut-grass
Leersia	*virginica*	white grass
Lespedeza	*cuneata*	Chinese bush clover
Lespedeza	*hirta*	hairy bush clover
Lespedeza	*procumbens*	trailing bush clover
Lilium	*superbum*	Turk's-cap lily
Lindera	*benzoin*	spicebush
Liparis	*liliifolia*	purple twayblade
Liparis	*loeselii*	yellow widelip orchid
Lobelia	*inflata*	Indian tobacco
Lobelia	*siphilitica*	great blue lobelia
Lonicera	*maackii*	amur honeysuckle
Lonicera	*japonica*	Japanese honeysuckle
Luzula	*echinata*	hedgehog woodrush
Lycopus	*virginicus*	Virginia bugleweed
Lysimachia	*ciliatata*	fringed loosestrife
Lysimachia	*lanceolata*	lance-leaved loosestrife
Lysimachia	*quadrifolia*	whorled loosestrife
Maianthemum	*racemosum*	false Solomon's seal
Medeola	*virginiana*	Indian cucumber root
Menispermum	*canadense*	moonseed
Mertensia	*virginica*	Virginia bluebells
Microstegium	*vimineum*	Japanese stiltgrass
Mitchella	*repens*	partridgeberry
Mitella	*diphylla*	mitrewort
Monarda	*clinopodia*	basil balm, white bergamot
Monarda	*fistulosa*	wild bergamot
Monotropa	*hypopithys*	pinesap
Monotropa	*uniflora*	Indian pipe
Muhlenbergi	*sobolifera*	rock muhly
Muhlenbergi	*tenuiflora*	slender satin grass or slender muhly grass
Narcissus	*paeudonarcissus*	daffodil
Obolaria	*virginica*	pennywort
Oenothera	*biennis*	common evening primrose
Onoclea	*sensibilis*	sensitive fern

Genus	Species	Common Name
Osmorhiza	*claytonii*	sweet cicely
Osmorhiza	*longistylis*	aniseroot
Osmunda	*claytoniana*	interrupted fern
Oxalis	*fontana*	lady's wood sorrel
Oxalis	*grandis*	big yellow wood sorrel
Oxalis	*stricta*	upright yellow wood sorrel
Oxalis	*violacea*	violet wood sorrel
Packera	*aurea*	heart-leaved golden ragwort
Packera	*glabella*	butterweed
Packera	*obovatus*	roundleaf golden ragwort
Panax	*quinquefolius*	ginseng
Parietaria	*pensylvanica*	Pennsylvania pellitory
Parthenocissus	*quinquefolia*	Virginia creeper
Passiflora	*lutea*	yellow passion flower
Pedicularis	*canadensis*	wood betony
Penthorum	*sedoides*	ditch stonecrop
Perilla	*frutescens*	beefsteak plant
Persicaria	*hydropiper*	water pepper
Persicaria	*longiseta*	creeping smartweed
Persicaria	*punctata*	dotted smartweed
Phacelia	*bipinnatifida*	loose-flowered phacelia
Phegopteris	*hexagonoptera*	broad beech fern
Phlox	*bifida*	cleft phlox
Phlox	*divaricata*	blue phlox
Phryma	*leptostachya*	lopseed
Physalis	*heterophylla*	clammy ground-cherry
Phytolacca	*americana*	pokeweed
Pilea	*pumila*	clearweed
Plantago	*major*	broadleaf plantain
Plantago	*major*	common plantain
Poa	*sylvestris*	woodland bluegrass
Podophyllum	*peltatum*	May apple
Polemonium	*reptans*	Jacob's ladder
Polygonatum	*biflorum*	smooth Solomon's seal
Polygonum	*buxiforme*	boxwood knotweed
Polygonum	*sagittatum*	arrow-leaved tearthumb
Polygonum	*virginianum*	Virginia knotweed or jumpseed
Polystichum	*acrostichoides*	Christmas fern
Potentilla	*simplex*	old field cinquefoil
Prenanthes	*altissima*	tall white lettuce
Prenanthes	*sp.*	white lettuces
Prenanthes	*crepidinea*	great white lettuce
Prunella	*vulgaris*	heal-all, self-heal
Pycnanthemum	*incanum*	hoary mountain mint
Pycnanthemum	*tenuifolium*	slender mountain mint
Ranunculus	*arbortivus*	kidney-leaved buttercup
Ranunculus	*hispidus*	rough buttercup
Ranunculus	*recurvatus*	hooked buttercup
Ranunculus	*septentrionalis*	swamp buttercup
Ribes	*cynosbati*	pasture gooseberry
Rosa	*multiflora*	multiflora rose
Rosa	*satigera*	climbing wild rose

Genus	Species	Common Name
Rosa	*carolina*	pasture rose
Rubus	*allegheniensis*	common blackberry
Rubus	*avipes*	blackberry
Rubus	*flagellaris*	northern dewberry
Rubus	*occidentalis*	black raspberry
Rubus	*pensilvanicus*	Pennsylvania blackberry
Rumex	*obtusifolius*	bitter dock
Sabatia	*angularis*	common marsh pink
Salmolus	*floridanus*	brookweed
Sambucus	*canadensis*	elderberry
Sanguinaria	*canadensis*	bloodroot
Sanicula	*canadensis*	Canada black snakeroot
Sanicula	*odorata*	clustered black snakeroot
Sanicula	*trifoliata*	large-fruited black snakeroot
Sceptridium	*dissectum*	cut-leaved grape fern
Scirpus	*atrovirens*	green bulrush
Scirpus	*georgianus*	Georgia bulrush
Scrophularia	*marilandica*	late figwort
Scutellaria	*incana*	downy skullcap
Scutellaria	*ovata*	heart-leaved skullcap
Sedum	*ternatum*	wild stonecrop
Silene	*stellata*	starry catchfly
Silene	*virginica*	fire pink
Sisyrinchium	*angustifolium*	stout blue-eyed grass
Smilax	*bona-nox*	fringed greenbrier
Smilax	*rotundifolia*	roundleaf greenbrier
Smilax	*tamnoides*	bristly greenbrier
Solanum	*ptycanthum*	eastern black nightshade
Solidago	*caesia*	blue-stemmed goldenrod
Solidago	*canadensis*	Canadian goldenrod
Solidago	*flexicaulis*	zigzag goldenrod
Solidago	*gigantea*	giant goldenrod
Solidago	*graminifolia*	grass-leaved goldenrod
Solidago	*ulmifolia*	elm-leaved goldenrod
Sonchus	*asper*	spiny sow thistle
Sphenopholis	*intermedia*	slender wedge grass
Spiranthes	*ovalis*	lady's tresses
Stachys	*nuttallii*	nuttall's hedge nettle
Stachys	*tenuifolia*	smooth hedge nettle
Stellaria	*pubera*	star chickweed
Stylophorum	*diphyllum*	wood poppy
Symphyotrichum	*cordifolium*	heart-leaved aster or common blue wood aster
Symphyotrichum	*lateriflorum*	calico aster
Symphyotrichum	*pilosus*	hairy aster
Symphyotrichum	*shortii*	Short's aster
Synandra	*hispidula*	synandra
Taraxacum	*officinale*	dandelion
Thalictrum	*thalictoides*	rue anemone
Thalictrum	*dioicum*	early meadow rue
Thaspium	*trifoliatum*	purple meadow parsnip
Thaspium	*barbinode*	meadow parsnip
Thelypteris	*noveboracensis*	New York fern

Appendix 1

Genus	Species	Common Name
Tipularia	discolor	crane-fly orchid
Toxicodendron	radicans	poison ivy
Tradescantia	subaspera	zigzag spiderwort
Trifolium	pretense	red clover
Trillium	recurvatum	prairie trillium
Trillium	sessile	toadshade or sessile trillium
Trillium	flexipes	drooping trillium
Triodanis	perfoliata	Venus's looking glass
Triosteum	aurantiacum	early horse gentian
Triphora	trianthophora	three birds
Typha	augustifolia	narrow-leaved cattail
Uvularia	grandiflora	large-flowered bellwort
Vaccinium	pallidum	dryland blueberry
Valeriana	pauciflora	large-flowered valerian
Verbena	urticifolia	white vervain
Verbesina	alternifolia	wingstem
Vernonia	gigantea	tall ironweed
Viburnum	acerifolium	maple-leaved viburnum
Viburnum	dentatum	arrowwood viburnum
Viburnum	prunifolium	black haw
Vinca	minor	periwinkle
Viola	canadensis	Canada violet
Viola	palmata	three-lobed violet
Viola	pubescens	downy yellow violet
Viola	rostrata	long-spurred violet
Viola	sororia	common blue violet
Viola	striata	striped white violet
Vitis	aestivalis	summer grape
Vitis	riparia	riverbank grape
Vitis	vulpina	frost grape

MOSSES AND LIVERWORTS

Genus	Species	Common Name
Anacampton	splachnoides	knothole moss
Anomodon	attenuatus	poodle moss
Anomodon	minor	rounded tongue moss
Anomodon	rostratus	yellow yarn moss
Anomodon	tristus	threadbare moss
Anomodon	viticulosis	greater tongue moss
Arrhenopterum	heterostichum	goose egg moss
Atrichum	altecristatum	wavy starburst moss
Atrichum	angustatum	slender starburst moss
Brachythecium	ratabulum	rough foxtail moss
Brachythecium	salebrosum	golden foxtail moss
Brotherella	recurvans	satin moss
Bryhnia	graminicolor	bryhnia moss
Bryhnia	novae-angliae	bonsai moss
Bryoandersonia	illecebra	worm moss
Callicladium	haldanianum	sword moss
Campyliadelphus	chrysophyllus	bristle star moss
Campylophyllum	hispidulum	tiny star moss
Ctenidium	molluscum	feathered comb moss
Dicranella	heteromalla	fine hair moss

Genus	Species	Common Name
Dicranella	*montanum*	crispy broom moss
Dicranum	*scoparium*	windswept broom moss
Entodon	*seductrix*	cord glaze moss
Fissidens	*bryoides*	pixie pocket moss
Herzogiella	*striatella*	tassel moss
Hygroamblystegium	*varium*	tangled thread moss
Hypnum	*imponens*	brocade moss
Hypnum	*pallescens*	lesser plait moss
Hypnum	*curvifolium*	greater plait moss
Leskea	*gracilescens*	necklace chain moss
Leskea	*polycarpa*	curled chain moss
Leskeella	*nervosa*	frayed string moss
Leucobryum	*glaucum*	pincushion moss
Oncophorus	*wahlenbergii*	goiter moss
Orthotrichum	*soridium*	umbrella bristle moss
Oxyrrnchium	*hians*	spare rug moss
Plagiocethium	*cavifolium*	round silk moss
Plagiomnium	*ciliare*	saber tooth moss
Plagiomnium	*cuspidatum*	baby tooth moss
Platydictya	*subtillis*	algal thread moss
Platygerium	*repens*	oil spill moss rock
Polytrichastrum	*pallidisetum*	mountain haircap moss
Polytrichum	*juniperinum*	juniper haircap moss
Polytrichum	*piliferum*	bristly haircap moss
Pylaisia	*selwynii*	paintbrush moss
Rhizomnium	*punctatum*	red penny moss
Rhynchostegium	*serrulatum*	beaked comb moss
Thelia	*hirtella*	train tracks moss
Thuidium	*delicatulam*	delicate fern moss
Thuidium	*recognitum*	kilt fern moss

FUNGI

Genus	Species
Agaricus	*cf. auricolor*
Agaricus	*cf. pattersonae*
Agaricus	*placomyces*
Agaricus	*pocillator*
Albatrellus	*cristatus*
Amanita	*abrupta*
Amanita	*albocreata*
Amanita	*Amerirubescens*
Amanita	*Banningiana*
Amanita	*bisporigera*
Amanita	*Brunnescens*
Amanita	*canescens*
Amanita	*cokeri*
Amanita	*daucipes*
Amanita	*Elliptosperma*
Amanita	*flavoconia*
Amanita	*flavorubens*
Amanita	*Fulva*
Amanita	*jacksonii*
Amanita	*Multisquamosa*

FUNGI *(continued)*

Genus	Species	Common Name
Amanita	*onusta*	
Amanita	*Parcivolvata*	
Amanita	*ravenelii*	
Amanita	*rhacopus*	amanita borealisorora, cecileae
Amanita	*rubescens*	var. alba
Amanita	*sect.*	vaginatae
Amanita	*sinicoflava*	
Amanita	*sp-To1*	
Amanita	*spp.*	
Amanita	*sp.*	#1
Amanita	*sp.*	#2
Amanita	*spreta*	
Amanita	*subcokeri*	
Amanita	*velatipes*	
Artomyces	*pyxidatus*	
Bisporella	*citrina*	
Boletellus	*chrysenteroides*	
Boletinellus	*merulioides*	
Boletus	*auriflammeus*	
Boletus	*auriporus*	
Boletus	*bicolor*	
Boletus	*campestris*	
Boletus	*chrysenteron*	
Boletus	*firmus*	
Boletus	*illudens*	
Boletus	*innixus*	
Boletus	*miniato-olivaceus*	
Boletus	*pallidus*	
Boletus	*pseudo-olivaceus*	
Boletus	*sensibilis*	
Boletus	*sp.*	
Boletus	*spadiceus*	var. gracilis
Bulgaria	*inquinans*	
Callistosporium	*luteo-olivaceum*	
Callistosporium	*purpureomarginatum*	
Calocera	*cornea*	
Cantharellus	*appalachiensis*	
Cantharellus	*cinnabarinus*	
Cantharellus	*lateritius*	
Cantharellus	*minor*	
Ceratiomyxa	*fruticulosa*	
Ceriporia	*spissa*	
Chalciporus	*piperatoides*	
Clauvinopsis	*fusciformis*	
Clavaria	*vermicularis*	
Clavaria	*zolleringii*	
Clitocybe	*americana*	
Clitocybe	*candicans*	
Clitocybe	*cf. gibba*	
Clitocybe	*cf. truncicola*	
Clitocybe	*odora*	
Clitocybe	*robusta*	

Complete Species List

FUNGI *(continued)*

Genus	Species	Common Name
Clitocybe	*sp.*	
Clitocybula	*lacerate*	
Coltricia	*cinnamomea*	
Coprinellus	*disseminatus*	
Coprinellus	*domesticus*	
Coprinopsis	*atramentaria*	
Cortinarius	*collinitus*	
Cortinarius	*corrugatus*	
Cortinarius	*spp.*	
Cortinarius	*vibratilis*	
Cortinarius	*violaceus*	
Craterellus	*calyculus*	
Craterellus	*cornucopioides*	
Craterellus	*fallax*	
Crepidotus	*applanatus*	
Crepidotus	*crocophyllus*	
Crinipellis	*zonata*	
Crucibulum	*laeve*	
Cuphophyllus	*pratensis*	
Cyathus	*striatus*	
Dacrymyces	*palmatus*	
Dacryopinax	*spathularia*	
Daedalopsis	*confragosa*	
Ductifera	*pululahuana*	
Elaphomyces	*granulatus*	
Entoloma	*griseum*	
Entoloma	*murrayi*	
Entoloma	*rhodopolium*	
Entoloma	*spp.*	
Entoloma	*vernum*	
Exidia	*resica*	
Flammulaster	*erinaceella*	
Flammulina	*velutipes*	
Fomitopsis	*pinicola*	
Fomitopsis	*spraguei*	
Fuligo	*septica*	
Galerina	*marginata*	
Galiella	*rufa*	
Ganoderma	*applanatum*	
Geastrum	*elegans*	
Geastrum	*saccatum*	
Geastrum	*sp.*	
Gerronema	*strombodes*	
Gliophorus	*psittacinus*	
Globifomes	*graveolens*	
Gymnopus	*alkalivirens*	
Gymnopus	*dichrous*	
Gymnopus	*dryophilus*	
Gymnopus	*junonius*	
Gymnopus	*semihirtipes*	
Gymnopus	*sp.*	
Gymnopus	*subnudus*	

FUNGI (*continued*)

Genus	Species	Common Name
Gyrodon	*meruloides*	
Gyroporus	*castaneus*	
Hebeloma	*albidulum*	
Heimioporus	*betula*	
Helvella	*crispa*	
Hericium	*erinaceus*	
Hohenbuehelia	*grisea*	
Hohenbuehelia	*sp.*	
Hydnellum	*scrobiculatum*	
Hydnellum	*spongiosipes*	
Hydnochaete	*olivacea*	
Hydnum	*repandum*	
Hydnum	*umbilicatum*	
Hygrocybe	*aurantiosplendens*	
Hygrocybe	*cantharellus*	
Hygrocybe	*chlorophana*	
Hygrocybe	*conica*	
Hygrocybe	*flavescens*	
Hygrocybe	*marginata*	
Hygrocybe	*miniata*	
Hygrocybe	*virginea*	
Hygrocybe	*sp.*	
Hygrophoropsis	*aurantiaca*	
Hygrophorus	*pudorinus*	
Hymenopellis	*megalospora*	
Hymenopellis	*sp.*	
Hypholoma	*fasciculare*	
Hypomyces	*chrysospermus*	
Hypomyces	*hyalinus*	
Hypoxylon	*multiforme*	
Infundibulicybe	*gibba*	
Inocybe	*sp.*	
Irpex	*lacteus*	
Kretzschmaria	*deusta*	
Laccaria	*amethystine*	
Laccaria	*laccata*	
Laccaria	*longipes*	
Lachnum	*virgineum*	
Lactarius	*camphoratus*	
Lactarius	*chrysorreus*	
Lactarius	*corrugis*	
Lactarius	*deceptivus*	
Lactarius	*fumosus*	
Lactarius	*hygrophoroides*	
Lactarius	*imperceptus*	
Lactarius	*indigo*	
Lactarius	*luteolus*	
Lactarius	*pipperatus*	
Lactarius	*psammicola*	
Lactarius	*psammicola*	var. glaber
Lactarius	*quietus*	var. incanus
Lactarius	*sp.*	

Complete Species List

FUNGI (*continued*)

Genus	Species	Common Name
Lactarius	*subplinthogalus*	
Lactarius	*subserifluus*	
Lactarius	*subvellereus*	var. subdistans
Lactarius	*subvernalis*	var. cokeri
Lactarius	*vinaceorufescens*	
Lactarius	*volemus*	
Laetiporus	*cincinnatus*	
Laetiporus	*sulphereus*	
Leccinum	*albellum*	
Leccinum	*pseudoscabrum*	
Leccinum	*scabrum*	
Leccinum	*sp.*	
Lentinellus	*micheneri*	
Lentinellus	*ursinus*	
Lenzites	*betulina*	
Leotia	*lubrica*	
Lepiota	*atrodisca*	
Lepiota	*clypeolaria*	
Lepiota	*rubrotincta*	
Lepiota	*sp.*	
Leucoagaricus	*leucothites*	
Lycogala	*epidendrum*	
Lycoperdon	*perlatum*	
Lycoperdon	*pyriforme*	
Lycoperdon	*sp.*	
Macrolepiota	*procera*	
Marasmiellus	*candidus*	
Marasmius	*capillaris*	
Marasmius	*cohaerens*	
Marasmius	*delectans*	
Marasmius	*nigrodiscus*	
Marasmius	*pulcherripes*	
Marasmius	*rotula*	
Marasmius	*siccus*	
Marasmius	*sp.*	
Marasmius	*sullivantii*	
Megacollybia	*rodmanii*	
Meripilus	*sumstinei*	
Microstoma	*floccosum*	
Mycena	*niveipes*	
Mycena	*galericulata*	
Mycena	*haematopus*	
Mycena	*leaiana*	
Mycena	*luteopallens*	
Mycena	*spp.*	
Mycena	*subcaerulea*	
Mycorrhaphium	*adustum*	
Oxyporus	*populinus*	
Panellus	*stipticus*	
Panus	*rudis*	
Parasola	*cf.*	plicatilis
Phellinus	*gilvus*	

Genus	Species	Common Name
Phlebia	*incarnata*	
Pholiota	*veris*	
Phylloporus	*leucomycelinus*	
Phylloporus	*rhodoxanthus*	
Phyllotopsis	*nidulans*	
Pleurotus	*ostreatus*	
Pleurotus	*pulmonarius*	
Pluteus	*americanus*	
Pluteus	*cervinus*	
Pluteus	*chrysophlebius*	
Pluteus	*flavofuligineus*	
Pluteus	*longistriatus*	
Polyporus	*alveolaris*	
Polyporus	*leptocephalus*	
Polyporus	*varius*	
Porodisculis	*pendulus*	
Psathyrella	*candolleana*	
Psathyrella	*cf.*	pseudovernalis
Psathyrella	*delineata*	
Puccinia	*podophyli*	
Pycnoporus	*cinnabarinus*	
Pyronema	*omphalodes*	
Ramaria	*aurea*	
Ramaria	*fennica*	
Ramaria	*formosa*	
Ramaria	*sp.*	
Ramaria	*stricta*	
Ramariopsis	*kunzei*	
Reitboletus	*griseus*	
Resupinatus	*alboniger*	
Retiboletus	*ornatipes*	
Rickenella	*ibula*	
Russula	*aeruginea*	
Russula	*amenolens*	
Russula	*amoenolens*	
Russula	*ballouii*	
Russula	*compacta*	
Russula	*densifolia*	
Russula	*emetic*	
Russula	*flavida*	
Russula	*flavisiccans*	
Russula	*mariae*	
Russula	*parvovirescens*	
Russula	*sp.*	
Russula	*sp.*	
Russula	*sp.*	emetica group
Russula	*sp.*	virescens-crustosa group
Russula	*spp.*	
Russula	*variata*	
Russula	*vinacea*	
Sarcoscypha	*occidentalis*	
Schizophyllum	*commune*	

FUNGI (continued)

Genus	Species	Common Name
Scutellinia	*scutellata*	eyelash cup
Spongipellis	*pachyodon*	
Stereum	*complicatum*	
Stereum	*hirsutum*	
Stereum	*ostrea*	
Strobilomyces	*spp.*	
Tetrapyrgos	*nigripes*	
Thelephora	*terrestris*	
Thelephora	*vialis*	
Tolypocladium	*longisegmentum*	
Tolypocladium	*ophioglossoides*	
Trametes	*aesculi*	
Trametes	*gibbosa*	
Trametes	*hirsuta*	
Trametes	*versicolor*	
Tremella	*foliacea*	
Tremella	*mesenterica*	
Tremellodendron	*pallidum*	
Trichaptum	*biforme*	
Tubifera	*ferruginosa*	
Tylopilus	*alboater*	
Tylopilus	*felleus*	
Tylopilus	*ferrugineus*	
Tylopilus	*indecisus*	
Tyromyces	*chioneus*	
Xeromphalina	*kauffmanii*	
Xeromphalina	*tenuipes*	
Xylaria	*polymorpha*	
Xylaria	*sp.*	

LICHEN

Genus	Species
Acrocordia	*megalospora*
Amandinea	*polyspora*
Anaptychia	*palmulata*
Anisomeridium	*leucochlorum*
Anisomeridium	*polypori*
Arthonia	*apatetica*
Arthonia	*caesia*
Arthonia	*helvola*
Arthonia	*quintaria*
Bacidia	*purpurans*
Bacidia	*schweinitzii*
Bacidia	*sorediata*
Biatora	*printzenii*
Buellia	*wheeleri*
Candelaria	*concolor*
Candelariella	*cf. efflorescens*
Canoparmelia	*texana*
Catillaria	*nigroclavata*
Chaenothecopsis	*debilis*
Cladonia	*caespiticia*

Genus	Species
Cladonia	*macilenta*
Cladonia	*ochrochlora*
Cladonia	*parasitica*
Cladonia	*petrophila*
Cladonia	*peziziformis*
Cladonia	*ramulosa*
Coenogonium	*pineti*
Collema	*subflaccidum*
Crespoa	*crozalsiana*
Dictyocatenulata	*alba*
Fellhanera	*silicis*
Flavoparmelia	*caperata*
Graphis	*scripta*
Heterodermia	*obscurata*
Heterodermia	*speciosa*
Hypotrachyna	*livida*
Julella	*fallaciosa*
Lecania	*croatica*
Lecanora	*appalachensis*
Lecanora	*hybocarpa*
Lecanora	*layana*
Lecanora	*nothocaesiella*
Lecanora	*strobilina*
Lecanora	*thysanophora*
Lecidea	*cyrtidia*
Lecidea	*erythrophaea*
Lepra	*pustulata*
Lepraria	*caesiella*
Lepraria	*finkii*
Lepraria	*harrisiana*
Lepraria	*hodkinsoniana*
Lepraria	*sp.*
Leptogium	*cyanescens*
Leptogium	*dactylinum*
Lithothelium	*hyalosporum*
Micarea	*micrococca*
Micarea	*peliocarpa*
Micarea	*prasina*
Micarea	*soralifera*
Myelochroa	*aurulenta*
Myelochroa	*galbina*
Nadvonikia	*sorediata*
Nectriopsis	*sp.*
Opegrapha	*varia*
Opegrapha	*vulgata*
Parmelia	*squarrosa*
Parmotrema	*gardneri*
Parmotrema	*hypotropum*
Parmotrema	*reticulatum*
Pertusaria	*pustulata*
Phaeocalicium	*polyporaeum*
Phaeophyscia	*adiastola*

Genus	Species
Phaeophyscia	*pusilloides*
Phaeophyscia	*rubropulchra*
Phaeophyscia	*squarrosa*
Physcia	*americana*
Physcia	*millegrana*
Physcia	*stellaris*
Piccolia	*nannaria*
Placynthiella	*icmalea*
Porpidia	*albocaerulescens*
Pseudosagedia	*cestrensis*
Pseudosagedia	*isidiata*
Punctelia	*caseana*
Punctelia	*graminicola*
Punctelia	*missouriensis*
Punctelia	*rudecta*
Pyrenidium	*aggregatum*
Pyrenula	*laevigata*
Pyrenula	*pseudobufonia*
Pyrenula	*subelliptica*
Pyrrhospora	*varians*
Pyxine	*sorediata*
Pyxine	*subcinerea*
Rinodina	*papillata*
Rinodina	*pyrina*
Ropalospora	*viridis*
Sarea	*difformis*
Sarea	*resinae*
Scoliciosporum	*chlorococcum*
Scoliciosporum	*pensylvanicum*
Thelidium	*minutulum*
Trapelia	*placodioides*
Trapeliopsis	*flexuosa*
Trypethelium	*virens*
Verrucaria	*phloeophila*
Violella	*fucata*
Xanthomendoza	*weberi*

BIRDS

Genus	Species	Common Name
Meleagris	*gallopavo*	wild turkey
Cathartes	*aura)*	turkey vulture
Buteo	*lineatus*	red-shouldered hawk
Buteo	*platypterus*	broad-winged hawk
Buteo	*jamaicensis*	red-tailed hawk
Zenaida	*macroura*	mourning dove
Coccyzus	*americanus*	yellow-billed cuckoo
Strix	*varia*	barred owl
Caprimulgus	*vociferus*	eastern whip-poor-will
Chaetura	*pelagica*	chimney swift
Archilochus	*colubris*	ruby-throated hummingbird
Megaceryle	*alcyon*	belted kingfisher
Melanerpes	*erythrocephalus*	redheaded woodpecker

Genus	Species	Common Name
Melanerpes	*carolinus*	red-bellied woodpecker
Picoides	*pubescens*	downy woodpecker
Leuconotopicus	*villosus*	hairy woodpecker
Colaptes	*auratus*	northern flicker
Dryocopus	*pileatus*	pileated woodpecker
Contopus	*virens*	eastern wood pewee
Empidonax	*virescens*	Acadian flycatcher
Sayornis	*phoebe*	eastern Phoebe
Myiarchus	*crinitus*	great crested flycatcher
Vireo	*griseus*	white-eyed vireo
Vireo	*solitarius*	blue-headed vireo
Vireo	*flavifrons*	yellow-throated vireo
Vireo	*olivaceus*	red-eyed vireo
Tachycineta	*bicolor*	tree swallow
Cyanocitta	*cristata*	blue jay
Corvus	*brachyrhynchos*	American crow
Poecile	*carolinensis*	Carolina chickadee
Baeolophus	*bicolor*	tufted titmouse
Sitta	*carolinensis*	white-breasted nuthatch
Certhia	*americana*	brown creeper
Thryothorus	*ludovicianus*	Carolina wren
Regulus	*satrapa*	golden-crowned kinglet
Regulus	*calendula*	Ruby-crowned kinglet
Polioptila	*caerulea*	blue-gray gnatcatcher
Catharus	*ustulatus*	Swainson's thrush
Catharus	*guttatus*	hermit thrush
Catharus	*fuscescens*	veery
Hylocichla	*mustelina*	wood thrush
Turdus	*migratorius*	American robin
Dumetella	*carolinensis*	gray catbird
Bombycilla	*cedrorum*	cedar waxwing
Vermivora	*cyanoptera*	blue-winged warbler
Vermivora	*chrysoptera*	golden-winged warbler
Leiothlypis	*peregrina*	Tennessee warbler
Leiothlypis	*ruficapilla*	Nashville warbler
Setophaga	*americana*	northern parula
Setophaga	*coronata*	yellow-rumped warbler
Setophaga	*virens*	black-throated green warbler
Setophaga	*dominica*	yellow-throated warbler
Setophaga	*pinus*	pine warbler
Setophaga	*castanea*	bay-breasted warbler
Setophaga	*fusca*	blackburnian warbler
Setophaga	*petechia*	yellow warbler
Setophaga	*striata*	black-poll warbler
Setophaga	*cerulean*	cerulean warbler
Mniotilta	*varia*	black-and-white warbler
Setophaga	*ruticilla*	American redstart
Helmitheros	*vermivorum*	worm-eating warbler
Seiurus	*aurocapilla*	ovenbird
Parkesia	*motacilla*	Louisiana water thrush
Geothlypis	*formosa*	Kentucky warbler
Geothlypis	*trichas*	common yellowthroat

BIRDS (continued)

Genus	Species	Common Name
Setophaga	*citrina*	hooded warbler
Cardellina	*pusilla*	Wilson's warbler
Cardellina	*canadensis*	Canada warbler
Icteria	*virens*	yellow-breasted chat
Piranga	*rubra*	summer tanager
Piranga	*olivacea*	scarlet tanager
Cardinalis	*cardinalis*	northern cardinal
Pheucticus	*ludovicianus*	rose-breasted grosbeak
Passerina	*cyanea*	indigo bunting
Pipilo	*erythrophthalmus*	eastern towhee
Spizella	*passerina*	chipping sparrow
Spizella	*pusilla*	field sparrow
Zonotrichia	*albicollis*	white-throated sparrow
Zonotrichia	*leucophrys*	white-crowned sparrow
Molothrus	*ater*	brown-headed cowbird
Spinus	*tristis*	American goldfinch

BATS

Genus	Species	Common Name
Lasiurus	*borealis*	eastern red bat
Myotis	*septentrionalis*	northern long-eared bat
Eptesicus	*fuscus*	big brown bat
Myotis	*sodalis*	Indiana bat
Perimyotis	*subflavus*	tricolored bat or eastern pipistrelle
Myotis	*lucifugus*	little brown bat
Lasiurus	*cinereus*	hoary bat
Nycticeius	*humeralis*	evening bat

INSECTS

Order	Family	Genus	Species
Beetles			
Coleoptera	Anthribidae	*Eurymycter*	*sp.*
Coleoptera	Anthribidae	*Euparius*	*marmoreus*
Coleoptera	Artematopodidae	*Eurypogon*	*niger*
Coleoptera	Attelabidae	*Synolabus*	*bipustulatus*
Coleoptera	Attelabidae	*Eugnamptus*	*angustatus*
Coleoptera	Bostrichidae	*Lichenophanes*	*bicornis*
Coleoptera	Bostrichidae	*Xylobiops*	*basilaris*
Coleoptera	Brentidae	*Arrhenodes*	*minutus*
Coleoptera	Buprestidae	*Agrilus*	*arcuatus*
Coleoptera	Buprestidae	*Agrilus*	*bilineatus*
Coleoptera	Buprestidae	*Agrilus*	*putillus*
Coleoptera	Buprestidae	*Agrilus*	*sp.*
Coleoptera	Buprestidae	*Pachyschelus*	*confusus/laevigatus*
Coleoptera	Buprestidae	*Chrysobothris*	*rugosicepts*
Coleoptera	Buprestidae	*Dicerca*	*divaricata*
Coleoptera	Buprestidae	*Acmaeodera*	*tubulus*
Coleoptera	Buprestidae	*Chalcophora*	*virginiensis*
Coleoptera	Buprestidae	*Chrysobothris*	*azurea*
Coleoptera	Buprestidae	*Agrilus*	*anxius*
Coleoptera	Buprestidae	*Chrysobothris*	*adelpha*
Coleoptera	Buprestidae	*Chrysobothris*	*femorata*

Order	Family	Genus	Species
Beetles			
Coleoptera	Buprestidae	*Brachys*	*tesselatus*
Coleoptera	Buprestidae	*Taphrocerus*	*gracilis*
Coleoptera	Buprestidae	*Taphrocerus*	*schaefferi*
Coleoptera	Buprestidae	*Chrysobothris*	*sp. 1*
Coleoptera	Buprestidae	*Chrysobothris*	*sp. 2*
Coleoptera	Buprestidae	*Chrysobothris*	*sp. 3*
Coleoptera	Buprestidae	*Agrilus*	*obsoletoguttatus*
Coleoptera	Buprestidae	*Chrysobothris*	*sexsignata*
Coleoptera	Buprestidae	*Agrilus*	*ruficolllis*
Coleoptera	Buprestidae	*Agrilus*	*sp. 1*
Coleoptera	Buprestidae	*Agrilus*	*sp. 2*
Coleoptera	Cantharidae	*Rhagonycha*	*angulata*
Coleoptera	Cantharidae	*Podabrus*	*tricostatus*
Coleoptera	Cantharidae	*Trypherus*	*latipennis*
Coleoptera	Cantharidae	*Podabrus*	*brunnicollis*
Coleoptera	Cantharidae	*Podabrus*	*rugosulus*
Coleoptera	Cantharidae	*Podabrus*	*flavicollis*
Coleoptera	Cantharidae	*Rhagonycha*	*imbecillis*
Coleoptera	Cantharidae	*Podabrus*	*brevicollis*
Coleoptera	Carabidae	*Cicindela*	*sexguttata*
Coleoptera	Carabidae	*Galerita*	*bicolor*
Coleoptera	Carabidae	*Anisodactylus*	*sp.*
Coleoptera	Carabidae	*Notiobia*	*sp.*
Coleoptera	Carabidae	*Harpalus*	*calliginosus*
Coleoptera	Carabidae	*Coptodera*	*aerata*
Coleoptera	Carabidae	*Cymindis*	*limbata*
Coleoptera	Carabidae	Undetermined	*sp.*
Coleoptera	Carabidae	*Chlaenius*	*sp.*
Coleoptera	Carabidae	*Cyclotrachelus*	*sp.*
Coleoptera	Carabidae	*Myas*	*coracinus*
Coleoptera	Carabidae	*Pterostichus*	*sp.*
Coleoptera	Carabidae	*Nebria*	*sp.*
Coleoptera	Carabidae	*Clivina*	*sp.*
Coleoptera	Carabidae	*Lebia (Lebia)*	*solea*
Coleoptera	Carabidae	*Lebia (Lebia)*	*viridis*
Coleoptera	Cerambycidae	*Lepturges*	*symmetricus*
Coleoptera	Cerambycidae	*Cyrtophorus*	*verrucosus*
Coleoptera	Cerambycidae	*Knulliana*	*cincta*
Coleoptera	Cerambycidae	*Clytus*	*ruricola*
Coleoptera	Cerambycidae	*Neoclytus*	*acuminatus*
Coleoptera	Cerambycidae	*Neoclytus*	*scutellaris*
Coleoptera	Cerambycidae	*Plagionotus*	*floralis*
Coleoptera	Cerambycidae	*Xylotrechus*	*colonus*
Coleoptera	Cerambycidae	*Anelaphus*	*villosus*
Coleoptera	Cerambycidae	*Elaphidion*	*mucronatum*
Coleoptera	Cerambycidae	*Parelaphidion*	*incertum*
Coleoptera	Cerambycidae	*Heterachthes*	*quadrimaculatus*
Coleoptera	Cerambycidae	*Obrium*	*maculatum*
Coleoptera	Cerambycidae	*Euderces*	*picipes*
Coleoptera	Cerambycidae	*Purpuricenus*	*axillaris*
Coleoptera	Cerambycidae	*Astylopsis*	*macula*

Complete Species List

Order	Family	Genus	Species
Beetles			

Coleoptera	Cerambycidae	*Astylopsis*	*sexguttata*
Coleoptera	Cerambycidae	*Graphisurus*	*fasciatus*
Coleoptera	Cerambycidae	*Leptostylus*	*transversus*
Coleoptera	Cerambycidae	*Urgleptes*	*querci*
Coleoptera	Cerambycidae	*Aegomorphus*	*modestus*
Coleoptera	Cerambycidae	*Astyleiopus*	*variegatus*
Coleoptera	Cerambycidae	*Microgoes*	*oculatus*
Coleoptera	Cerambycidae	*Saperda*	*lateralis*
Coleoptera	Cerambycidae	*Anoplodera/* *Anoploderomorpha*	*pubera*
Coleoptera	Cerambycidae	*Brachyleptura*	*rubrica/champlaini*
Coleoptera	Cerambycidae	*Neoalosterna*	*capitata*
Coleoptera	Cerambycidae	*Strangalia*	*luteicornis*
Coleoptera	Cerambycidae	*Strophiona*	*nitens*
Coleoptera	Cerambycidae	*Trachysida*	*mutabilis*
Coleoptera	Cerambycidae	*Typocerus*	*lugubris*
Coleoptera	Cerambycidae	*Typocerus*	*velutinus*
Coleoptera	Cerambycidae	*Gaurotes*	*cyanipennis*
Coleoptera	Cerambycidae	*Metacmaeops*	*vittata*
Coleoptera	Cerambycidae	*Stenocorus*	*cinnamopterus*
Coleoptera	Cerambycidae	*Necydalis*	*mellita*
Coleoptera	Cerambycidae	*Orthosoma*	*brunneum*
Coleoptera	Cerambycidae	*Prionus*	*laticollis*
Coleoptera	Cerambycidae	*Sternidius*	*alpha*
Coleoptera	Cerambycidae	*Hippopsis*	*lemniscata*
Coleoptera	Cerambycidae	*Prionus (Homaesthesis)*	*sp.*
Coleoptera	Cerambycidae	*Neandra*	*brunnea*
Coleoptera	Cerambycidae	*Analeptura*	*lineola*
Coleoptera	Cerambycidae	*Centrodera*	*decolorata*
Coleoptera	Cerylonidae	*Cerylon*	*sp.*
Coleoptera	Chrysomelidae	*Charidotella*	*sexpunctata*
Coleoptera	Chrysomelidae	*Sumitrosis*	*rosea*
Coleoptera	Chrysomelidae	*Brachypnoea*	*clypealis*
Coleoptera	Chrysomelidae	*Kuschelina*	*vians*
Coleoptera	Chrysomelidae	*Kuschelina/Capriata*	
Coleoptera	Chrysomelidae	*Palaeolontha*	*picta*
Coleoptera	Chrysomelidae	*Cerotoma*	*trifurcata*
Coleoptera	Chrysomelidae	*Diabrotica*	*undecimpunctata*
Coleoptera	Chrysomelidae	*Phyllobrotica*	*limbata*
Coleoptera	Chrysomelidae	*Sumitrosis*	*inaequalis*
Coleoptera	Chrysomelidae	*Plagiometriona*	*clavata*
Coleoptera	Cleridae	*Enoclerus*	*nigripes*
Coleoptera	Cleridae	*Madoniella*	*dislocata*
Coleoptera	Cleridae	*Phyllobaenus*	*humeralis*
Coleoptera	Cleridae	*Phyllobaenus*	*pallipennis*
Coleoptera	Cleridae	*Neorthopleura*	*thoracica*
Coleoptera	Cleridae	*Chariessa*	*pilosa*
Coleoptera	Cleridae	*Cymatodera*	*sp. 1*
Coleoptera	Cleridae	*Cymatodera*	*sp. 2*
Coleoptera	Cleridae	*Enoclerus*	*analis/nigripes*
Coleoptera	Cleridae	*Cregya*	*oculata*

INSECTS *(continued)*

Order	Family	Genus	Species
Beetles			
Coleoptera	Coccinellidae	*Anatis*	*labiculata*
Coleoptera	Coccinellidae	*Anatis*	*mali*
Coleoptera	Coccinellidae	*Cycloneda*	*munda*
Coleoptera	Coccinellidae	*Harmonia*	*axyridis*
Coleoptera	Coccinellidae	*Psyllobora*	*vigintimaculata*
Coleoptera	Coccinellidae	*Scymnus*	*indianensis*
Coleoptera	Coccinellidae	*Scymnus*	*sp.*
Coleoptera	Coccinellidae	*Coleomegilla*	*maculata*
Coleoptera	Coccinellidae	*Brachiacantha*	*ursina*
Coleoptera	Coccinellidae	*Brachiacantha*	*sp.*
Coleoptera	Cucujidae	Undetermined	*sp.*
Coleoptera	Curculionidae	*Cossonus*	*corticola*
Coleoptera	Curculionidae	*Apteromechus*	*ferratus*
Coleoptera	Curculionidae	*Eubulus*	*bisignatus*
Coleoptera	Curculionidae	*Eubulus*	*obliquefasciatus*
Coleoptera	Curculionidae	*Curculio*	*caryae*
Coleoptera	Curculionidae	*Curculio*	*pardalis*
Coleoptera	Curculionidae	*Rhodobaenus*	*quinquepunctatus*
Coleoptera	Curculionidae	*Cyrtepistomus*	*castaneus*
Coleoptera	Curculionidae	*Pandeleteius*	*hilaris*
Coleoptera	Curculionidae	*Conotrachelus*	*anaglypticus*
Coleoptera	Curculionidae	*Monarthrum*	*fasciatum*
Coleoptera	Curculionidae	*Ips*	*grandicollis*
Coleoptera	Curculionidae	*Anisandrus*	*sayi*
Coleoptera	Curculionidae	*Euwallacea*	*validus*
Coleoptera	Curculionidae	*Xyleborinus*	*saxeseni*
Coleoptera	Curculionidae	*Xyleborus*	*affinus*
Coleoptera	Curculionidae	*Xyleborus*	*celsus*
Coleoptera	Curculionidae	*Xylosandrus*	*crassiusculus*
Coleoptera	Curculionidae	*Xylosandrus*	*germanus*
Coleoptera	Curculionidae	*Linogeraeus*	*neglectus*
Coleoptera	Curculionidae	*Unknown*	*sp.*
Coleoptera	Curculionidae	*Curculio*	*sp 1*
Coleoptera	Curculionidae	*Curculio*	*sp 2*
Coleoptera	Dryopidae	*Helichus*	*basalis*
Coleoptera	Dryopidae	*Helichus*	*striatus*
Coleoptera	Dytiscidae	*Agabus*	*sp.*
Coleoptera	Dytiscidae	*Agabus*	*sp.*
Coleoptera	Dytiscidae	*Acilius*	*mediatus*
Coleoptera	Dytiscidae	*Hydaticus*	*sp.*
Coleoptera	Dytiscidae	*Heterosternuta*	*wickhami*
Coleoptera	Dytiscidae	*Hydroporus*	*sp.*
Coleoptera	Elateridae	*Lacon*	*avitus*
Coleoptera	Elateridae	*Lacon*	*discoideus*
Coleoptera	Elateridae	*Lacon*	*marmorata*
Coleoptera	Elateridae	*Alaus*	*oculatus*
Coleoptera	Elateridae	*Horistonotus*	*curiatus*
Coleoptera	Elateridae	*Athous*	*brightwelli*
Coleoptera	Elateridae	*Athous*	*cucullatus*
Coleoptera	Elateridae	*Athous*	*scapularis*
Coleoptera	Elateridae	*Limonius*	*basillaris*

Complete Species List

INSECTS *(continued)*

Order	Family	Genus	Species
Beetles			
Coleoptera	Elateridae	*Hemicrepidius*	*memnonius*
Coleoptera	Elateridae	*Hypoganus*	*sulcicollis*
Coleoptera	Elateridae	*Anchastus*	*binus*
Coleoptera	Elateridae	*Ampedus*	*melantoides*
Coleoptera	Elateridae	*Ampedus*	*semicinctus*
Coleoptera	Elateridae	*Melanotus*	*sp.*
Coleoptera	Elateridae	*Melanotus*	*sp.*
Coleoptera	Elateridae	*Diplostethus*	*carolinensis*
Coleoptera	Elateridae	*Elater*	*abruptus*
Coleoptera	Elateridae	*Parallelostethus*	*attenuatus*
Coleoptera	Elateridae	*Megapenthes*	*insignis*
Coleoptera	Elateridae	*Megapenthes*	*limbalis*
Coleoptera	Elateridae	*Drapetes*	*exstriatus*
Coleoptera	Elateridae	*Dipropus*	*sp.*
Coleoptera	Elateridae	*Ctenicera/ Neopristilophus*	*aethiops*
Coleoptera	Elateridae	*Ampedus*	*militarus*
Coleoptera	Elateridae	*Dolerosomus*	*silaceus*
Coleoptera	Elateridae	*Lacon*	*impressicollis*
Coleoptera	Elateridae	*Glyphonyx*	*recticollis*
Coleoptera	Elateridae	*Ampedus*	*luteolus*
Coleoptera	Elateridae	*Ampedus*	*areolatus*
Coleoptera	Elateridae	*Ampedus*	*rubricollis*
Coleoptera	Elateridae	*Ampedus*	*militaris*
Coleoptera	Elateridae	*Ampedus*	*pusio*
Coleoptera	Elateridae	*Cardiophorus*	*convexus*
Coleoptera	Elateridae	*Limonius*	*quercinus*
Coleoptera	Elateridae	*Limonius*	*griceus*
Coleoptera	Elmidae	*Stenelmis*	*sp.*
Coleoptera	Endomychidae	*Endomychus*	*biguttatus*
Coleoptera	Erotylidae	*Microsternus*	*ulkei*
Coleoptera	Erotylidae	*Triplax*	*festiva*
Coleoptera	Erotylidae	*Triplax*	*sp.*
Coleoptera	Erotylidae	*Triplax*	*flavicollis*
Coleoptera	Erotylidae	*Triplax*	*frosti*
Coleoptera	Erotylidae	*Tritoma*	*biguttata*
Coleoptera	Erotylidae	*Tritoma*	*sanguinipennis*
Coleoptera	Erotylidae	*Tritoma*	*humeralis*
Coleoptera	Erotylidae	*Tritoma*	*tenebrosa*
Coleoptera	Erotylidae	*Tritoma*	*biguttata biguttata*
Coleoptera	Erotylidae	*Megalodacne*	*heros*
Coleoptera	Erotylidae	*Megalodacne*	*fasciata*
Coleoptera	Erotylidae	*Tritoma*	*angulata/erythrocephala*
Coleoptera	Erotylidae	*Tritoma*	*mimetica*
Coleoptera	Eucinetidae	*Nycteus*	*oviformis*
Coleoptera	Eucnemidae	*Dromaeolus*	*sp.*
Coleoptera	Eucnemidae	*Isarthrus*	*sp.*
Coleoptera	Eucnemidae	*Onichodon*	*orchesides*
Coleoptera	Eucnemidae	*Hylis*	*sp.*
Coleoptera	Eucnemidae	*Isorhipis*	*obliqua*
Coleoptera	Eucnemidae	*Perothops*	*muscida*

Order	Family	Genus	Species
Beetles			
Coleoptera	Eucnemidae	*Onichodon*	*downiei*
Coleoptera	Geotrupidae	*Bulbocerosoma*	*farctum/bruneri*
Coleoptera	Geotrupidae	*Odonteus*	*sp.*
Coleoptera	Histeridae	*Platylomalus*	*aequalis*
Coleoptera	Histeridae	*Hololepta*	*aequalis*
Coleoptera	Histeridae	*Hololepta*	*lucida*
Coleoptera	Histeridae	*Platysoma*	*aequalis*
Coleoptera	Histeridae	*Platysoma*	*aurelianum*
Coleoptera	Histeridae	*Platysoma*	*leconti*
Coleoptera	Hydrophilidae	Undetermined	*sp.*
Coleoptera	Hydrophilidae	*Helocombus*	*bifidus*
Coleoptera	Laemophloeidae	*Laemophloeus*	*biguttatus*
Coleoptera	Laemophloeidae	*Placonotus*	*sp.*
Coleoptera	Lampyridae	*Lucidota*	*atra*
Coleoptera	Lampyridae	*Photinus*	*marginellus*
Coleoptera	Lampyridae	*Photinus*	*pyralis*
Coleoptera	Lampyridae	*Photinus*	*sp.*
Coleoptera	Lampyridae	*Photuris*	*fairchildi*
Coleoptera	Lampyridae	*Photuris*	*sp.*
Coleoptera	Lampyridae	*Ellychnia*	*corrusca*
Coleoptera	Lampyridae	*Pyractomena*	*linearis*
Coleoptera	Lampyridae	*Pyropyga*	*decipians*
Coleoptera	Latridiidae	*Cortinicara*	*gibbosa*
Coleoptera	Leiodidae	*Prionochaeta*	*opaca*
Coleoptera	Leiodidae	Undetermined	*sp.*
Coleoptera	Leiodidae	*Anisotoma*	*sp.*
Coleoptera	Lucanidae	*Ceruchus*	*piceus*
Coleoptera	Lycidae	*Caenia*	*dimidiata*
Coleoptera	Lycidae	*Calopteron*	*discrepans*
Coleoptera	Lycidae	*Calopteron*	*reticulatum*
Coleoptera	Lycidae	*Calopteron*	*terminale*
Coleoptera	Lycidae	*Leptoceletes*	*basalis*
Coleoptera	Lycidae	*Plateros*	*sp.*
Coleoptera	Lycidae	*Plateros*	*sp.*
Coleoptera	Lycidae	*Erotides*	*sculptilis*
Coleoptera	Lycidae	*Eropterus*	*sp.*
Coleoptera	Lymexylidae	*Melittoma*	*sericeum*
Coleoptera	Melandryidae	*Dircaea*	*liturata*
Coleoptera	Melandryidae	*Melandrya*	*striata*
Coleoptera	Melandryidae	*Enchodes*	*sericea*
Coleoptera	Melyridae	*Trichochrous*	*egenus*
Coleoptera	Mordellidae	*Glipa*	*hiralis*
Coleoptera	Mordellidae	*Glipa*	*oculata*
Coleoptera	Mordellidae	*Paramordellaria*	*triloba*
Coleoptera	Mordellidae	*Tomoxia*	*lineella*
Coleoptera	Mordellidae	*Yakuhananomia*	*bidentata*
Coleoptera	Mordellidae	*Glipostenoda*	*ambusta*
Coleoptera	Mordellidae	*Mordellistena*	*trifasciata*
Coleoptera	Mordellidae	*Mordellistena/ Mordellina*	*spp.*
Coleoptera	Mordellidae	*Tomoxia*	*inclusa*
Coleoptera	Mordellidae	*Mordellistena*	*attenuata*

Complete Species List   289

INSECTS *(continued)*

Order	Family	Genus	Species
Beetles			
Coleoptera	Mordellidae	*Hoshihananomia*	*octopunctata*
Coleoptera	Mordellidae	*Glipodes*	*sericans*
Coleoptera	Mordellidae	*Mordellaria*	*serval*
Coleoptera	Mordellidae	*Falsemordellistena*	*bihamata*
Coleoptera	Mordellidae	*Falsemordellistena*	*pubescens*
Coleoptera	Mordellidae	*Falsemordellistena*	*discolor*
Coleoptera	Mordellidae	*Toidomordella*	*discoidea*
Coleoptera	Mordellidae	*Mordellaria*	*serval*
Coleoptera	Mordellidae	*Mordella*	*marginata*
Coleoptera	Mycetophagidae	*Litargus*	*balteatus*
Coleoptera	Mycetophagidae	*Mycetophagus*	*flexuosus*
Coleoptera	Mycetophagidae	*Mycetophagus*	*pluripunctatus*
Coleoptera	Mycetophagidae	*Mycetophagus*	*punctatus*
Coleoptera	Nitidulidae	*Amphicrossus*	*ciliatus*
Coleoptera	Nitidulidae	*Carpophilus*	*sp.*
Coleoptera	Nitidulidae	*Colopterus*	*niger*
Coleoptera	Nitidulidae	*Cryptarcha*	*ampla*
Coleoptera	Nitidulidae	*Glischrochilus*	*fasciatus*
Coleoptera	Nitidulidae	*Glischrochilus*	*obtusus*
Coleoptera	Nitidulidae	*Glischrochilus*	*quadrisignatus*
Coleoptera	Nitidulidae	*Glischrochilus*	*sanguinolentus*
Coleoptera	Nitidulidae	*Pallodes*	*pallidus*
Coleoptera	Nitidulidae	*Pallodes*	*pallidus*
Coleoptera	Passandridae	*Catogenus*	*rufus*
Coleoptera	Phengodidae	*Phengodes sensu stricto*	*sp. 1*
Coleoptera	Phengodidae	*Phengodes sensu stricto*	*sp. 2*
Coleoptera	Phengodidae	*Phengodes sensu stricto*	*sp. 3*
Coleoptera	Phengodidae	*Phengodes sensu stricto*	*sp. 4*
Coleoptera	Ptilodactylidae	*Ptilodactyla*	*sp.*
Coleoptera	Ptinidae	*Priobium*	*sericeum*
Coleoptera	Ptinidae	*Trichodesma*	*sp.*
Coleoptera	Ptinidae	*Ernobius*	*mollis*
Coleoptera	Ptinidae	*Hadrobregmus*	*sp.*
Coleoptera	Ptinidae	*Protheca*	*hispida*
Coleoptera	Ptinidae	*Sculptotheca*	*pubera*
Coleoptera	Pyrochroidae	*Dendroides*	*canadensis*
Coleoptera	Pyrochroidae	*Dendroides*	*concolor*
Coleoptera	Pyrochroidae	*Neopyrochroa*	*flabellata*
Coleoptera	Pyrochroidae	*Neopyrochroa*	*femoralis*
Coleoptera	Rhipiceridae	*Sandalus*	*niger*
Coleoptera	Ripiphoridae	*Ripiphorus*	*fasciatus-complex*
Coleoptera	Scarabaeidae	*Euphoria*	*fulgida*
Coleoptera	Scarabaeidae	*Trichiotinus*	*affinis*
Coleoptera	Scarabaeidae	*Trichiotinus*	*lunulatus*
Coleoptera	Scarabaeidae	*Valgus*	*canaliculatus*
Coleoptera	Scarabaeidae	*Dichelonyx*	*sp.*
Coleoptera	Scarabaeidae	*Macrodactylus*	*subspinosus*
Coleoptera	Scarabaeidae	*Phyllophaga*	*marginalis*
Coleoptera	Scarabaeidae	*Serica*	*sp.*
Coleoptera	Scarabaeidae	*Popillia*	*japonica*
Coleoptera	Scarabaeidae	*Ateuchus*	*histeroides*

Order	Family	Genus	Species
Beetles			
Coleoptera	Scarabaeidae	*Onthophagus*	*hecate*
Coleoptera	Scarabaeidae	*Onthophagus*	*striatulus*
Coleoptera	Scarabaeidae	*Callistethus*	*marginatus*
Coleoptera	Scarabaeidae	*Macrodactylus*	*angustatus*
Coleoptera	Scirtidae	*Prionocyphon*	*discoideus*
Coleoptera	Scirtidae	*Sacodes*	*pulchella*
Coleoptera	Silphidae	*Necrodes*	*surinamensis*
Coleoptera	Silphidae	*Necrophila*	*americana*
Coleoptera	Silphidae	*Nicrophorus*	*orbicollis*
Coleoptera	Silphidae	*Nicrophorus*	*sayi*
Coleoptera	Silphidae	*Nicrophorus*	*tomentosus*
Coleoptera	Silvanidae	*Uleiota*	*dubius*
Coleoptera	Staphylinidae	*Oxyporus*	*quinquemaculatus*
Coleoptera	Staphylinidae	*Medon/Sunius*	*sp./sp.*
Coleoptera	Staphylinidae	*Scaphidium*	*piceum*
Coleoptera	Staphylinidae	*Hesperus*	*apiciallis*
Coleoptera	Staphylinidae	*Philonthus*	*caeruleipennis*
Coleoptera	Staphylinidae	*Philonthus*	*sp.*
Coleoptera	Staphylinidae	*Ontholestes*	*cingulatus*
Coleoptera	Staphylinidae	*Platydracus*	*maculosus*
Coleoptera	Staphylinidae	*Platydracus*	*praetermissus*
Coleoptera	Staphylinidae	*Lordithon*	*cinctus*
Coleoptera	Staphylinidae	*Sepedophilus*	*sp.*
Coleoptera	Staphylinidae	*Tachinus*	*fimbriatus*
Coleoptera	Staphylinidae	Undetermined	*sp. 1*
Coleoptera	Staphylinidae	Undetermined	*sp. 2*
Coleoptera	Staphylinidae	*Oxyporus*	*stygicus*
Coleoptera	Staphylinidae	*Siagonium*	*americanum*
Coleoptera	Staphylinidae	*Tachinus*	*sp.*
Coleoptera	Staphylinidae	*Nitidotachinus*	*sp.*
Coleoptera	Staphylinidae	*Lathrobium*	*sp.*
Coleoptera	Stenotrachelidae	*Cephaloon*	*lepturides*
Coleoptera	Synchroidae	*Synchroa*	*punctata*
Coleoptera	Tenebrionidae	*Hymenorus*	*sp.*
Coleoptera	Tenebrionidae	*Lobopoda*	*sp.*
Coleoptera	Tenebrionidae	*Androchirus*	*erythropus*
Coleoptera	Tenebrionidae	*Capnochroa*	*fuliginosa*
Coleoptera	Tenebrionidae	*Isomira*	*quadristriata*
Coleoptera	Tenebrionidae	*Pseudocistela*	*brevis*
Coleoptera	Tenebrionidae	*Mycetochara*	*binotata*
Coleoptera	Tenebrionidae	*Diaperis*	*maculata*
Coleoptera	Tenebrionidae	*Neomida*	*bicornis*
Coleoptera	Tenebrionidae	*Platydema*	*laevipes*
Coleoptera	Tenebrionidae	*Anaedus*	*brunneus*
Coleoptera	Tenebrionidae	*Paratenetus*	*punctatus*
Coleoptera	Tenebrionidae	*Arthromacra*	*aenea*
Coleoptera	Tenebrionidae	*Alobates*	*pennsylvanicus*
Coleoptera	Tenebrionidae	*Haplandrus*	*fulvipes*
Coleoptera	Tenebrionidae	*Strongylium*	*tenuicolle*
Coleoptera	Tenebrionidae	*Meracantha*	*contracta*
Coleoptera	Tenebrionidae	*Bolitotherus*	*cornutus*

Order	Family	Genus	Species
Beetles			
Coleoptera	Tenebrionidae	*Tenebrio*	*molitor*
Coleoptera	Tetratomidae	*Eustrophopsis*	*bicolor*
Coleoptera	Tetratomidae	*Eustrophus*	*tomentosus*
Coleoptera	Tetratomidae	*Synstrophus*	*repandus*
Coleoptera	Tetratomidae	*Penthe*	*obliquata*
Coleoptera	Tetratomidae	*Penthe*	*pimelia*
Coleoptera	Throscidae	*Trixagus*	*sp.*
Coleoptera	Trogossitidae	*Tenebroides*	*sp.*
Flies			
Diptera	Asilidae	*Holcocephala*	*fusca*
Diptera	Asilidae	*Holcocephala*	*calva*
Diptera	Asilidae	*Holopogon*	*phaenonotus*
Diptera	Asilidae	*Cerotainia*	*macrocera*
Diptera	Asilidae	*Apachekolos*	*tenuipes*
Diptera	Asilidae	*Tipulogaster*	*glabrata*
Diptera	Asilidae	*Leptogaster*	*flavipes*
Diptera	Asilidae	*Laphria*	*winnemana/sicula*
Diptera	Asilidae	*Laphria*	*canis complex*
Diptera	Asilidae	*Laphria*	*aktis*
Diptera	Asilidae	*Laphria*	*sericea*
Diptera	Asilidae	*Laphria*	*index*
Diptera	Asilidae	*Laphria*	*flavicollis*
Diptera	Asilidae	*Laphria*	*divisor*
Diptera	Asilidae	*Laphria*	*thoracica*
Diptera	Asilidae	*Lampria*	*bicolor*
Diptera	Asilidae	*Ommatius*	*gemma*
Diptera	Pyrgotidae	*Sphecomyiella*	*valida*
Diptera	Tipulidae	*Tanyptera*	*dorsalis*
Diptera	Tipulidae	Undetermined	*sp.*
Diptera	Rhagionidae	*Rhagio*	*mystaceus*
Diptera	Rhagionidae	*Chrysopilus*	*proximus*
Diptera	Rhagionidae	*Chrysopilus*	*thoracicus/davisi*
Diptera	Rhagionidae	*Symphoromyia*	*hirta*
Diptera	Syrphidae	*Ocyptamus*	*fuscipennis*
Diptera	Syrphidae	*Chrysotoxum*	*perplexum*
Diptera	Syrphidae	*Chrysotoxum*	*sp.*
Diptera	Syrphidae	*Sphaerophoria*	*sp.*
Diptera	Syrphidae	*Temnostoma*	*trifasciatum*
Diptera	Syrphidae	*Temnostoma*	*balyras*
Diptera	Syrphidae	*Temnostoma*	*barberi*
Diptera	Syrphidae	*Temnostoma*	*obscurum*
Diptera	Syrphidae	*Temnostoma*	*sp.*
Diptera	Syrphidae	*Temnostoma*	*excentrica*
Diptera	Syrphidae	*Temnostoma*	*daochus*
Diptera	Syrphidae	*Melanostoma*	*mellinum*
Diptera	Syrphidae	*Ferdinandea*	*croesus*
Diptera	Syrphidae	*Pterallastes*	*thoracicus*
Diptera	Syrphidae	*Neoascia*	*sp.*
Diptera	Syrphidae	*Eupeodes*	*sp.*
Diptera	Syrphidae	*Paragus*	*sp.*

Order	Family	Genus	Species
Flies			
Diptera	Syrphidae	*Tropidia*	*albistylum*
Diptera	Syrphidae	*Meligramma*	*cincta*
Diptera	Syrphidae	*Xanthogramma*	*flavipes*
Diptera	Syrphidae	*Milesia*	*virginiensis*
Diptera	Syrphidae	*Toxomerus*	*geminatus*
Diptera	Syrphidae	*Toxomerus*	*marginatus*
Diptera	Syrphidae	*Toxomerus*	*politus*
Diptera	Syrphidae	*Eristalis*	*tenax*
Diptera	Syrphidae	*Cheilosia*	*sp.*
Diptera	Syrphidae	*Microdon*	*sp.*
Diptera	Syrphidae	*Chalcosyrphus*	*anthreas*
Diptera	Syrphidae	*Chalcosyrphus*	*libo*
Diptera	Syrphidae	*Chalcosyrphus*	*nemorum*
Diptera	Syrphidae	*Chalcosyrphus*	*inarmatus*
Diptera	Syrphidae	*Chalcosyrphus*	*chalybeus*
Diptera	Syrphidae	*Sphiximorpha*	*willistoni*
Diptera	Syrphidae	*Xylota*	*sp.*
Diptera	Syrphidae	*Xylota*	*quadrimaculata*
Diptera	Syrphidae	*Sphecomyia*	*sp.*
Diptera	Syrphidae	*Myolepta*	*varipes*
Diptera	Syrphidae	*Blera*	*confusa*
Diptera	Syrphidae	*Sphegina*	*sp.*
Diptera	Tachinidae	*Zelia*	*vertebrata*
Diptera	Tachinidae	*Hemyda*	*aurata*
Diptera	Tachinidae	*Xanthomelanodes*	*arcuatus*
Diptera	Tachinidae	*Trichopoda (T)*	*plumipes*
Diptera	Tachinidae	*Trichopoda (G)*	*pennipes*
Diptera	Tachinidae	Undetermined	*sp. 1*
Diptera	Tachinidae	Undetermined	*sp. 2*
Diptera	Tachinidae	Undetermined	*sp. 3*
Diptera	Tachinidae	Undetermined	*sp. 4*
Diptera	Tachinidae	Undetermined	*sp. 5*
Diptera	Bibionidae	Undetermined	*sp. 6*
Diptera	Bibionidae	Undetermined	*sp. 7*
Diptera	Acroceridae	*Turbopsabius*	*sulphuripes*
Diptera	Dolichopodidae	*Condylostylus*	*sp.*
Diptera	Dolichopodidae	Undetermined	*sp. 1*
Diptera	Dolichopodidae	Undetermined	*sp. 2*
Diptera	Dolichopodidae	Undetermined	*sp. 3*
Diptera	Dolichopodidae	Undetermined	*sp. 4*
Diptera	Dolichopodidae	Undetermined	*sp. 5*
Diptera	Dolichopodidae	Undetermined	*sp. 6*
Diptera	Heleomyzidae	Undetermined	*sp.*
Diptera	Therevidae	Undetermined	*sp.*
Diptera	Lauxaniidae	Undetermined	*sp.*
Diptera	Mycetophilidae	Undetermined	*sp.*
Diptera	Scathophagidae	*Cordilura*	*scapularis*
Diptera	Pipunculidae	Undetermined	*sp.*
Diptera	Sciomyzidae	*Tetanocera*	*clara*
Diptera	Sciomyzidae	Undetermined	*sp. 2*
Diptera	Sciomyzidae	Undetermined	*sp. 3*

Complete Species List   293

Order	Family	Genus	Species
Flies			
Diptera	Ceratopogonidae	Undetermined	*sp.*
Diptera	Sciaridae	Undetermined	*sp. 1*
Diptera	Sciaridae	Undetermined	*sp. 2*
Diptera	Stratiomyidae	*Ptecticus*	*trivittatus*
Diptera	Stratiomyidae	*Cephalochrysa*	*nigricornis*
Diptera	Stratiomyidae	*Oxycera*	*variegata*
Diptera	Stratiomyidae	Undetermined	*sp. 1*
Diptera	Stratiomyidae	Undetermined	*sp. 2*
Diptera	Xylomyidae	*Xylomya*	*tenthredinoides*
Diptera	Xylomyidae	*Xylomya*	*pallidifemur*
Diptera	Xylomyidae	*Xylomya*	*simillima*
Diptera	Xylomyidae	*Xylomya*	*americana*
Diptera	Xylophagidae	*Coenomiya*	*ferruginea*
Diptera	Ulidiidae	*Pseudotephritina*	*vau*
Diptera	Ulidiidae	*Seioptera*	*vibrans*
Diptera	Ulidiidae	*Callopistromyia*	*annulipes*
Diptera	Platystomatidae	*Rivellia*	*pallida/imitabilis*
Diptera	Conopidae	*Stylogaster*	*neglecta*
Diptera	Tabanidae	*Tabanus*	*pumilus*
Diptera	Tabanidae	*Tabanus*	*sulcifrons*
Diptera	Tabanidae	*Tabanus*	*fulvulus*
Diptera	Tabanidae	*Tabanus*	*calens*
Diptera	Tabanidae	*Tabanus*	*lineola*
Diptera	Tabanidae	*Tabanus*	*sackeni*
Diptera	Tabanidae	*Tabanus*	*similis*
Diptera	Tabanidae	*Tabanus*	*quinquevittatus*
Diptera	Tabanidae	*Hybomitra*	*lasiophthalma*
Diptera	Tabanidae	*Chrysops*	*montanus*
Diptera	Tabanidae	*Chrysops*	*upsilon*
Diptera	Tabanidae	*Chrysops*	*impunctus*
Diptera	Tabanidae	*Chrysops*	*delicatulus*
Diptera	Tabanidae	*Chrysops*	*macquarti*
Diptera	Limoniidae	Undetermined	*sp.*
Diptera	Sepsidae	*Sepsis*	*sp. 1*
Diptera	Sepsidae	*Sepsis*	*sp. 2*
Diptera	Chloropidae	*Parectecephala*	*sp.*
Diptera	Micropezidae	Undetermined	Undetermined
Diptera	Fanniidae	Many undetermined	Many undetermined
Diptera	Muscidae	Many undetermined	Many undetermined
Diptera	Calliphoridae	*Lucilia*	*silvarum*
Diptera	Calliphoridae	*Lucilia*	*sericata*
Diptera	Sarcophagidae	Many undetermined	Many undetermined

True Bugs

Hemiptera	Aphrophoridae	*Lepyronia*	*quadrangularis*
Hemiptera	Cercopidae	*Prosapia*	*bicincta*
Hemiptera	Clastopteridae	*Clastoptera*	*arborina*
Hemiptera	Clastopteridae	*Clastoptera*	*obtusa*
Hemiptera	Clastopteridae	*Clastoptera*	*proteus*
Hemiptera	Cicadellidae	*sp.*	
Hemiptera	Cicadellidae	*Draeculacephala*	*sp.*

INSECTS *(continued)*

Order	Family	Genus	Species
True Bugs			
Hemiptera	Cicadellidae	*Graphocephala*	*coccinea*
Hemiptera	Cicadellidae	*Provancherana*	*tripunctata*
Hemiptera	Cicadellidae	*Tylozygus*	*bifidus*
Hemiptera	Cicadellidae	*Tylozygus*	*geometricus*
Hemiptera	Cicadellidae	*Colladonus*	*clitellarius*
Hemiptera	Cicadellidae	*Graminella*	*cognita*
Hemiptera	Cicadellidae	*Paraphlepsius*	*irroratus*
Hemiptera	Cicadellidae	*Scaphoideus*	*sp.*
Hemiptera	Cicadellidae	*Ponana*	*puncticollis*
Hemiptera	Cicadellidae	*Agallia*	*constricta*
Hemiptera	Cicadellidae	*Paraulacizes*	*irrorata*
Hemiptera	Membracidae	*Acutalis*	*tartarea*
Hemiptera	Membracidae	*Strictocephala*	*sp.*
Hemiptera	Membracidae	*Entylia*	*carinata*
Hemiptera	Membracidae	*Carynota*	*mera*
Hemiptera	Cixiidae	*Cixius*	*sp.*
Hemiptera	Cixiidae	*Cixius*	*meridionalis*
Hemiptera	Derbidae	*Apache*	*degeeri*
Hemiptera	Miridae	*Deraeocoris*	*sp.*
Hemiptera	Miridae	*Adelphocoris*	*lineolatus*
Hemiptera	Miridae	*Lygus*	*lineolaris*
Hemiptera	Miridae	*Tropidosteptes*	*sp.*
Hemiptera	Reduviidae	*Rhiginia*	*cinctiventris*
Hemiptera	Reduviidae	*Zelus*	*luridus*
Hemiptera	Reduviidae	*Zelus*	*tetracanthus*
Hemiptera	Reduviidae	*Phymata*	*pennsylvanica*
Hemiptera	Reduviidae	*Melanolestes*	*picipes*
Hemiptera	Reduviidae	*Reduvius*	*personatus*
Hemiptera	Corixidae	*Sigara*	*alternata*
Hemiptera	Corixidae	*Trichocorixa*	*calva*
Hemiptera	Coreidae	*Piezogaster*	*calcarator*
Hemiptera	Geocoridae	*Geocoris*	*uliginosus*
Hemiptera	Rhyparochromidae	*Drymus*	*unus*
Hemiptera	Rhyparochromidae	*Myodocha*	*serripes*
Hemiptera	Rhyparochromidae	*Ozophora*	*picturata*
Hemiptera	Cydnidae	*Cyrtomenus*	*ciliatus*
Hemiptera	Pentatomidae	*Euschistus*	*tristigmus*
Hemiptera	Pentatomidae	*Mcphersonarcys*	*aequalis*
Hemiptera	Pentatomidae	*Menecles*	*insertus*
Hemiptera	Pentatomidae	*Mormidea*	*lugens*
Hemiptera	Pentatomidae	*Chinavia*	*hilaris*
Hemiptera	Thyreocoridae	*Corimelaena*	*lateralis*

Wasps, Ants, and Bees

Order	Family	Genus	Species
Hymenoptera	Bethylidae		
Hymenoptera	Braconidae	*Phanerotoma*	*sp.*
Hymenoptera	Braconidae	*Morphotype 1*	*sp.*
Hymenoptera	Braconidae	*Morphotype 2*	*sp.*
Hymenoptera	Braconidae	*Morphotype 3*	*sp.*
Hymenoptera	Braconidae	*Morphotype 4*	*sp.*
Hymenoptera	Braconidae	*Morphotype 5*	*sp.*

Complete Species List

Order	Family	Genus	Species
Wasps, Ants, and Bees			
Hymenoptera	Braconidae	*Morphotype 6*	*sp.*
Hymenoptera	Braconidae	*Morphotype 7*	*sp.*
Hymenoptera	Braconidae	*Morphotype 8*	*sp.*
Hymenoptera	Braconidae	*Morphotype 9*	*sp.*
Hymenoptera	Braconidae	*Morphotype 10*	*sp.*
Hymenoptera	Braconidae	*Morphotype 11*	*sp.*
Hymenoptera	Braconidae	*Morphotype 12*	*sp.*
Hymenoptera	Crabronidae	*Cerceris*	*clypeata*
Hymenoptera	Crabronidae	*Cerceris*	*halone*
Hymenoptera	Crabronidae	*Crossocerus*	*nitidiventris*
Hymenoptera	Crabronidae	*Ectemnius*	*continuus*
Hymenoptera	Crabronidae	*Ectemnius*	*dives*
Hymenoptera	Crabronidae	*Lestica*	*confluenta*
Hymenoptera	Crabronidae	*Trypoxylon*	*sp. 1*
Hymenoptera	Crabronidae	*Trypoxylon*	*politum*
Hymenoptera	Chrysididae	*Caenochrysus*	*carinata*
Hymenoptera	Chrysididae	*Chrysis*	*sp. 1*
Hymenoptera	Chrysididae	*Chrysis*	*sp. 2*
Hymenoptera	Chrysididae	*Hedychrum*	*confusus*
Hymenoptera	Chrysididae	*Omalus*	*iridiscens*
Hymenoptera	Diapriidae	Undetermined	*sp.*
Hymenoptera	Evaniidae	Undetermined	*sp.*
Hymenoptera	Figitidae	Undetermined	*sp.*
Hymenoptera	Ibaliidae	Undetermined	*sp.*
Hymenoptera	Ichneumonidae	Undetermined	At least 150 species
Hymenoptera	Ormyridae	Undetermined	*sp.*
Hymenoptera	Orussidae	*Orussus*	*sp.*
Hymenoptera	Pamphiliidae	Undetermined	*sp.*
Hymenoptera	Pelecinidae	*Pelecinus*	*sp.*
Hymenoptera	Pergidae	Undetermined	*sp.*
Hymenoptera	Perilampidae	Undetermined	*sp.*
Hymenoptera	Platygastridae	Undetermined	*sp.*
Hymenoptera	Pompilidae	Undetermined	At least 20 species
Hymenoptera	Proctotrupidae	Undetermined	*sp.*
Hymenoptera	Siricidae	Undetermined	*sp.*
Hymenoptera	Sphecidae	*Eremnophila*	*aureonotata*
Hymenoptera	Sphecidae	*Isodontia*	*auripes*
Hymenoptera	Sphecidae	*Ammophila*	*sp.*
Hymenoptera	Tenthredinidae	Undetermined	At least 10 species
Hymenoptera	Tiphiidae	Undetermined	*sp.*
Hymenoptera	Trigonalidae	Undetermined	*sp.*
Hymenoptera	Vespidae	*Ancistrocerus*	*adiabatus*
Hymenoptera	Vespidae	*Ancistrocerus*	*albophaleratus*
Hymenoptera	Vespidae	*Ancistrocerus*	*catskill*
Hymenoptera	Vespidae	*Ancistrocerus*	*gazella*
Hymenoptera	Vespidae	*Ancistrocerus*	*univasciatus*
Hymenoptera	Vespidae	*Ancistrocerus*	*spinolae*
Hymenoptera	Vespidae	*Dolichovespula*	*arenosa*
Hymenoptera	Vespidae	*Dolichovespula*	*maculata*
Hymenoptera	Vespidae	*Vespula*	*maculifrons*
Hymenoptera	Vespidae	*Vespula*	*squamosa*

INSECTS *(continued)*

Order	Family	Genus	Species
Wasps, Ants, and Bees			

Order	Family	Genus	Species
Hymenoptera	Vespidae	*Vespula*	*flavopilosa*
Hymenoptera	Vespidae	*Polistes*	*metricus*
Hymenoptera	Vespidae	*Polistes*	*fuscatus*
Hymenoptera	Vespidae	Undetermined	*sp.*
Hymenoptera	Xiphydriidae	Undetermined	*sp.*
Orthoptera	Acrididae	Melanoplus	*sp.*

BEES

Order	Family	Genus	Species
Andrenidae (Solitary, Ground-Nesting Bees)			

Order	Family	Genus	Species
Hymenoptera	Andrenidae	*Andrena*	*aliciae*
Hymenoptera	Andrenidae	*Andrena*	*carlini*
Hymenoptera	Andrenidae	*Andrena*	*crataegi*
Hymenoptera	Andrenidae	*Andrena*	*cressonii*
Hymenoptera	Andrenidae	*Andrena*	*distans*
Hymenoptera	Andrenidae	*Andrena*	*erigeniae*
Hymenoptera	Andrenidae	*Andrena*	*fenningeri*
Hymenoptera	Andrenidae	*Andrena*	*Aforbesii*
Hymenoptera	Andrenidae	*Andrena*	*gardineri*
Hymenoptera	Andrenidae	*Andrena*	*geranii*
Hymenoptera	Andrenidae	*Andrena*	*heraclei*
Hymenoptera	Andrenidae	*Andrena*	*hilaris*
Hymenoptera	Andrenidae	*Andrena*	*illini*
Hymenoptera	Andrenidae	*Andrena*	*imitatrix*
Hymenoptera	Andrenidae	*Andrena*	*mandibularis*
Hymenoptera	Andrenidae	*Andrena*	*nasonii*
Hymenoptera	Andrenidae	*Andrena*	*nubecula*
Hymenoptera	Andrenidae	*Andrena*	*nuda*
Hymenoptera	Andrenidae	*Andrena*	*perplexa*
Hymenoptera	Andrenidae	*Andrena*	*phaceliae*
Hymenoptera	Andrenidae	*Andrena*	*polemonii*
Hymenoptera	Andrenidae	*Andrena*	*pruni*
Hymenoptera	Andrenidae	*Andrena*	*robertsonii*
Hymenoptera	Andrenidae	*Andrena*	*rugosa*
Hymenoptera	Andrenidae	*Andrena*	*sayi*
Hymenoptera	Andrenidae	*Andrena*	*spiraeana*
Hymenoptera	Andrenidae	*Andrena*	*tridens*
Hymenoptera	Andrenidae	*Andrena*	*violae*
Hymenoptera	Andrenidae	*Pseudopanurgus*	*andrenoides*
Hymenoptera	Andrenidae	*Pseudopanurgus*	*labrosus*

Apidae (Cuckoo, Carpenter, and Digger Bees, Bumblebees, and Honeybees)

Hymenoptera	Apidae	*Anthophora*	*terminalis*
Hymenoptera	Apidae	*Apis*	*mellifera*
Hymenoptera	Apidae	*Bombus*	*bimaculatus*
Hymenoptera	Apidae	*Bombus*	*citrinus*
Hymenoptera	Apidae	*Bombus*	*griseocollis*
Hymenoptera	Apidae	*Bombus*	*impatiens*
Hymenoptera	Apidae	*Bombus*	*pensylvanicus*
Hymenoptera	Apidae	*Bombus*	*vagans*
Hymenoptera	Apidae	*Ceratina*	*calcarata*

BEES *(continued)*

Order	Family	Genus	Species

Apidae *(Cuckoo, Carpenter, and Digger Bees, Bumblebees, and Honeybees)*

Hymenoptera	Apidae	*Ceratina*	*dupla*
Hymenoptera	Apidae	*Ceratina*	*mikmaqi*
Hymenoptera	Apidae	*Ceratina*	*strenua*
Hymenoptera	Apidae	*Epeolus*	*bifasciatus*
Hymenoptera	Apidae	*Melissodes*	*bimaculatus*
Hymenoptera	Apidae	*Melissodes*	*denticulatus*
Hymenoptera	Apidae	*Melissodes*	*dentiventris*
Hymenoptera	Apidae	*Melissodes*	*desponsus*
Hymenoptera	Apidae	*Melissodes*	*druriellus*
Hymenoptera	Apidae	*Nomada*	*cressonii*
Hymenoptera	Apidae	*Nomada*	*cuneata*
Hymenoptera	Apidae	*Nomada*	*denticulata*
Hymenoptera	Apidae	*Nomada*	*depressa*
Hymenoptera	Apidae	*Nomada*	*heiligbrodtii*
Hymenoptera	Apidae	*Nomada*	*imbricata*
Hymenoptera	Apidae	*Nomada*	*lepida*
Hymenoptera	Apidae	*Nomada*	*luteoloides*
Hymenoptera	Apidae	*Nomada*	*maculata*
Hymenoptera	Apidae	*Nomada*	*ovata*
Hymenoptera	Apidae	*Nomada*	*pygmaea*
Hymenoptera	Apidae	*Nomada*	*sayi*
Hymenoptera	Apidae	*Xylocopa*	*virginica*

Colletidae *(Plasterer Bees)*

Hymenoptera	Colletidae	*Colletes*	*inaequalis*
Hymenoptera	Colletidae	*Hylaeus*	*affinis*
Hymenoptera	Colletidae	*Hylaeus*	*fedorica*
Hymenoptera	Colletidae	*Hylaeus*	*illinoisensis*
Hymenoptera	Colletidae	*Hylaeus*	*modestus*
Hymenoptera	Colletidae	*Hylaeus*	*modestus group*
Hymenoptera	Colletidae	*Hylaeus*	*sp. A*
Hymenoptera	Colletidae	*Hylaeus*	*sparsus*

Halictidae *(Sweat Bees)*

Hymenoptera	Halictidae	*Agapostemon*	*sericeus*
Hymenoptera	Halictidae	*Augochlora*	*pura*
Hymenoptera	Halictidae	*Augochlorella*	*aurata*
Hymenoptera	Halictidae	*Augochloropsis*	*fulgida*
Hymenoptera	Halictidae	*Halictus*	*confusus*
Hymenoptera	Halictidae	*Halictus*	*ligatus*
Hymenoptera	Halictidae	*Lasioglossum*	*abanci*
Hymenoptera	Halictidae	*Lasioglossum*	*atwoodi*
Hymenoptera	Halictidae	*Lasioglossum*	*birkmanni*
Hymenoptera	Halictidae	*Lasioglossum*	*bruneri*
Hymenoptera	Halictidae	*Lasioglossum*	*cattellae*
Hymenoptera	Halictidae	*Lasioglossum*	*coeruleum*
Hymenoptera	Halictidae	*Lasioglossum*	*coriaceum*
Hymenoptera	Halictidae	*Lasioglossum*	*cressonii*
Hymenoptera	Halictidae	*Lasioglossum*	*ephialtum*
Hymenoptera	Halictidae	*Lasioglossum*	*foxii*
Hymenoptera	Halictidae	*Lasioglossum*	*fuscipenne*

Appendix 1

BEES (continued)

Order	Family	Genus	Species
Halictidae (Sweat Bees)			
Hymenoptera	Halictidae	*Lasioglossum*	*hitchensi*
Hymenoptera	Halictidae	*Lasioglossum*	*imitatum*
Hymenoptera	Halictidae	*Lasioglossum*	*nigroviride*
Hymenoptera	Halictidae	*Lasioglossum*	*obscurum*
Hymenoptera	Halictidae	*Lasioglossum*	*paradmirandum*
Hymenoptera	Halictidae	*Lasioglossum*	*subviridatum*
Hymenoptera	Halictidae	*Lasioglossum*	*taylorae*
Hymenoptera	Halictidae	*Lasioglossum*	*truncatum*
Hymenoptera	Halictidae	*Lasioglossum*	*versans*
Hymenoptera	Halictidae	*Lasioglossum*	*versatum*
Hymenoptera	Halictidae	*Lasioglossum*	*weemsi*
Hymenoptera	Halictidae	*Lasioglossum*	*zephyrum*
Hymenoptera	Halictidae	*Lasioglossum*	*spp.*

Order	Family	Genus	Species
Megachilidae (Leafcutting, Mason, and Resin Bees)			
Hymenoptera	Megachilidae	*Hoplitis*	*nemophilae*
Hymenoptera	Megachilidae	*Megachile*	*campanulae*
Hymenoptera	Megachilidae	*Megachile*	*gemula*
Hymenoptera	Megachilidae	*Megachile*	*mendica*
Hymenoptera	Megachilidae	*Megachile*	*petulans*
Hymenoptera	Megachilidae	*Osmia*	*atriventris*
Hymenoptera	Megachilidae	*Osmia*	*bucephala*
Hymenoptera	Megachilidae	*Osmia*	*cornifrons*
Hymenoptera	Megachilidae	*Osmia*	*georgica*
Hymenoptera	Megachilidae	*Osmia*	*pumila*
Hymenoptera	Megachilidae	*Osmia*	*taurus*

MOTHS

Order	Family	Genus	Species	Common Name
Lepidoptera	Acrolophidae	*Acrolophus*	*popeanella*	grass tubeworm moth
Lepidoptera	Acrolophidae	*Cameraria*	*guttifinitella*	poison ivy leafminer
Lepidoptera	Acrolophidae	*Niditinae*	*orleansella*	fungus moth
Lepidoptera	Acrolophidae	*Tinea*	*croceoverticella*	clothes moth
Lepidoptera	Adelidae	*Adela*	*ridingsella*	Ridings's fairy moth
Lepidoptera	Argyresthiidae	*Argyresthia*	*oreasella*	cherry shoot borer moth
Lepidoptera	Blastobasidae	*Dryoperia*	*tenebrella*	common plain neb
Lepidoptera	Blastobasidae	*Gerdana*	*caritella*	moth
Lepidoptera	Bombycoidea	*Apatelodes*	*torrefacta*	spotted apatelodes moth
Lepidoptera	Choreutidae	*Prochoreutis*	*inflatella*	skullcap skeletonizer moth
Lepidoptera	Choreutidae	*Tebenna*	*gnapheliella*	everlasting tebenna moth
Lepidoptera	Coleophoridae	*Coleophora*	*trifolii*	large clover casebearer moth
Lepidoptera	Copromorphoidea	*Bondia*	*crescentella*	crescent-marked bondia
Lepidoptera	Copromorphoidea	*Carposina*	*sasakii*	peach fruit moth
Lepidoptera	Copromorphoidea	*Glyphipterix*	*quadragintapunctata*	sedge moth
Lepidoptera	Cosmopterigidae	*Euclemensia*	*bassettella*	kermes scale moth
Lepidoptera	Cosmopterigidae	*Limnaecia*	*phragmitella*	shy cosmet moth
Lepidoptera	Cosmopterigidae	*Stagmatophora*	*sexnotella*	
Lepidoptera	Cosmopterigidae	*Walshia*	*miscecolorella*	sweetclover root borer moth
Lepidoptera	Cossidae	*Givira*	*anna*	anna carpenterworm moth
Lepidoptera	Cossidae	*Inguromorpha*	*basalis*	black-lined carpenterworm moth
Lepidoptera	Cossidae	*Prionoxystus*	*macmurtrei*	little carpenterworm moth

Order	Family	Genus	Species	Common Name
Lepidoptera	Cossidae	*Prionoxystus*	*robiniae*	Robin's carpenterworm moth
Lepidoptera	Crambidae	*Achyra*	*rantalis*	garden webworm moth
Lepidoptera	Crambidae	*Aethiophysa*	*invisalis*	crambid snout moth
Lepidoptera	Crambidae	*Agriphila*	*vulgivagellus*	vagabond sod webworm moth
Lepidoptera	Crambidae	*Anageshna*	*primordialis*	yellow-spotted webworm moth
Lepidoptera	Crambidae	*Anania*	*coronata*	elderberry pearl moth
Lepidoptera	Crambidae	*Argyria*	*critica*	straight-lined argyria moth
Lepidoptera	Crambidae	*Blepharomastix*	*ranalis*	hollow-spotted blepharomastix moth
Lepidoptera	Crambidae	*Chalcoela*	*iphitalis*	sooty-winged chalcoela moth
Lepidoptera	Crambidae	*Chrysendeton*	*medicinalis*	bold medicine moth
Lepidoptera	Crambidae	*Cliniodes*	*ostreonalis*	oystershell metrea moth
Lepidoptera	Crambidae	*Colomychus*	*talis*	distinguished colomychus
Lepidoptera	Crambidae	*Compacta*	*capitalis*	crambid snout moth
Lepidoptera	Crambidae	*Conchylodes*	*ovulalis*	Zebra conchylodes moth
Lepidoptera	Crambidae	*Crambus*	*agitatellus*	double-banded grass-veneer moth
Lepidoptera	Crambidae	*Crambus*	*caliginosellus*	black grass-veneer
Lepidoptera	Crambidae	*Crocidophora*	*serratissimalis*	angelic crocidophora moth
Lepidoptera	Crambidae	*Crocidophora*	*tuberculalis*	pale-winged crocidophora moth
Lepidoptera	Crambidae	*Desmia*	*funeralis*	grape leaffolder moth
Lepidoptera	Crambidae	*Diacme*	*elealis*	paler diacme moth
Lepidoptera	Crambidae	*Diathrausta*	*reconditalis*	recondite webworm moth
Lepidoptera	Crambidae	*Dicymolomia*	*julianalis*	Julia's dicymolomioa moth
Lepidoptera	Crambidae	*Donacaula*	*tripunctella*	crambid snout moth
Lepidoptera	Crambidae	*Ecpyrrhoerrhoe*	*puralis*	crambid snout moth
Lepidoptera	Crambidae	*Elophila*	*icciusalis*	pondside pyralid moth
Lepidoptera	Crambidae	*Elophila*	*obliteralis*	waterlily leafcutter moth
Lepidoptera	Crambidae	*Eoreuma*	*densella*	wainscot grass-veneer moth
Lepidoptera	Crambidae	*Eudonia*	*heterosalis*	eudonia heterosalis
Lepidoptera	Crambidae	*Eudonia*	*strigalis*	striped eudonia moth
Lepidoptera	Crambidae	*Eustixia*	*pupula*	spotted peppergrass moth
Lepidoptera	Crambidae	*Evergestis*	*pallidata*	purple-backed cabbageworm moth
Lepidoptera	Crambidae	*Fissicrambus*	*mutabilis*	changeable grass-veneer moth
Lepidoptera	Crambidae	*Glaphyria*	*fulminalis*	black-patched glaphyria moth
Lepidoptera	Crambidae	*Glaphyria*	*sequistrialis*	white-roped glaphyria moth
Lepidoptera	Crambidae	*Hahncappsia*	*marculenta*	crambid moth
Lepidoptera	Crambidae	*Helvibotys*	*pucilla*	crambid snout moth
Lepidoptera	Crambidae	*Herpetogramma*	*thestealis*	zigzag herpetogramma moth
Lepidoptera	Crambidae	*Hileithia*	*rehamalis*	crambid snout moth
Lepidoptera	Crambidae	*Hymenia*	*perspectalis*	spotted beet webworn moth
Lepidoptera	Crambidae	*Lineodes*	*integra*	eggplant leafroller moth
Lepidoptera	Crambidae	*Lipocosma*	*sicalis*	crambid snout moth
Lepidoptera	Crambidae	*Lipocosmodes*	*fuliginosalis*	sooty lipocosmodes moth
Lepidoptera	Crambidae	*Microcrambus*	*biguttellus*	gold-stripe grass-veneer moth
Lepidoptera	Crambidae	*Mimoschinia*	*rufofascialis*	rufous-banded crambid moth
Lepidoptera	Crambidae	*Nomophila*	*nearctica*	lucerne moth
Lepidoptera	Crambidae	*Palpita*	*freemanalis*	Freeman's palpita moth
Lepidoptera	Crambidae	*Pantographa*	*limata*	basswood leafroller moth
Lepidoptera	Crambidae	*Pilocrocis*	*ramentalis*	scraped pilocrocis moth
Lepidoptera	Crambidae	*Psara*	*obscuralis*	crambid snout moth

Order	Family	Genus	Species	Common Name
Lepidoptera	Crambidae	*Pyrausta*	*acrionalis*	mint-loving pyrausta moth
Lepidoptera	Crambidae	*Pyrausta*	*bicoloralis*	bicolored pyrausta moth
Lepidoptera	Crambidae	*Pyrausta*	*generosa*	crambid snout moth
Lepidoptera	Crambidae	*Pyrausta*	*inveterascalis*	crambid snout moth
Lepidoptera	Crambidae	*Pyrausta*	*niveicilialis*	white-fringed pyrausta moth
Lepidoptera	Crambidae	*Samea*	*ecclesialis*	assembly moth
Lepidoptera	Crambidae	*Sitochroa*	*palealis*	crambid snouth moth
Lepidoptera	Crambidae	*Udea*	*rubigalis*	celery leaftier moth
Lepidoptera	Crambidae	*Urola*	*nivalis*	snowy urola moth
Lepidoptera	Crambidae	*Xanthophysa*	*psychialis*	xanthophysa moth
Lepidoptera	Drepanoidae	*Drepana*	*arcuata*	arched hooktip moth
Lepidoptera	Drepanoidae	*Eudeilinia*	*herminiata*	northern eudeilinia
Lepidoptera	Drepanoidae	*Euthyatira*	*pudens*	dogwood thyatirid moth
Lepidoptera	Drepanoidae	*Habrosyne*	*gloriosa*	glorious habrosyne
Lepidoptera	Drepanoidae	*Habrosyne*	*scripta*	lettered habrosyne moth
Lepidoptera	Drepanoidae	*Oreta*	*rosea*	rose hooktip moth
Lepidoptera	Elachistidae	*Agonopterix*	*alstroemeriana*	poison hemlock moth
Lepidoptera	Elachistidae	*Agonopterix*	*robiniella*	four-dotted agonopterix moth
Lepidoptera	Elachistidae	*Cosmiotes*	*illectella*	grass minor moth
Lepidoptera	Elachistidae	*Ethmia*	*orestella*	echelon
Lepidoptera	Elachistidae	*Ethmia*	*trifurcella*	ethmia trifurcella
Lepidoptera	Elachistidae	*Ethmia*	*zelleriella*	coptotriche zelleriella
Lepidoptera	Epiplemidae	*Callizzia*	*amorata*	gray swooping moth
Lepidoptera	Erebidae	*Alabama*	*argillacea*	cotton leafworm moth
Lepidoptera	Erebidae	*Allotria*	*elonympha*	false underwing moth
Lepidoptera	Erebidae	*Anomis*	*erosa*	yellow scallop moth
Lepidoptera	Erebidae	*Anticarsia*	*gemmatalis*	velvet bean caterpillar moth
Lepidoptera	Erebidae	*Apantesis*	*anna*	anna tiger moth
Lepidoptera	Erebidae	*Apantesis*	*arge*	arge moth
Lepidoptera	Erebidae	*Apantesis*	*carlotta*	Carlotta's tiger moth
Lepidoptera	Erebidae	*Apantesis*	*figurata*	figured tiger moth
Lepidoptera	Erebidae	*Apantesis*	*nais*	nais tiger moth
Lepidoptera	Erebidae	*Apantesis*	*parthenice*	parthenice tiger moth
Lepidoptera	Erebidae	*Apantesis*	*phalerata*	harnessed tiger moth
Lepidoptera	Erebidae	*Apantesis*	*phyrilla*	Philip's tiger moth
Lepidoptera	Erebidae	*Apantesis*	*virgo*	virgin tiger moth
Lepidoptera	Erebidae	*Apantesis*	*virguncula*	little virgin tiger moth
Lepidoptera	Erebidae	*Apantesis*	*vittata*	banded tiger moth
Lepidoptera	Erebidae	*Argyrostrotis*	*anilis*	short-lined chocolate
Lepidoptera	Erebidae	*Arugisa*	*latiorella*	common arugisa
Lepidoptera	Erebidae	*Bleptina*	*caradrinalis*	bent-winged owlet moth
Lepidoptera	Erebidae	*Bleptina*	*sangamonia*	owlet moth
Lepidoptera	Erebidae	*Caenurgia*	*chloropha*	vetch looper moth
Lepidoptera	Erebidae	*Caenurgia*	*crassiuscula*	clover looper moth
Lepidoptera	Erebidae	*Caenurgia*	*erechtea*	forage looper moth
Lepidoptera	Erebidae	*Calyptra*	*canadensis*	Canadian owlet moth
Lepidoptera	Erebidae	*Catocala*	*amatrix*	sweetheart underwing
Lepidoptera	Erebidae	*Catocala*	*amica*	girlfriend underwing
Lepidoptera	Erebidae	*Catocala*	*angusii*	Angus's underwing
Lepidoptera	Erebidae	*Catocala*	*cara*	darling underwing moth
Lepidoptera	Erebidae	*Catocala*	*cerogama*	yellow-banded underwing moth
Lepidoptera	Erebidae	*Catocala*	*coccinata*	scarlet underwing

Order	Family	Genus	Species	Common Name
Lepidoptera	Erebidae	*Catocala*	*connubialis*	connubial underwing
Lepidoptera	Erebidae	*Catocala*	*dejecta*	dejected underwing
Lepidoptera	Erebidae	*Catocala*	*dulciola*	quiet or sweet underwing
Lepidoptera	Erebidae	*Catocala*	*epione*	epione underwing
Lepidoptera	Erebidae	*Catocala*	*flebilis*	mournful underwing
Lepidoptera	Erebidae	*Catocala*	*grynea*	woody underwing moth
Lepidoptera	Erebidae	*Catocala*	*habilis*	habilis underwing
Lepidoptera	Erebidae	*Catocala*	*ilia*	ilia underwing moth
Lepidoptera	Erebidae	*Catocala*	*illecta*	magdalen underwing
Lepidoptera	Erebidae	*Catocala*	*innubens*	betrothed underwing
Lepidoptera	Erebidae	*Catocala*	*insolabilis*	inconsolable underwing
Lepidoptera	Erebidae	*Catocala*	*judith*	Judith's underwing
Lepidoptera	Erebidae	*Catocala*	*junctura*	joined underwing moth
Lepidoptera	Erebidae	*Catocala*	*lacrymosa*	Lincoln underwing
Lepidoptera	Erebidae	*Catocala*	*lineella*	litlle lined underwing
Lepidoptera	Erebidae	*Catocala*	*micronympha*	little nymph underwing
Lepidoptera	Erebidae	*Catocala*	*minuta*	little underwing
Lepidoptera	Erebidae	*Catocala*	*mira*	wonderful underwing
Lepidoptera	Erebidae	*Catocala*	*nebulosa*	clouded underwing
Lepidoptera	Erebidae	*Catocala*	*neogama*	the bride underwing
Lepidoptera	Erebidae	*Catocala*	*obscura*	obscure underwing
Lepidoptera	Erebidae	*Catocala*	*palaeogama*	oldwife underwing
Lepidoptera	Erebidae	*Catocala*	*parta*	mother underwing moth
Lepidoptera	Erebidae	*Catocala*	*piatrix*	penitent underwing
Lepidoptera	Erebidae	*Catocala*	*relicta*	white underwing moth
Lepidoptera	Erebidae	*Catocala*	*residua*	residua underwing
Lepidoptera	Erebidae	*Catocala*	*retecta*	yellow-gray underwing moth
Lepidoptera	Erebidae	*Catocala*	*robinsonii*	Robinson's underwing
Lepidoptera	Erebidae	*Catocala*	*subnata*	youthful underwing
Lepidoptera	Erebidae	*Catocala*	*ultronia*	ultronia underwing moth
Lepidoptera	Erebidae	*Catocala*	*vidua*	widow underwing
Lepidoptera	Erebidae	*Celiptera*	*frustulum*	black bit moth
Lepidoptera	Erebidae	*Chytolita*	*morbidalis*	morbid owlet
Lepidoptera	Erebidae	*Cisseps*	*fulvicollis*	yellow-collared scape moth
Lepidoptera	Erebidae	*Cissusa*	*spadix*	black-dotted brown
Lepidoptera	Erebidae	*Cisthene*	*packardii*	Packard's lichen moth
Lepidoptera	Erebidae	*Cisthene*	*plumbea*	lead-colored lichen moth
Lepidoptera	Erebidae	*Cisthene*	*subjecta*	subject lichen moth
Lepidoptera	Erebidae	*Clemensia*	*albata*	little white lichen moth
Lepidoptera	Erebidae	*Colobochula*	*interpuncta*	yellow-lined owlet moth
Lepidoptera	Erebidae	*Comachara*	*cadburyi*	Cadbury's lichen moth
Lepidoptera	Erebidae	*Crambidia*	*casta*	pearly-winged lichen moth
Lepidoptera	Erebidae	*Crambidia*	*lithosioides*	dark gray lichen moth
Lepidoptera	Erebidae	*Crambidia*	*pallida*	pale lichen moth
Lepidoptera	Erebidae	*Crambidia*	*pura*	pure lichen moth
Lepidoptera	Erebidae	*Crambidia*	*uniformis*	uniform lichen moth
Lepidoptera	Erebidae	*Cycnia*	*oregonensis*	yellow shore crab
Lepidoptera	Erebidae	*Cycnia*	*tenera*	gim or nori
Lepidoptera	Erebidae	*Dasychira*	*antiqua*	onion fly
Lepidoptera	Erebidae	*Dasychira*	*basiflava*	yellow-based tussock
Lepidoptera	Erebidae	*Dasychira*	*manto*	manto tussock moth
Lepidoptera	Erebidae	*Dasychira*	*obliquata*	purple cat's paw pearly mussel

Order	Family	Genus	Species	Common Name
Lepidoptera	Erebidae	*Dasychira*	*plagiata*	the treble-bar
Lepidoptera	Erebidae	*Dasychira*	*tephra*	hellinsia tephradactyla
Lepidoptera	Erebidae	*Dasychira*	*vagans*	Mexican red rump
Lepidoptera	Erebidae	*Dyspyralis*	*illocata*	visitation moth
Lepidoptera	Erebidae	*Dyspyralis*	*nigellus*	slaty dyspyralis moth
Lepidoptera	Erebidae	*Dyspyralis*	*puncicosta*	spot-edged dyspyralis moth
Lepidoptera	Erebidae	*Ecpantheria*	*scribonia*	giant leopard
Lepidoptera	Erebidae	*Estigmene*	*acrea*	salt marsh moth
Lepidoptera	Erebidae	*Euchaetes*	*egle*	milkweed tiger moth
Lepidoptera	Erebidae	*Euclidia*	*cuspidea*	toothed somberwing
Lepidoptera	Erebidae	*Euparthenos*	*nubilis*	locust underwing
Lepidoptera	Erebidae	*Gabara*	*subnivosella*	owlet moth
Lepidoptera	Erebidae	*Halysidota*	*harrisii*	sycamore tussock moth
Lepidoptera	Erebidae	*Halysidota*	*tessellaris*	banded tussock moth
Lepidoptera	Erebidae	*Haploa*	*clymene*	clymene moth
Lepidoptera	Erebidae	*Haploa*	*colona*	colona moth
Lepidoptera	Erebidae	*Haploa*	*contigua*	neighbor moth
Lepidoptera	Erebidae	*Haploa*	*lecontei*	Leconte's haploa moth
Lepidoptera	Erebidae	*Hemeroplanis*	*scopulepes*	variable tropic
Lepidoptera	Erebidae	*Hypena*	*abalienalis*	white-lined bomolocha moth
Lepidoptera	Erebidae	*Hypena*	*baltimoralis*	Baltimore bomolocha moth
Lepidoptera	Erebidae	*Hypena*	*bijugalis*	dimorphic bomolocha moth
Lepidoptera	Erebidae	*Hypena*	*deceptalis*	deceptive bomolocha moth
Lepidoptera	Erebidae	*Hypena*	*eductalis*	red-footed bomolocha moth
Lepidoptera	Erebidae	*Hypena*	*humuli*	hopvine moth
Lepidoptera	Erebidae	*Hypena*	*madefactalis*	grey-eyed bomolocha
Lepidoptera	Erebidae	*Hypena*	*manalis*	flowing-line bomolocha moth
Lepidoptera	Erebidae	*Hypena*	*palparia*	mottled bomolocha moth
Lepidoptera	Erebidae	*Hypena*	*scabra*	green cloverworm moth
Lepidoptera	Erebidae	*Hypena*	*sordidula*	sordid bomolocha
Lepidoptera	Erebidae	*Hypenodes*	*fractilinea*	broken-line hypenodes moth
Lepidoptera	Erebidae	*Hyphantria*	*cunea*	fall webworm moth
Lepidoptera	Erebidae	*Hypoprepia*	*fucosa*	painted lichen moth
Lepidoptera	Erebidae	*Hypoprepia*	*miniata*	scarlet-winged lichen moth
Lepidoptera	Erebidae	*Hypsoropha*	*hormos*	small necklace moth
Lepidoptera	Erebidae	*Hypsoropha*	*monilis*	large necklace moth
Lepidoptera	Erebidae	*Idia*	*aemula*	commonn idia moth
Lepidoptera	Erebidae	*Idia*	*americalis*	American idia moth
Lepidoptera	Erebidae	*Idia*	*denticulalis*	toothed idia moth
Lepidoptera	Erebidae	*Idia*	*diminuendis*	orange-spotted idia moth
Lepidoptera	Erebidae	*Idia*	*forbesi*	idia moth
Lepidoptera	Erebidae	*idia*	*julia*	idia moth
Lepidoptera	Erebidae	*Idia*	*lubricalis*	glossy black idia moth
Lepidoptera	Erebidae	*Idia*	*rotundalis*	rotund idia
Lepidoptera	Erebidae	*Idia*	*scobialis*	smoky idia
Lepidoptera	Erebidae	*Isogona*	*tenuis*	thin-lined owlet moth
Lepidoptera	Erebidae	*Lascoria*	*ambigualis*	ambiguous moth
Lepidoptera	Erebidae	*Ledaea*	*perditalis*	lost owlet
Lepidoptera	Erebidae	*Lophocampa*	*caryae*	hickory tussock moth
Lepidoptera	Erebidae	*Lophocampa*	*maculata*	spotted tussock moth
Lepidoptera	Erebidae	*Lycomorpha*	*pholus*	black-and-yellow lichen moth
Lepidoptera	Erebidae	*Manulea*	*bicolor*	bicolored moth

Order	Family	Genus	Species	Common Name
Lepidoptera	Erebidae	*Mascrochilo*	*absorptalis*	slant-lined owlet moth
Lepidoptera	Erebidae	*Mascrochilo*	*hypocritalis*	twin-dotted macrochilo moth
Lepidoptera	Erebidae	*Mascrochilo*	*litophora*	brown-lined owlet moth
Lepidoptera	Erebidae	*Mascrochilo*	*orciferalis*	bronzy macrochilo moth
Lepidoptera	Erebidae	*Melipotis*	*jucunda*	merry melipotis moth
Lepidoptera	Erebidae	*Metalectra*	*discalis*	common fungus moth
Lepidoptera	Erebidae	*Metalectra*	*quadrisignata*	four-spotted fungus moth
Lepidoptera	Erebidae	*Metalectra*	*richardsi*	Richard's fungus moth
Lepidoptera	Erebidae	*Metalectra*	*tanillus*	black fungus moth
Lepidoptera	Erebidae	*Mocis*	*texana*	Texas mocis moth
Lepidoptera	Erebidae	*Nigetia*	*formosalis*	thin-winged owlet
Lepidoptera	Erebidae	*Orgyia*	*definita*	definite tussock moth
Lepidoptera	Erebidae	*Palthis*	*angulalis*	dark-spotted palthis moth
Lepidoptera	Erebidae	*Palthis*	*asopialis*	faint-spotted palthis moth
Lepidoptera	Erebidae	*Pangrapta*	*decoralis*	decorated owlet moth
Lepidoptera	Erebidae	*Panopoda*	*carneicosta*	brown panopoda moth
Lepidoptera	Erebidae	*Panopoda*	*repanda*	orange panopoda
Lepidoptera	Erebidae	*Panopoda*	*rufimargo*	red-lined panopoda moth
Lepidoptera	Erebidae	*Paraga*	*simplex*	mouse-colored lichen moth
Lepidoptera	Erebidae	*Parallelia*	*bistriaris*	maple looper moth
Lepidoptera	Erebidae	*Phalaenophana*	*pyramusalis*	dark-banded owlet moth
Lepidoptera	Erebidae	*Phalaenostola*	*eumelusalis*	dark phalaenostola moth
Lepidoptera	Erebidae	*Phalaenostola*	*larentioides*	black-banded owlet moth
Lepidoptera	Erebidae	*Phalaenostola*	*metonalis*	tufted snout moth
Lepidoptera	Erebidae	*Phoberia*	*atomaris*	common oak moth
Lepidoptera	Erebidae	*Phyprosopus*	*callitrichoides*	curve-lined owlet
Lepidoptera	Erebidae	*Phytometra*	*ernestinana*	Ernestine's moth
Lepidoptera	Erebidae	*Phytometra*	*rhodarialis*	pink-bordered yellow moth
Lepidoptera	Erebidae	*Plusiodonta*	*compressipalpis*	moonseed moth
Lepidoptera	Erebidae	*Pyrrharctia*	*isabella*	isabella tiger moth
Lepidoptera	Erebidae	*Redectis*	*vitrea*	white-spotted redectis moth
Lepidoptera	Erebidae	*Renia*	*discoloralis*	discolored renia moth
Lepidoptera	Erebidae	*Renia*	*factiosalis*	sociable renia moth
Lepidoptera	Erebidae	*Renia*	*flavipunctalis*	yellow-spotted renia moth
Lepidoptera	Erebidae	*Renia*	*nemoralis*	chocolate renia moth
Lepidoptera	Erebidae	*Renia*	*salusalis*	noctuid moth
Lepidoptera	Erebidae	*Renia*	*sobrialis*	sober renia moth
Lepidoptera	Erebidae	*Rivula*	*propinqualis*	spotted grass moth
Lepidoptera	Erebidae	*Scolecocampa*	*liburna*	Deadwood borer moth
Lepidoptera	Erebidae	*Scoliopteryx*	*libatrix*	herald moth
Lepidoptera	Erebidae	*Spargaloma*	*sexpunctata*	six-spotted gray moth
Lepidoptera	Erebidae	*Spiloloma*	*lunilinea*	moon-lined moth
Lepidoptera	Erebidae	*Spilosoma*	*congrua*	agreeable tiger moth
Lepidoptera	Erebidae	*Spilosoma*	*dubia*	dubious tiger moth
Lepidoptera	Erebidae	*Spilosoma*	*latipennis*	pink-legged tiger moth
Lepidoptera	Erebidae	*Spilosoma*	*virginica*	Virginia tiger moth
Lepidoptera	Erebidae	*Tathorhynchus*	*exsiccata*	alfalfa looper moth
Lepidoptera	Erebidae	*Tetanolita*	*floridana*	Florida tetanolita moth
Lepidoptera	Erebidae	*Tetanolita*	*mynesalis*	smoky tetanolita
Lepidoptera	Erebidae	*Utethesia*	*bella*	cenometra bella
Lepidoptera	Erebidae	*Virbia*	*aurantiaca*	orange holomelina moth
Lepidoptera	Erebidae	*Virbia*	*ferruginosa*	rusty holomelina moth

Order	Family	Genus	Species	Common Name
Lepidoptera	Erebidae	Virbia	immaculata	immaculate holomelina moth
Lepidoptera	Erebidae	Virbia	laeta	joyful holomelina moth
Lepidoptera	Erebidae	Virbia	opella	tawny holomelina
Lepidoptera	Erebidae	Zale	aeruginosa	green-dusted zale
Lepidoptera	Erebidae	Zale	galbanata	maple zale moth
Lepidoptera	Erebidae	Zale	helata	brown-spotted zale
Lepidoptera	Erebidae	Zale	horrida	horrid zale moth
Lepidoptera	Erebidae	Zale	lunata	lunate zale moth
Lepidoptera	Erebidae	Zale	lunifera	bold-based zale moth
Lepidoptera	Erebidae	Zale	metata	zale moth
Lepidoptera	Erebidae	Zale	metatoides	washed-out zale moth
Lepidoptera	Erebidae	Zale	minerea	colorful zale moth
Lepidoptera	Erebidae	Zale	obliqua	oblique zale moth
Lepidoptera	Erebidae	Zale	phaeocapna	zale moth
Lepidoptera	Erebidae	Zale	undularis	black zale moth
Lepidoptera	Erebidae	Zale	unilineata	one-lined zale
Lepidoptera	Erebidae	Zanclognatha	cruralis	early zanclognatha moth
Lepidoptera	Erebidae	Zanclognatha	jacchusalis	wavy-lined zanclognatha moth
Lepidoptera	Erebidae	Zanclognatha	laevigata	variable zanclognatha moth
Lepidoptera	Erebidae	Zanclognatha	lituralis	lettered zanclognatha moth
Lepidoptera	Erebidae	Zanclognatha	marcidilinea	yellowish zanclognatha moth
Lepidoptera	Erebidae	Zanclognatha	martha	pine barrens zanclognatha moth
Lepidoptera	Erebidae	Zanclognatha	obscuripennis	dark zanclognatha moth
Lepidoptera	Erebidae	Zanclognatha	pedipilalis	grayish zanclognatha moth
Lepidoptera	Erebidae	Zanclognatha	protumnsalis	conifer zanclognatha moth
Lepidoptera	Geometroidae	Anacamptodes	defectaria	brown-shaded gray moth
Lepidoptera	Geometroidae	Anacamptodes	humaria	small purplish gray moth
Lepidoptera	Geometroidae	Anagoga	occiduaria	American barred umber moth
Lepidoptera	Geometroidae	Anavitrinella	pampinaria	common gray moth
Lepidoptera	Geometroidae	Antepione	thisoaria	variable antipione
Lepidoptera	Geometroidae	Anticlea	multiferata	many-lined carpet moth
Lepidoptera	Geometroidae	Besma	endropiaria	straw besma
Lepidoptera	Geometroidae	Besma	quercivoraria	oak besma moth
Lepidoptera	Geometroidae	Biston	betularia	pepper and salt geometer moth
Lepidoptera	Geometroidae	Campaea	perlata	pale beauty moth
Lepidoptera	Geometroidae	Caripeta	aretaria	southern pine looper moth
Lepidoptera	Geometroidae	Cepphis	armataria	scallop moth
Lepidoptera	Geometroidae	Chlorochlamys	chloroleucaria	blackberry looper moth
Lepidoptera	Geometroidae	Chlorochlamys	tepperaria	angle-winged emerald moth
Lepidoptera	Geometroidae	Cladara	anguilineata	angle-lined carpet moth
Lepidoptera	Geometroidae	Cladara	atroliturata	scribbler moth
Lepidoptera	Geometroidae	Cladara	limitaria	mottled gray carpet moth
Lepidoptera	Geometroidae	Cleora	sublunaria	double-lined gray
Lepidoptera	Geometroidae	Cyclophora	packardi	Vernal pool tadpole shrimp
Lepidoptera	Geometroidae	Dichorda	iridaria	showy emerald moth
Lepidoptera	Geometroidae	Disclisioprocta	stellata	somber carpet
Lepidoptera	Geometroidae	Dyspteris	abortivaria	the bad-wing
Lepidoptera	Geometroidae	Ecliptopera	atricolorata	dark-banded geometer moth
Lepidoptera	Geometroidae	Ectropis	crepuscularia	small engrailed moth
Lepidoptera	Geometroidae	Ennomos	magnaria	maple spanworm moth
Lepidoptera	Geometroidae	Epimecis	hortaria	tulip tree beauty
Lepidoptera	Geometroidae	Erannis	tiliaria	linden looper moth

Order	Family	Genus	Species	Common Name
Lepidoptera	Geometroidae	*Eubaphe*	*mendica*	muslin moth
Lepidoptera	Geometroidae	*Euchlaena*	*amoenaria*	deep yellow euchlaena
Lepidoptera	Geometroidae	*Euchlaena*	*irraria*	least-marked euchlaena
Lepidoptera	Geometroidae	*Euchlaena*	*johnsonaria*	Johnson's euchlaena moth
Lepidoptera	Geometroidae	*Euchlaena*	*madusaria*	scrub euchlaena moth
Lepidoptera	Geometroidae	*Euchlaena*	*obtusaria*	obtuse euchlaena moth
Lepidoptera	Geometroidae	*Euchlaena*	*pectinaria*	Gould's trumpet worm
Lepidoptera	Geometroidae	*Euchlaena*	*serrata*	saw-wing moth
Lepidoptera	Geometroidae	*Euchlaena*	*tiginaria*	barn funnel weaver
Lepidoptera	Geometroidae	*Eulithis*	*diversilineata*	lesser grapevine looper
Lepidoptera	Geometroidae	*Eulithis*	*gracilineata*	greater grapevine looper
Lepidoptera	Geometroidae	*Euphyia*	*unangulata*	sharp-angled carpet
Lepidoptera	Geometroidae	*Eupithecia*	*jejunata*	eupithecia jejunata
Lepidoptera	Geometroidae	*Eupithecia*	*matheri*	eupithecia matheri rindge
Lepidoptera	Geometroidae	*Eupithecia*	*miserulata*	common eupithecia
Lepidoptera	Geometroidae	*Eupithecia*	*swettii*	eupithecia swettii grossbeck
Lepidoptera	Geometroidae	*Eusarca*	*confusaria*	confused eusarca
Lepidoptera	Geometroidae	*Eutrapela*	*clemataria*	curve-toothed geometer moth
Lepidoptera	Geometroidae	*Glena*	*cribrataria*	dotted gray
Lepidoptera	Geometroidae	*Glenoides*	*texanaria*	Texas gray
Lepidoptera	Geometroidae	*Haematopis*	*grataria*	chickweed geometer moth
Lepidoptera	Geometroidae	*Heliomata*	*cycladata*	common spring moth
Lepidoptera	Geometroidae	*Heterophleps*	*triguttaria*	three-spotted fillip moth
Lepidoptera	Geometroidae	*Hethemia*	*pistasciaria*	pistachio emerald moth
Lepidoptera	Geometroidae	*Horisme*	*intestinata*	brown bark carpet moth
Lepidoptera	Geometroidae	*Hydrelia*	*inornata*	unadorned carpet moth
Lepidoptera	Geometroidae	*Hydria*	*prunivorata*	cherry scallop shell moth
Lepidoptera	Geometroidae	*Hydriomena*	*divisaria*	black-dashed hydriomena moth
Lepidoptera	Geometroidae	*Hydriomena*	*pluviata*	sharp green hydriomena moth
Lepidoptera	Geometroidae	*Hydriomena*	*transfigurata*	transfigured hydriomena
Lepidoptera	Geometroidae	*Hypagyrtis*	*unipunctata*	one-spotted variant moth
Lepidoptera	Geometroidae	*Idaea*	*demissaria*	red-boardered wave
Lepidoptera	Geometroidae	*Idaea*	*obfusaria*	rippled wave moth
Lepidoptera	Geometroidae	*Iridopsis*	*larvaria*	bent-line gray moth
Lepidoptera	Geometroidae	*Itame*	*pustularia*	lesser maple spanworm moth
Lepidoptera	Geometroidae	*Itame*	*subcessaria*	barred itame
Lepidoptera	Geometroidae	*Lambdina*	*fervidaria*	curve-lined looper moth
Lepidoptera	Geometroidae	*LambdINa*	*pellucidaria*	yellow-headed looper moth
Lepidoptera	Geometroidae	*Leptostales*	*rubromarginaria*	dark-ribboned wave
Lepidoptera	Geometroidae	*Lobocleta*	*ossularia*	drab brown wave
Lepidoptera	Geometroidae	*Lomographa*	*glomeraria*	gray spring moth
Lepidoptera	Geometroidae	*Lomographa*	*vestaliata*	white spring moth
Lepidoptera	Geometroidae	*Lytrosis*	*unitaria*	common lytrosis moth
Lepidoptera	Geometroidae	*Melanolophia*	*canadaria*	Canadian melanolophia moth
Lepidoptera	Geometroidae	*Melanolophia*	*signataria*	signate melanolophia moth
Lepidoptera	Geometroidae	*Metanema*	*determinata*	dark metanema moth
Lepidoptera	Geometroidae	*Metarranthis*	*angularia*	angled metarranthis moth
Lepidoptera	Geometroidae	*Metarranthis*	*homuraria*	purplish metarranthis moth
Lepidoptera	Geometroidae	*Metarranthis*	*hypochraria*	common metarranthis moth
Lepidoptera	Geometroidae	*Nacophora*	*quernaria*	oak beauty moth
Lepidoptera	Geometroidae	*Nematocampa*	*limbata*	filament bearer
Lepidoptera	Geometroidae	*Nemoria*	*bistriaria*	red-fringed emerald moth

Order	Family	Genus	Species	Common Name
Lepidoptera	Geometroidae	*Nemoria*	*mimosaria*	white-fringed emerald moth
Lepidoptera	Geometroidae	*Orthonama*	*centrostrigaria*	traveller or bent-line carpet
Lepidoptera	Geometroidae	*Orthonama*	*obstipata*	gem moth
Lepidoptera	Geometroidae	*Paleacrita*	*vernata*	spring cankerworm moth
Lepidoptera	Geometroidae	*Patalene*	*olyzonaria*	juniper geometer
Lepidoptera	Geometroidae	*Pero*	*honestaria*	honest pero moth
Lepidoptera	Geometroidae	*Pero*	*hubneraria*	Hubner's pero moth
Lepidoptera	Geometroidae	*Pero*	*morrisonaria*	Morrison's pero moth
Lepidoptera	Geometroidae	*Phigalia*	*denticulata*	toothed phigalia
Lepidoptera	Geometroidae	*Phigalia*	*strigataria*	small phigalia
Lepidoptera	Geometroidae	*Phigalia*	*titea*	half-wing moth
Lepidoptera	Geometroidae	*Plagodis*	*alcoolaria*	hollow-spotted plagodis moth
Lepidoptera	Geometroidae	*Plagodis*	*fervidaria*	fervid plagodis
Lepidoptera	Geometroidae	*Plagodis*	*kuetzingi*	purple plagodis moth
Lepidoptera	Geometroidae	*Plagodis*	*phlogosaria*	straight-lined plagodis moth
Lepidoptera	Geometroidae	*Plagodis*	*serinaria*	lemon plagodis moth
Lepidoptera	Geometroidae	*Pleuroprucha*	*insulsaria*	common tan ave
Lepidoptera	Geometroidae	*Probole*	*amicaria*	friendly probole moth
Lepidoptera	Geometroidae	*Probole*	*nyssaria*	dogwood probole moth
Lepidoptera	Geometroidae	*Prochoerodes*	*transversata*	large maple spanworm moth
Lepidoptera	Geometroidae	*Protoboarmia*	*porcelaria*	porcelain gray moth
Lepidoptera	Geometroidae	*Scopula*	*inductata*	soft-lined wave moth
Lepidoptera	Geometroidae	*Scopula*	*limboundata*	large lace-border moth
Lepidoptera	Geometroidae	*Semiothisa*	*aemulataria*	common angle moth
Lepidoptera	Geometroidae	*Semiothisa*	*aequiferaria*	common angle
Lepidoptera	Geometroidae	*Semiothisa*	*bicolorata*	bicolored angle moth
Lepidoptera	Geometroidae	*Semiothisa*	*bisignata*	redheaded inchworm moth
Lepidoptera	Geometroidae	*Semiothisa*	*continuata*	curve-lined angle moth
Lepidoptera	Geometroidae	*Semiothisa*	*gnophosaris*	hollow-spotted angle moth
Lepidoptera	Geometroidae	*Semiothisa*	*granitata*	granite moth
Lepidoptera	Geometroidae	*Semiothisa*	*multilineata*	many-lined angle
Lepidoptera	Geometroidae	*Semiothisa*	*ocellinata*	faint-spotted angle moth
Lepidoptera	Geometroidae	*Semiothisa*	*promiscuata*	promiscuous angle
Lepidoptera	Geometroidae	*Semiothisa*	*quadrinotaria*	four-spotted angle moth
Lepidoptera	Geometroidae	*Semiothisa*	*transitaria*	blurry chocolate angle moth
Lepidoptera	Geometroidae	*Synchlora*	*aerata*	wavy-lined emerald moth
Lepidoptera	Geometroidae	*Tetracis*	*cachexiata*	white slant-line moth
Lepidoptera	Geometroidae	*Tetracis*	*crocallata*	yellow slant-line moth
Lepidoptera	Geometroidae	*Timandra*	*amaturaria*	cross-lined wave
Lepidoptera	Geometroidae	*Tornos*	*scolopacinaria*	dimorphic gray moth
Lepidoptera	Geometroidae	*Trichodezia*	*albovittata*	white-stripped black moth
Lepidoptera	Geometroidae	*Venusia*	*comptaria*	brown-shaped carpet moth
Lepidoptera	Geometroidae	*Xanthotype*	*sospeta*	crocus geometer moth
Lepidoptera	Geometroidae	*Xanthotype*	*urticaria*	false crocus geometer moth
Lepidoptera	Lasiocampidae	*Artace*	*cribraria*	dot-lined white moth
Lepidoptera	Lasiocampidae	*Malacosoma*	*americanum*	eastern tent caterpillar moth
Lepidoptera	Lasiocampidae	*Malacosoma*	*disstria*	forest tent caterpillar moth
Lepidoptera	Lasiocampidae	*Olceclostera*	*angelica*	angel moth
Lepidoptera	Lasiocampidae	*Phyllodesma*	*americana*	lappet moth
Lepidoptera	Lasiocampidae	*Tolype*	*notialis*	small tolype moth
Lepidoptera	Lasiocampidae	*Tolype*	*velleda*	large tolype moth
Lepidoptera	Megalopygidae	*Pyromorpha*	*dimidiata*	orange-patched smoky moth

Order	Family	Genus	Species	Common Name
Lepidoptera	Mimallonoidae	Cicinnus	melsheimeri	Melsheimer's sack-bearer
Lepidoptera	Mimallonoidae	Lacoasoma	chiridota	scalloped sack-bearer moth
Lepidoptera	Noctuidae	Achatia	distincta	distinct Quaker moth
Lepidoptera	Noctuidae	Achatodes	zeae	elder shoot borer moth
Lepidoptera	Noctuidae	Acontia	aprica	exposed bird-dropping moth
Lepidoptera	Noctuidae	Acontia	delecta	delightful bird-dropping moth
Lepidoptera	Noctuidae	Acronicta	afflicta	afflicted dagger moth
Lepidoptera	Noctuidae	Acronicta	americana	American dagger moth
Lepidoptera	Noctuidae	Acronicta	betulae	birch dagger moth
Lepidoptera	Noctuidae	Acronicta	clarescens	clear dagger moth
Lepidoptera	Noctuidae	Acronicta	connecta	connected dagger moth
Lepidoptera	Noctuidae	Acronicta	dactylina	fingered dagger moth
Lepidoptera	Noctuidae	Acronicta	falcula	corylus dagger moth
Lepidoptera	Noctuidae	Acronicta	fallax	green marvel moth
Lepidoptera	Noctuidae	Acronicta	fragilis	fragile dagger moth
Lepidoptera	Noctuidae	Acronicta	funeralis	funerary dagger moth
Lepidoptera	Noctuidae	Acronicta	haesitata	hesitant dagger moth
Lepidoptera	Noctuidae	Acronicta	hasta	forked dagger moth
Lepidoptera	Noctuidae	Acronicta	impleta	yellow-haired dagger moth
Lepidoptera	Noctuidae	Acronicta	inclara	unclear dagger moth
Lepidoptera	Noctuidae	Acronicta	increta	southern oak dagger moth
Lepidoptera	Noctuidae	Acronicta	innotata	unmarked dagger moth
Lepidoptera	Noctuidae	Acronicta	Insularis	marsh dagger
Lepidoptera	Noctuidae	Acronicta	interrupta	interrupted dagger moth
Lepidoptera	Noctuidae	Acronicta	laetifica	pleasant dagger moth
Lepidoptera	Noctuidae	Acronicta	lepusculina	cottonwood dagger moth
Lepidoptera	Noctuidae	Acronicta	lithospila	streaked dagger moth
Lepidoptera	Noctuidae	Acronicta	lobeliae	greater oak dagger moth
Lepidoptera	Noctuidae	Acronicta	longa	long-winged dagger moth
Lepidoptera	Noctuidae	Acronicta	modica	medium dagger moth
Lepidoptera	Noctuidae	Acronicta	morula	ochre dagger moth
Lepidoptera	Noctuidae	Acronicta	oblinita	smeared dagger moth
Lepidoptera	Noctuidae	Acronicta	ovata	ovate dagger moth
Lepidoptera	Noctuidae	Acronicta	radcliffei	Radcliffe's dagger moth
Lepidoptera	Noctuidae	Acronicta	retardata	retarded dagger moth
Lepidoptera	Noctuidae	Acronicta	rubricoma	ruddy dagger moth
Lepidoptera	Noctuidae	Acronicta	sprinigera	nondescript dagger moth
Lepidoptera	Noctuidae	Acronicta	tristis	sad dagger moth
Lepidoptera	Noctuidae	Acronicta	vinnula	delightful dagger moth
Lepidoptera	Noctuidae	Adita	chionanthi	fringe-tree sallow moth
Lepidoptera	Noctuidae	Alypia	octomaculata	eight-spotted forester moth
Lepidoptera	Noctuidae	Amolita	fessa	feeble grass moth
Lepidoptera	Noctuidae	Amphipoea	americana	American ear moth
Lepidoptera	Noctuidae	Amphipoea	erepta	dart moth
Lepidoptera	Noctuidae	Amphipoea	interoceanica	strawberry cutworm moth
Lepidoptera	Noctuidae	Amphipoea	velata	veiled ear moth
Lepidoptera	Noctuidae	Amphipyra	pyramidoides	copper underwing moth
Lepidoptera	Noctuidae	Amyna	bullula	hook-tipped amyna moth
Lepidoptera	Noctuidae	Anathix	ralla	dotted sallow moth
Lepidoptera	Noctuidae	Anterastria	teratophora	gray marvel moth
Lepidoptera	Noctuidae	Apamea	amputarix	yellow-headed cutworm moth
Lepidoptera	Noctuidae	Apamea	cristata	noctuid moth

Order	Family	Genus	Species	Common Name
Lepidoptera	Noctuidae	*Apamea*	*devastator*	glassy cutworm moth
Lepidoptera	Noctuidae	*Apamea*	*helva*	yellow three-spot moth
Lepidoptera	Noctuidae	*Apamea*	*indocilis*	ignorant apamea moth
Lepidoptera	Noctuidae	*Apamea*	*lignicolora*	wood-colored Quaker moth
Lepidoptera	Noctuidae	*Apamea*	*mixta*	coastal plain apamea moth
Lepidoptera	Noctuidae	*Apamea*	*plutonia*	dusky apamea moth
Lepidoptera	Noctuidae	*Apamea*	*sordens*	bordered apamea moth
Lepidoptera	Noctuidae	*Apamea*	*vulgaris*	common apamea moth
Lepidoptera	Noctuidae	*Archanara*	*oblonga*	oblong sedge borer
Lepidoptera	Noctuidae	*Athetis*	*tarda*	slowpoke moth
Lepidoptera	Noctuidae	*Azenis*	*obtusa*	obtuse yellow moth
Lepidoptera	Noctuidae	*Bagisara*	*rectifascia*	straight-lined mallow moth
Lepidoptera	Noctuidae	*Balsa*	*labecula*	white-blotched balsa moth
Lepidoptera	Noctuidae	*Balsa*	*malana*	many-dotted apple worm moth
Lepidoptera	Noctuidae	*Balsa*	*tristrigella*	three-lined balsa moth
Lepidoptera	Noctuidae	*Basilodes*	*peptia*	gold moth
Lepidoptera	Noctuidae	*Bellura*	*gortynoides*	white-tailed diver moth
Lepidoptera	Noctuidae	*Bellura*	*obliqua*	cattail borer moth
Lepidoptera	Noctuidae	*Callopistria*	*cordata*	silver-spotted fern moth
Lepidoptera	Noctuidae	*Callopistria*	*mollissima*	pink-shaded fern moth
Lepidoptera	Noctuidae	*Cerma*	*cerintha*	tufted bird-dropping moth
Lepidoptera	Noctuidae	*Cerma*	*cora*	bird-dropping moth
Lepidoptera	Noctuidae	*Chaetaglaea*	*cerata*	waxed sallow moth
Lepidoptera	Noctuidae	*Chaetaglaea*	*sericea*	silky sallow moth
Lepidoptera	Noctuidae	*Charadra*	*deridens*	laughter moth
Lepidoptera	Noctuidae	*Cirrhophanus*	*triangulifer*	goldenrod stowaway moth
Lepidoptera	Noctuidae	*Colocasia*	*flavicornis*	yellowhorn moth
Lepidoptera	Noctuidae	*Colocasia*	*propinquilnea*	closebranded yellowhorn moth
Lepidoptera	Noctuidae	*Condica*	*confederate*	confederate moth
Lepidoptera	Noctuidae	*Condica*	*mobilis*	mobile groundling
Lepidoptera	Noctuidae	*Condica*	*sutor*	cobbler moth
Lepidoptera	Noctuidae	*Condica*	*vecors*	dusky groundling moth
Lepidoptera	Noctuidae	*Condica*	*videns*	white-dotted groundling moth
Lepidoptera	Noctuidae	*Copivaleria*	*grotei*	Grote's sallow moth
Lepidoptera	Noctuidae	*Cosmia*	*calami*	American dun-bar moth
Lepidoptera	Noctuidae	*Crambodes*	*talidiformis*	verbena moth
Lepidoptera	Noctuidae	*Cucullia*	*asteroides*	tiny lazy daisy
Lepidoptera	Noctuidae	*Cucullia*	*convexipennis*	brown-hooded owlet
Lepidoptera	Noctuidae	*Cucullia*	*florea*	dwarf honey bee
Lepidoptera	Noctuidae	*Cucullia*	*intermedia*	nievitas
Lepidoptera	Noctuidae	*Deltote*	*bellicula*	bog glyph moth
Lepidoptera	Noctuidae	*Discestra*	*trifolii*	American serpentine leafminer
Lepidoptera	Noctuidae	*Elaphria*	*georgei*	chalcedony midget moth
Lepidoptera	Noctuidae	*Elaphria*	*versicolor*	festive midget moth
Lepidoptera	Noctuidae	*Enargia*	*decolor*	aspen twoleaf tier moth
Lepidoptera	Noctuidae	*Epiglaea*	*decliva*	sloping sallow moth
Lepidoptera	Noctuidae	*Eucrirroedia*	*pampinaria*	common gray
Lepidoptera	Noctuidae	*Eudryas*	*grata*	grateful midget moth
Lepidoptera	Noctuidae	*Eudryas*	*octomaculata*	eight-spotted forester
Lepidoptera	Noctuidae	*Euplexia*	*benesimilis*	American angle shades
Lepidoptera	Noctuidae	*Eupsilia*	*cirripalea*	Franclemont's sallow moth
Lepidoptera	Noctuidae	*Eupsilia*	*devia*	lost sallow moth

Order	Family	Genus	Species	Common Name
Lepidoptera	Noctuidae	*Eupsilia*	*morrisoni*	Morrison's sallow
Lepidoptera	Noctuidae	*Eupsilia*	*sidus*	sidus sallow moth
Lepidoptera	Noctuidae	*Eupsilia*	*tristigmata*	three-spotted sallow moth
Lepidoptera	Noctuidae	*Eupsilia*	*vinulenta*	straight-toothed sallow moth
Lepidoptera	Noctuidae	*Fagitana*	*littera*	marsh fern moth
Lepidoptera	Noctuidae	*Faronta*	*diffusa*	punarnava
Lepidoptera	Noctuidae	*Faronta*	*rubripennus*	redhook pacu
Lepidoptera	Noctuidae	*Feralia*	*comstocki*	Comstock's sallow moth
Lepidoptera	Noctuidae	*Feralia*	*jocosa*	jocose sallow moth
Lepidoptera	Noctuidae	*Feralia*	*major*	major sallow moth
Lepidoptera	Noctuidae	*Galgula*	*partita*	wedgling moth
Lepidoptera	Noctuidae	*Hadena*	*ectypa*	starry campion moth
Lepidoptera	Noctuidae	*Harrisimemna*	*trisignata*	Harris's three-spot moth
Lepidoptera	Noctuidae	*Helotropha*	*reniformis*	kidney-spotted rustic moth
Lepidoptera	Noctuidae	*Homohedena*	*infixa*	broad-lined sallow moth
Lepidoptera	Noctuidae	*Homophoberia*	*apicosa*	black wedge-spot moth
Lepidoptera	Noctuidae	*Homophoberia*	*cristata*	waterlily owlet moth
Lepidoptera	Noctuidae	*Hydraecia*	*stramentosa*	figwort borer moth
Lepidoptera	Noctuidae	*Hyperstrotia*	*secta*	black-patched graylet moth
Lepidoptera	Noctuidae	*Hyperstrotia*	*villificans*	white-lined graylet
Lepidoptera	Noctuidae	*Iodopepla*	*u-album*	white-eyed borer moth
Lepidoptera	Noctuidae	*Lacanobia*	*subjuncta*	speckled cutworm moth
Lepidoptera	Noctuidae	*Lacinipolia*	*implicata*	implicit arches moth
Lepidoptera	Noctuidae	*Lemmeria*	*digitalis*	fingered lemmeria moth
Lepidoptera	Noctuidae	*Leucania*	*adjuta*	adjutant wainscot moth
Lepidoptera	Noctuidae	*Leucania*	*commoides*	two-lined wainscot moth
Lepidoptera	Noctuidae	*Leucania*	*inermis*	unarmed wainscot
Lepidoptera	Noctuidae	*Leucania*	*linda*	linda wainscot
Lepidoptera	Noctuidae	*Leucania*	*multilinea*	many-lined wainscot moth
Lepidoptera	Noctuidae	*Leucania*	*phragmitidicola*	phragmites wainscot moth
Lepidoptera	Noctuidae	*Leucania*	*pseudargyria*	false wainscot
Lepidoptera	Noctuidae	*Leucania*	*ursula*	ursula wainscot
Lepidoptera	Noctuidae	*Leuconycta*	*diphteroides*	green leuconycta moth
Lepidoptera	Noctuidae	*Leuconycta*	*lepidula*	marbled-green leuconycta moth
Lepidoptera	Noctuidae	*Lithacodia*	*muscosula*	large mossy lithacodia moth
Lepidoptera	Noctuidae	*Lithacodia*	*musta*	smally mossy lithacodia moth
Lepidoptera	Noctuidae	*Lithophane*	*antennata*	ashen pinion moth
Lepidoptera	Noctuidae	*Lithophane*	*bethunei*	Bethune's pinion moth
Lepidoptera	Noctuidae	*Lithophane*	*disposita*	dashed gray pinion moth
Lepidoptera	Noctuidae	*Lithophane*	*grotei*	Grote's pinion moth
Lepidoptera	Noctuidae	*Lithophane*	*hemina*	hemina pinion moth
Lepidoptera	Noctuidae	*Lithophane*	*innominata*	nameless pinion moth
Lepidoptera	Noctuidae	*Lithophane*	*joannis*	pinion moth
Lepidoptera	Noctuidae	*Lithophane*	*laticunerea*	broad ashen pinion moth
Lepidoptera	Noctuidae	*Lithophane*	*patefacta*	dimorphic pinion moth
Lepidoptera	Noctuidae	*Lithophane*	*petulca*	wanton pinion moth
Lepidoptera	Noctuidae	*Lithophane*	*querquera*	shivering pinion moth
Lepidoptera	Noctuidae	*Lithophane*	*signosa*	sycamore pinion moth
Lepidoptera	Noctuidae	*Lithophane*	*unimoda*	dowdy pinion moth
Lepidoptera	Noctuidae	*Luperina*	*passer*	dock rustic moth
Lepidoptera	Noctuidae	*Macronoctua*	*onusta*	iris borer moth
Lepidoptera	Noctuidae	*Magusa*	*divaricata*	orbed narrow-wing moth

Order	Family	Genus	Species	Common Name
Lepidoptera	Noctuidae	*Maliattha*	*concinnimacula*	red-spotted lithacodia
Lepidoptera	Noctuidae	*Maliattha*	*synochitis*	black-dotted lithacodia
Lepidoptera	Noctuidae	*Melanchra*	*adjuncta*	hitched arches moth
Lepidoptera	Noctuidae	*Melanchra*	*picta*	zebra caterpillar moth
Lepidoptera	Noctuidae	*Meropleon*	*ambifusa*	Newman's brocade
Lepidoptera	Noctuidae	*Meropleon*	*diversicolor*	multicolored sedgeminer moth
Lepidoptera	Noctuidae	*Metaxaglaea*	*inulta*	unsated sallow
Lepidoptera	Noctuidae	*Metaxaglaea*	*viatica*	roadside sallow
Lepidoptera	Noctuidae	*Micrathetis*	*triplex*	triplex cutworm moth
Lepidoptera	Noctuidae	*Mythimna*	*oxygala*	lesser wainscot moth
Lepidoptera	Noctuidae	*Mythimna*	*unipuncta*	armyworm moth
Lepidoptera	Noctuidae	*Neoligia*	*semicana*	northern brocade moth
Lepidoptera	Noctuidae	*Ogdoconta*	*cinereola*	common pinkband moth
Lepidoptera	Noctuidae	*Oligia*	*chlorostigma*	brocade moth
Lepidoptera	Noctuidae	*Oligia*	*exhausta*	exhausted brocade moth
Lepidoptera	Noctuidae	*Oligia*	*fractilnea*	broken-lined brocade moth
Lepidoptera	Noctuidae	*Oligia*	*illocata*	wandering brocade moth
Lepidoptera	Noctuidae	*Oligia*	*modica*	geissleria modica
Lepidoptera	Noctuidae	*Orthosia*	*alurina*	gray Quaker
Lepidoptera	Noctuidae	*Orthosia*	*garmani*	Garman's Quaker
Lepidoptera	Noctuidae	*Orthosia*	*revicta*	speckled green fruitworm moth
Lepidoptera	Noctuidae	*Oruza*	*albocostaliata*	white edge moth
Lepidoptera	Noctuidae	*Pachypolia*	*atricornis*	hunter lake moth
Lepidoptera	Noctuidae	*Panthea*	*furcilla*	eastern panthea moth
Lepidoptera	Noctuidae	*Papaipema*	*arctivorens*	northern burdock borer moth
Lepidoptera	Noctuidae	*Papaipema*	*baptisiae*	wild indigo borer moth
Lepidoptera	Noctuidae	*Papaipema*	*beeriana*	blazing star stem borer
Lepidoptera	Noctuidae	*Papaipema*	*cataphracta*	burdock borer moth
Lepidoptera	Noctuidae	*Papaipema*	*cerussata*	ironweed borer moth
Lepidoptera	Noctuidae	*Papaipema*	*circumlucens*	hop borer
Lepidoptera	Noctuidae	*Papaipema*	*eupatorii*	eupatorium borer moth
Lepidoptera	Noctuidae	*Papaipema*	*furcata*	ash borer moth
Lepidoptera	Noctuidae	*Papaipema*	*harrisii*	heracleum steam borer moth
Lepidoptera	Noctuidae	*Papaipema*	*impecuniosa*	aster borer moth
Lepidoptera	Noctuidae	*Papaipema*	*inquaesita*	sensitive fern borer moth
Lepidoptera	Noctuidae	*Papaipema*	*insulidens*	umbellifer borer moth
Lepidoptera	Noctuidae	*Papaipema*	*maritima*	maritime sunflower borer moth
Lepidoptera	Noctuidae	*Papaipema*	*nebris*	stalk borer moth
Lepidoptera	Noctuidae	*Papaipema*	*necopina*	sunflower borer moth
Lepidoptera	Noctuidae	*Papaipema*	*nelita*	coneflower borer moth
Lepidoptera	Noctuidae	*Papaipema*	*petrisii*	Peters's thin-toed frog
Lepidoptera	Noctuidae	*Papaipema*	*polymniae*	polymnia borer moth
Lepidoptera	Noctuidae	*Papaipema*	*rigida*	rigid sunflower borer moth
Lepidoptera	Noctuidae	*Papaipema*	*rutila*	mayapple borer moth
Lepidoptera	Noctuidae	*Papaipema*	*unimoda*	meadow rue borer moth
Lepidoptera	Noctuidae	*Parsapamea*	*buffaloensis*	buffalo moth
Lepidoptera	Noctuidae	*Perigea*	*xanthioides*	red groundling moth
Lepidoptera	Noctuidae	*Phosphila*	*miselioides*	spotted phosphila
Lepidoptera	Noctuidae	*Phosphila*	*turbulenta*	turbulent phosphila moth
Lepidoptera	Noctuidae	*Plagiomimicus*	*pityochromus*	black-barred brown
Lepidoptera	Noctuidae	*Polia*	*detracta*	disparaged arches moth
Lepidoptera	Noctuidae	*Polia*	*imbrifera*	cloudy arches moth

Order	Family	Genus	Species	Common Name
Lepidoptera	Noctuidae	Polia	nimbosa	stormy arches moth
Lepidoptera	Noctuidae	Polygrammate	hebraeicum	Hebrew moth
Lepidoptera	Noctuidae	Ponometia	binocula	prairie bird-dropping moth
Lepidoptera	Noctuidae	Ponometia	semiflava	half-yellow moth
Lepidoptera	Noctuidae	Psaphida	electilis	chosen sallow
Lepidoptera	Noctuidae	Psaphida	grandis	gray sallow moth
Lepidoptera	Noctuidae	Psaphida	resumens	figure-eight sallow
Lepidoptera	Noctuidae	Psaphida	rolandi	Roland's sallow
Lepidoptera	Noctuidae	Psaphida	styracis	fawn sallow moth
Lepidoptera	Noctuidae	Psaphida	thaxteriana	Thaxter's sallow
Lepidoptera	Noctuidae	Psychomorpha	epimenis	grapevine epimenis moth
Lepidoptera	Noctuidae	Pyreferra	citromra	citrine sallow moth
Lepidoptera	Noctuidae	Pyreferra	hesperidago	mustard sallow
Lepidoptera	Noctuidae	Pyreferra	pettiti	Pettit's sallow moth
Lepidoptera	Noctuidae	Raphia	frater	brother moth
Lepidoptera	Noctuidae	Sericaglaea	signata	variable sallow
Lepidoptera	Noctuidae	Spodoptera	exigua	beet armyworm moth
Lepidoptera	Noctuidae	Spodoptera	frugiperda	fall armyworm moth
Lepidoptera	Noctuidae	Spodoptera	ornithogalli	yellow-striped armyworm moth
Lepidoptera	Noctuidae	Spragueia	apicalis	yellow spragueia moth
Lepidoptera	Noctuidae	Spragueia	dama	southern spragueia moth
Lepidoptera	Noctuidae	Spragueia	leo	common spragueia moth
Lepidoptera	Noctuidae	Sturia	rugifrons	yellow sunflower moth
Lepidoptera	Noctuidae	Sunira	bicolorago	bicolored sallow moth
Lepidoptera	Noctuidae	Tarachidia	candefacta	olive-shaded bird-dropping moth
Lepidoptera	Noctuidae	Tarachidia	erastrioides	small bird-dropping moth
Lepidoptera	Noctuidae	Thioptera	nigrofimbria	black-bordered lemon moth
Lepidoptera	Noctuidae	Trichordestra	legitima	striped garden caterpillar moth
Lepidoptera	Noctuidae	Xystopeplus	rufago	red-winged sallow
Lepidoptera	Noctuidea	Abagrotis	alternata	greater red dart
Lepidoptera	Noctuidea	Abagrotis	anchoelioides	blueberry budworm moth
Lepidoptera	Noctuidea	Agnorisma	badinodis	pale-banded dart moth
Lepidoptera	Noctuidea	Agnorisma	bollii	noctuid moth
Lepidoptera	Noctuidea	Agnorisma	bugrai	collared dart moth
Lepidoptera	Noctuidea	Agrotis	gladiaria	swordsman dart moth
Lepidoptera	Noctuidea	Agrotis	ipsilon	dark sword grass moth
Lepidoptera	Noctuidea	Agrotis	malefida	rascal dart
Lepidoptera	Noctuidea	Agrotis	subterranean	subterranean cutworm moth
Lepidoptera	Noctuidea	Agrotis	venerabilis	venerable dart moth
Lepidoptera	Noctuidea	Anicla	illapsa	snowy dart
Lepidoptera	Noctuidea	Anicla	infecta	green cutworm
Lepidoptera	Noctuidea	Anicla	lubricans	slippery dart moth
Lepidoptera	Noctuidea	Cerastis	tenebrifera	reddish speckled dart
Lepidoptera	Noctuidea	Choephora	fungorum	pink star moth
Lepidoptera	Noctuidea	Chytonix	palliatricula	cloaked marvel moth
Lepidoptera	Noctuidea	Crocigrapha	normani	pterobranch
Lepidoptera	Noctuidea	Egira	alternans	alternate woodling moth
Lepidoptera	Noctuidea	Elaphria	chalcedonia	George's midget moth
Lepidoptera	Noctuidea	Elaphria	festivoides	variegated midget moth
Lepidoptera	Noctuidea	Eueretgagrotis	sigmoides	sigmoid dart
Lepidoptera	Noctuidea	Euxoa	campestris	flat dart moth
Lepidoptera	Noctuidea	Euxoa	messoria	reaper dart moth

Order	Family	Genus	Species	Common Name
Lepidoptera	Noctuidea	*Feltia*	*herilis*	Master's dart moth
Lepidoptera	Noctuidea	*Feltia*	*jaculifera*	dingy cutworm moth
Lepidoptera	Noctuidea	*Feltia*	*subgothica*	subgothic dart moth
Lepidoptera	Noctuidea	*Feltia*	*tricosa*	confused dart moth
Lepidoptera	Noctuidea	*Helicoverpa*	*zeae*	corn earworm moth
Lepidoptera	Noctuidea	*Heliothis*	*subflexa*	subflexus straw moth
Lepidoptera	Noctuidea	*Himella*	*interactata*	intractable Quaker moth
Lepidoptera	Noctuidea	*Homorthodes*	*furfurata*	northern scurfy Quaker moth
Lepidoptera	Noctuidea	*Lycophotia*	*phyllophora*	phyllophora dart moth
Lepidoptera	Noctuidea	*Morrisonia*	*confusa*	confused woodgrain moth
Lepidoptera	Noctuidea	*Morrisonia*	*evicta*	bicolored woodgrain moth
Lepidoptera	Noctuidea	*Morrisonia*	*latex*	fluid arches moth
Lepidoptera	Noctuidea	*Nephelodes*	*minians*	bronzed cutworm moth
Lepidoptera	Noctuidea	*Ochropleura*	*implecta*	flame-shouldered dart moth
Lepidoptera	Noctuidea	*Orthodes*	*crenulata*	Buxton gum
Lepidoptera	Noctuidea	*Orthodes*	*cynica*	cynical Quaker moth
Lepidoptera	Noctuidea	*Orthodes*	*goodelli*	Goodell's arches moth
Lepidoptera	Noctuidea	*Orthosia*	*hibisci*	subdued Quaker moth
Lepidoptera	Noctuidea	*Orthosia*	*rubescens*	ruby Quaker moth
Lepidoptera	Noctuidea	*Peridroma*	*saucia*	variegated cutworm moth
Lepidoptera	Noctuidea	*Protolampra*	*brunneicollis*	brown collared dart
Lepidoptera	Noctuidea	*Pseudohermanassa*	*bicarnea*	pink-spotted dart moth
Lepidoptera	Noctuidea	*Pseudorthodes*	*vectors*	small brown Quaker moth
Lepidoptera	Noctuidea	*Pyrrhia*	*adela*	bordered sallow moth
Lepidoptera	Noctuidea	*Pyrrhia*	*exprimens*	purple-lined sallow moth
Lepidoptera	Noctuidea	*Richia*	*acclivis*	switchgrass dart
Lepidoptera	Noctuidea	*Schinia*	*rivulosa*	ragweed flower moth
Lepidoptera	Noctuidea	*Schinia*	*trifascia*	three-lined flower moth
Lepidoptera	Noctuidea	*Spaelotis*	*clandestina*	clandestine dart moth
Lepidoptera	Noctuidea	*Tricholita*	*signata*	signate Quaker moth
Lepidoptera	Noctuidea	*Trichosilia*	*geniculata*	knee-joint dart moth
Lepidoptera	Noctuidea	*Trichosilia*	*manifesta*	dart moth
Lepidoptera	Noctuidea	*Ulolonche*	*culea*	sheathed Quaker moth
Lepidoptera	Noctuidea	*Xestia*	*dilucida*	dull reddish dart moth
Lepidoptera	Noctuidea	*Xestia*	*dolosa*	greater black-lettered dart
Lepidoptera	Noctuidea	*Xestia*	*elimata*	southern variable dart moth
Lepidoptera	Noctuidea	*Xestia*	*nomankana*	Norman's dart moth
Lepidoptera	Noctuidea	*Xestia*	*smithii*	Smith's dart moth
Lepidoptera	Noctuideae	*Lacinipolia*	*renigra*	bristly cutworm moth
Lepidoptera	Notodontidae	*Cerura*	*scitiscripta*	black-etched prominent (formerly *cerura scitiscripta*)
Lepidoptera	Notodontidae	*Clostera*	*albosigma*	sigmoid prominent moth
Lepidoptera	Notodontidae	*Clostera*	*inclusa*	angle-lined prominent moth
Lepidoptera	Notodontidae	*Dasylophia*	*anguina*	serpent gourd
Lepidoptera	Notodontidae	*Dasylophia*	*thyatiroides*	gray patched prominent
Lepidoptera	Notodontidae	*Datana*	*angusii*	Mona Vale onion orchid
Lepidoptera	Notodontidae	*Datana*	*contracta*	prairie cupgrass
Lepidoptera	Notodontidae	*Datana*	*drexelii*	Megalichthy's mullisoni
Lepidoptera	Notodontidae	*Datana*	*intergerrima*	spicy jatropha
Lepidoptera	Notodontidae	*Datana*	*ministra*	yellow-necked caterpillar
Lepidoptera	Notodontidae	*Datana*	*perspicua*	transparent lamellaria
Lepidoptera	Notodontidae	*Ellida*	*caniplaga*	linden prominent

Order	Family	Genus	Species	Common Name
Lepidoptera	Notodontidae	*Furcula*	*borealis*	white furcula moth
Lepidoptera	Notodontidae	*Furcula*	*cinerea*	gray furcula moth
Lepidoptera	Notodontidae	*Gluphisia*	*septentrionis*	common gluphisia moth
Lepidoptera	Notodontidae	*Heterocampa*	*biundata*	wavy-lined heterocampa moth
Lepidoptera	Notodontidae	*Heterocampa*	*guttivitta*	maple prominent moth
Lepidoptera	Notodontidae	*Heterocampa*	*obliqua*	oblique heterocampa
Lepidoptera	Notodontidae	*Heterocampa*	*subrotata*	colour sergeant
Lepidoptera	Notodontidae	*Heterocampa*	*umbrata*	band-winged dragonlet
Lepidoptera	Notodontidae	*Hyparpax*	*aurora*	pink prominent
Lepidoptera	Notodontidae	*Hyperaeschra*	*georgica*	Georgian prominent
Lepidoptera	Notodontidae	*Lochmaeus*	*bilineata*	double-lined prominent
Lepidoptera	Notodontidae	*Lochmaeus*	*manteo*	variable oakleaf caterpillar moth
Lepidoptera	Notodontidae	*Macrurocampa*	*marthesia*	mottled prominent
Lepidoptera	Notodontidae	*Misogada*	*unicolor*	drab prominent
Lepidoptera	Notodontidae	*Nadata*	*gibbosa*	white-dotted prominent moth
Lepidoptera	Notodontidae	*Nerice*	*binentata*	double-toothed prominent moth
Lepidoptera	Notodontidae	*Oligocentria*	*lignicolor*	white-streaked prominent
Lepidoptera	Notodontidae	*Oligocentria*	*semirufescens*	red-washed prominent moth
Lepidoptera	Notodontidae	*Peridea*	*angulosa*	angulose prominent
Lepidoptera	Notodontidae	*Peridea*	*basitriens*	oval-based prominent moth
Lepidoptera	Notodontidae	*Peridea*	*ferruginea*	chocolate prominent moth
Lepidoptera	Notodontidae	*Pheosia*	*rimosa*	black-rimmed prominent moth
Lepidoptera	Notodontidae	*Schizura*	*apicalis*	plain schizura
Lepidoptera	Notodontidae	*Schizura*	*badia*	chestnut schizura
Lepidoptera	Notodontidae	*Schizura*	*concinna*	red-humped caterpillar moth
Lepidoptera	Notodontidae	*Schizura*	*ipomoeae*	morning-glory prominent moth
Lepidoptera	Notodontidae	*Schizura*	*leptinoides*	black-blotched schizura moth
Lepidoptera	Notodontidae	*Schizura*	*unicornis*	unicorn caterpillar moth
Lepidoptera	Notodontidae	*Symmerista*	*albifrons*	white-headed prominent
Lepidoptera	Notodontidae	*Symmerista*	*canicosta*	red-humped oakworm moth
Lepidoptera	Notodontidae	*Symmerista*	*leucitys*	orange-humped oakworm moth
Lepidoptera	Oecophoridae	*Antaeotricha*	*osseella*	grass miner moth
Lepidoptera	Oecophoridae	*Antaeotricha*	*schlaegeri*	Schlaeger's fruitworm moth
Lepidoptera	Oecophoridae	*Decantha*	*boreasella*	decantha boreasella
Lepidoptera	Oecophoridae	*Epicallima*	*argenticinctella*	orange-headed epicallima moth
Lepidoptera	Oecophoridae	*Fabiola*	*edithella*	concealer moth
Lepidoptera	Oecophoridae	*Fabiola*	*shaleriella*	concealer moth
Lepidoptera	Plusiinae	*Abrostola*	*ovalis*	oval nettle moth
Lepidoptera	Plusiinae	*Abrostola*	*urentis*	spectacled nettle moth
Lepidoptera	Plusiinae	*Allagrapha*	*aerea*	unspotted looper moth
Lepidoptera	Plusiinae	*Anagrapha*	*falcifera*	celery looper moth
Lepidoptera	Plusiinae	*Argyrogramma*	*verruca*	golden looper moth
Lepidoptera	Plusiinae	*Autographa*	*californica*	alfalfa looper moth
Lepidoptera	Plusiinae	*Autographa*	*precationis*	common looper moth
Lepidoptera	Plusiinae	*Baileya*	*australis*	small baileya moth
Lepidoptera	Plusiinae	*Baileya*	*dormitans*	sleeping Bailey's moth
Lepidoptera	Plusiinae	*Baileya*	*frigidana*	frigid midget
Lepidoptera	Plusiinae	*Baileya*	*levitans*	pale baileya moth
Lepidoptera	Plusiinae	*Baileya*	*nilotica*	acacia nilotica
Lepidoptera	Plusiinae	*Baileya*	*ophthalmica*	eyed baileya moth
Lepidoptera	Plusiinae	*Chrysanympha*	*formosa*	formosa looper moth
Lepidoptera	Plusiinae	*Chrysodeixis*	*includens*	soybean looper moth

Order	Family	Genus	Species	Common Name
Lepidoptera	Plusiinae	*Diachrysia*	*balluca*	green-patched looper moth
Lepidoptera	Plusiinae	*Enigmogramma*	*basigera*	pink-washed looper moth
Lepidoptera	Plusiinae	*Eosphoropteryx*	*thyatyroides*	pink-patched looper moth
Lepidoptera	Plusiinae	*Eutelia*	*pulcherrimus*	beautiful eutelia
Lepidoptera	Plusiinae	*Marathyssa*	*basalis*	light marathyssa moth
Lepidoptera	Plusiinae	*Megaloprapha*	*biloba*	bilobed looper moth
Lepidoptera	Plusiinae	*Meganola*	*minuscula*	confused meganola moth
Lepidoptera	Plusiinae	*Nola*	*cereella*	sorghum webworm
Lepidoptera	Plusiinae	*Nola*	*cilicoides*	blurry-patched nola moth
Lepidoptera	Plusiinae	*Paectes*	*abrostoloides*	large paectes moth
Lepidoptera	Plusiinae	*Paectes*	*oculatrix*	eyed paectes moth
Lepidoptera	Plusiinae	*Paectes*	*pygmaea*	pygmy paetes moth
Lepidoptera	Plusiinae	*Trichoplusia*	*ni*	cabbage looper moth
Lepidoptera	Pterophoridae	*Adaina*	*ambrosiae*	ambrosia plume moth
Lepidoptera	Pterophoridae	*Emmelina*	*monodactyla*	morning-glory plume moth
Lepidoptera	Pterophoridae	*Geina*	*tenuidactylus*	Himmelman's plume moth
Lepidoptera	Pterophoridae	*Gillmeria*	*pallidactyla*	plume moth
Lepidoptera	Pterophoridae	*Hellinsia*	*inquinatus*	plume moth
Lepidoptera	Pterophoridae	*Paraplatyptillia*	*auriga*	pterophorid moth
Lepidoptera	Saturniidae	*Actias*	*luna*	luna moth
Lepidoptera	Saturniidae	*Anisota*	*senatoria*	orange-striped oakworm moth
Lepidoptera	Saturniidae	*Anisota*	*stigma*	spiny oakworm moth
Lepidoptera	Saturniidae	*Anisota*	*virginiensis*	pink-striped oakworm moth
Lepidoptera	Saturniidae	*Antheraea*	*polyphemus*	polyphemus moth
Lepidoptera	Saturniidae	*Automeris*	*io*	io moth
Lepidoptera	Saturniidae	*Callosamia*	*angulifera*	tulip tree silk moth
Lepidoptera	Saturniidae	*Callosamia*	*promethea*	promethea silk moth
Lepidoptera	Saturniidae	*Dryocampa*	*rubicunda*	rosy maple moth
Lepidoptera	Saturniidae	*Hyalophora*	*cecropia*	cecropia silk moth
Lepidoptera	Saturniidae	*Sphingicampa*	*bicolor*	honey locust moth
Lepidoptera	Saturniidae	*Sphingicampa*	*bisecta*	bisected honey locust moth
Lepidoptera	Sessiidae	*Albuna*	*fraxini*	Virginia creeper clearwing moth
Lepidoptera	Sessiidae	*Alcathoe*	*caudata*	clematis clearwing moth
Lepidoptera	Sessiidae	*Carmenta*	*bassiformis*	eupatorium borer moth
Lepidoptera	Sessiidae	*Paranthrene*	*dollii*	Doll's clearwing moth
Lepidoptera	Sessiidae	*Paranthrene*	*simulans*	hornet clearwing
Lepidoptera	Sessiidae	*Paranthrene*	*tabaniformis*	European poplar clearwing moth
Lepidoptera	Sessiidae	*Podosesia*	*aureocincta*	clearwing moth
Lepidoptera	Sessiidae	*Podosesia*	*syringae*	lilac borer moth
Lepidoptera	Sessiidae	*Synathedon*	*acerni*	maple callus borer moth
Lepidoptera	Sessiidae	*Synathedon*	*acerrubri*	maple clearwing moth
Lepidoptera	Sessiidae	*Synathedon*	*decipiens*	clearwing moth
Lepidoptera	Sessiidae	*Synathedon*	*exitiosa*	peach tree borer moth
Lepidoptera	Sessiidae	*Synathedon*	*pictipes*	lesser peach tree borer moth
Lepidoptera	Sessiidae	*Synathedon*	*rileyana*	Riley's clearwing moth
Lepidoptera	Sessiidae	*Synathedon*	*rubrofascia*	tupelo clearwing moth
Lepidoptera	Sessiidae	*Synathedon*	*scitula*	dogwood borer moth
Lepidoptera	Sessiidae	*Vitacea*	*polistiformis*	grape root borer moth
Lepidoptera	Sphingidae	*Amorpha or Laothoe*	*juglandis*	walnut sphinx moth
Lepidoptera	Sphingidae	*Amphion*	*floridensis*	Nessus sphinx moth
Lepidoptera	Sphingidae	*Argrius*	*cingulata*	pink-spotted hawk moth
Lepidoptera	Sphingidae	*Ceratomia*	*amyntor*	elm sphinx moth

Order	Family	Genus	Species	Common Name
Lepidoptera	Sphingidae	*Ceratomia*	*catalpae*	catalpa hornworm
Lepidoptera	Sphingidae	*Ceratomia*	*hageni*	Hagen's sphinx
Lepidoptera	Sphingidae	*Ceratomia*	*undulosa*	waved sphinx moth
Lepidoptera	Sphingidae	*Darapsa*	*myron*	Virginia creeper sphinx
Lepidoptera	Sphingidae	*Darapsa*	*versicolor*	Malassezia furfur
Lepidoptera	Sphingidae	*Deidamia*	*inscriptum*	lettered sphinx
Lepidoptera	Sphingidae	*Eumorpha*	*fasciata*	mottled sea hare
Lepidoptera	Sphingidae	*Eumorpha*	*pandorus*	pandora sphinx moth
Lepidoptera	Sphingidae	*Hemaris*	*diffinis*	snowberry clearwing
Lepidoptera	Sphingidae	*Hemaris*	*thysbe*	hummingbird clearwing
Lepidoptera	Sphingidae	*Lapara*	*coniferarum*	southern pine sphinx
Lepidoptera	Sphingidae	*Manduca*	*jasminearum*	ash sphinx
Lepidoptera	Sphingidae	*Manduca*	*quinquemaculata*	five-spotted hawk moth
Lepidoptera	Sphingidae	*Manduca*	*rustica*	rustic sphinx
Lepidoptera	Sphingidae	*Manduca*	*sexta*	Carolina sphinx
Lepidoptera	Sphingidae	*Pachysphinx*	*modesta*	big poplar sphinx moth
Lepidoptera	Sphingidae	*Paonias*	*excaecatus*	blinded sphinx moth
Lepidoptera	Sphingidae	*Paonias*	*myops*	small-eyed sphinx moth
Lepidoptera	Sphingidae	*Smerinthus*	*jamaicensis*	twin-spotted sphinx moth
Lepidoptera	Sphingidae	*Sphecodina*	*abbotti*	Abbott's sphinx
Lepidoptera	Sphingidae	*Sphinx*	*canadensis*	Canadian sphinx moth
Lepidoptera	Sphingidae	*Sphinx*	*chersis*	great ash sphinx moth
Lepidoptera	Sphingidae	*Sphinx*	*drupiferarum*	wild cherry sphinx moth
Lepidoptera	Sphingidae	*Sphinx*	*gordius*	apple sphinx moth
Lepidoptera	Thyrididae	*Dysodia*	*oculatana*	eyed dysodia moth
Lepidoptera	Thyrididae	*Pseudothyris*	*sepulchralis*	mournful thyris moth
Lepidoptera	Thyrididae	*Thyris*	*maculata*	spotted thyris moth
Lepidoptera	Tineoidae	*Acrolophus*	*arcanella*	Clemens's grass tubeworm moth
Lepidoptera	Tineoidae	*Astrotischeris*	*astericola*	trumpet leafminer moth
Lepidoptera	Tineoidae	*Dyseriocrania*	*griseocaptella*	chinquapin leafminer moth
Lepidoptera	Tineoidae	*Tegeticula*	*yuccasella*	yucca moth
Lepidoptera	Tortricidae	*Acleris*	*chalybeana*	lesser maple leafroller moth
Lepidoptera	Tortricidae	*Acleris*	*subnivana*	tortricid moth
Lepidoptera	Tortricidae	*Bactra*	*furfurana*	mottled marble
Lepidoptera	Tortricidae	*Bactra*	*verutana*	javelin moth
Lepidoptera	Tortricidae	*Chimoptesis*	*pennsylvaniana*	tortricid moth
Lepidoptera	Tortricidae	*Endothenia*	*heinrichi*	tortricid moth
Lepidoptera	Tortricidae	*Endothenia*	*montanana*	tortricid moth
Lepidoptera	Tortricidae	*Episimus*	*argutana*	sumac leaftier moth
Lepidoptera	Tortricidae	*Paralobesia*	*carduana*	paralobesia carduana
Lepidoptera	Tortricidae	*Paralobesia*	*liriodendrana*	tulip tree leaftier moth
Lepidoptera	Tortricidae	*Paralobesia*	*slingerlandana*	tortricid moth
Lepidoptera	Tortricidae	*Paralobesia*	*viteana*	grape-berry moth
Lepidoptera	Yponomeutidae	*Atteva*	*aurea*	ailanthus webworm moth
Lepidoptera	Yponomeutidae	*Yponomeuta*	*multipunctella*	American ermine moth
Lepidoptera	Zygaenidae	*Harrisina*	*americana*	grapeleaf skeletonizer moth

BUTTERFLIES

Order	Family	Genus	Species	Common Name
Lepidoptera	Hesperiidae	*Amblyscirtes*	*vialis*	common roadside skipper
Lepidoptera	Hesperiidae	*Ancyloxypha*	*numitor*	common least skipper
Lepidoptera	Hesperiidae	*Archalarus*	*lyciades*	hoary edge
Lepidoptera	Hesperiidae	*Atalopedes*	*campestris*	sachem

Order	Family	Genus	Species	Common Name
Lepidoptera	Hesperiidae	*Epargyreus*	*clarus*	silver-spotted skipper
Lepidoptera	Hesperiidae	*Erynnis*	*baptisiae*	wild indigo duskywing
Lepidoptera	Hesperiidae	*Erynnis*	*brizo*	sleepy duskywing
Lepidoptera	Hesperiidae	*Erynnis*	*horatius*	Horace's duskywing
Lepidoptera	Hesperiidae	*Erynnis*	*icelus*	dreamy duskywing
Lepidoptera	Hesperiidae	*Erynnis*	*juvenalis*	Juvenal's duskywing
Lepidoptera	Hesperiidae	*Euphyes*	*vestris*	dun skipper
Lepidoptera	Hesperiidae	*Hylephila*	*phyleus*	fiery skipper
Lepidoptera	Hesperiidae	*Lerema*	*accius*	clouded skipper
Lepidoptera	Hesperiidae	*Pholisora*	*catullus*	common sootywing
Lepidoptera	Hesperiidae	*Poanes*	*hobomok*	hobomok skipper
Lepidoptera	Hesperiidae	*Poanes*	*zabulon*	zabulon skipper
Lepidoptera	Hesperiidae	*Polites*	*origenes*	crossline skipper
Lepidoptera	Hesperiidae	*Polites*	*peckius*	Peck's skipper
Lepidoptera	Hesperiidae	*Polites*	*themistocles*	tawny-edged skipper
Lepidoptera	Hesperiidae	*Pompeius*	*verna*	little glassywing
Lepidoptera	Hesperiidae	*Thorybes*	*bathyllus*	southern cloudywing
Lepidoptera	Hesperiidae	*Thorybes*	*pylades*	northern cloudywing
Lepidoptera	Hesperiidae	*Wallengrenia*	*egeremet*	northern broken dash
Lepidoptera	Hesperiidae	*Wallengrenia*	*otho*	southern broken dash
Lepidoptera	Lycaenidae	*Celastrina*	*ladon*	spring azure
Lepidoptera	Lycaenidae	*Celastrina*	*neglecta*	summer azure
Lepidoptera	Lycaenidae	*Cupido*	*comyntas*	eastern tailed-blue
Lepidoptera	Lycaenidae	*Feniseca*	*tarquinius*	harvester
Lepidoptera	Lycaenidae	*Satyrium*	*calanus*	banded hairstreak
Lepidoptera	Lycaenidae	*Satyrium*	*liparops*	striped hairstreak
Lepidoptera	Nymphalidae	*Asterocampa*	*celtis*	hackberry emperor
Lepidoptera	Nymphalidae	*Boloria*	*bellona*	meadow fritillary
Lepidoptera	Nymphalidae	*Cercyonis*	*pegala*	common wood nymph
Lepidoptera	Nymphalidae	*Chlosyne*	*nycteis*	silvery checkerspot
Lepidoptera	Nymphalidae	*Danaus*	*plexippus*	monarch butterfly
Lepidoptera	Nymphalidae	*Junonia*	*coenia*	common buckeye
Lepidoptera	Nymphalidae	*Lethe*	*anthedon*	northern pearly-eye
Lepidoptera	Nymphalidae	*Limenitis*	*archippus*	viceroy
Lepidoptera	Nymphalidae	*Limenitis*	*arthemis*	red-spotted purple
Lepidoptera	Nymphalidae	*Megisto*	*cymela*	little wood satyr
Lepidoptera	Nymphalidae	*Nymphalis*	*antiopa*	mourning cloak
Lepidoptera	Nymphalidae	*Phyciodes*	*tharos*	pearl crescent
Lepidoptera	Nymphalidae	*Polygonia*	*comma*	eastern comma
Lepidoptera	Nymphalidae	*Polygonia*	*interrogationis*	question mark
Lepidoptera	Nymphalidae	*Speyeria*	*aphrodite*	Aphrodite fritillary
Lepidoptera	Nymphalidae	*Speyeria*	*cybele*	great spangled fritillary
Lepidoptera	Nymphalidae	*Vanessa*	*atalanta*	red admiral
Lepidoptera	Nymphalidae	*Vanessa*	*cardui*	painted lady
Lepidoptera	Nymphalidae	*Vanessa*	*virginiensis*	American lady
Lepidoptera	Papilionidae	*Battus*	*philenor*	pipe-vine swallowtail
Lepidoptera	Papilionidae	*Eurytides*	*marcellus*	zebra swallowtail
Lepidoptera	Papilionidae	*Papilio*	*glaucus*	eastern tiger swallowtail
Lepidoptera	Papilionidae	*Papilio*	*polyxenes*	black swallowtail
Lepidoptera	Papilionidae	*Papilio*	*troilus*	spicebush swallowtail
Lepidoptera	Pieridae	*Anthocharis*	*midea*	falcate orange tip
Lepidoptera	Pieridae	*Colias*	*eurytheme*	orange sulphur

BUTTERFLIES *(continued)*

Order	Family	Genus	Species	Common Name
Lepidoptera	Pieridae	*Colias*	*philodice*	clouded sulphur
Lepidoptera	Pieridae	*Pieris*	*rapae*	cabbage white
Lepidoptera	Pieridae	*Pieris*	*virginiensis*	West Virginia white

Orthoptera (Grasshoppers, Crickets, and Singing Insects)

Order	Family	Genus	Species	Common Name
Orthoptera	Trigonidiidae	*Allonemobius*	*socius*	Southern ground cricket
Orthoptera	Trigonidiidae	*Allonemobius*	*tinnulus*	Tinkling ground cricket
Orthoptera	Tettigoniidae	*Amblycorypha*	*rotundifolia*	Rattler round-winged katydid
Orthoptera	Trigonidiidae	*Anaxipha*	*exigua*	Say's trig
Orthoptera	Rhaphidophoridae	*Ceuthophilus*	*sp.*	Camel cricket
Orthoptera	Trigonidiidae	*Eunemobius*	*carolinus*	Carolina ground cricket
Orthoptera	Trigonidiidae	*Eunemobius*	*confusus*	Confused ground cricket
Orthoptera	Tettigoniidae	*Microcentrum*	*retinerve*	Lesser angle-winged katydid
Orthoptera	Tettigoniidae	*Neoconocephalus*	*nebrascensis*	Nebraska conehead
Orthoptera	Trigonidiidae	*Neonemobius*	*variegatus*	Variegated ground cricket
Orthoptera	Cicadidae	*Neotibicen*	*linnei*	Linne's cicada
Orthoptera	Cicadidae	*Neotibicen*	*tibicen*	Swamp cicada
Orthoptera	Trigonidiidae	*Neoxabea*	*bipunctata*	Two-spotted tree cricket
Orthoptera	Trigonidiidae	*Oecanthus*	*exclamationis*	Davis's tree cricket
Orthoptera	Trigonidiidae	*Oecanthus*	*niveus*	Narrow-winged tree cricket
Orthoptera	Tettigoniidae	*Orchelimum*	*silvaticum*	Long-spurred meadow katydid
Orthoptera	Trigonidiidae	*Orocharis*	*saltator*	Jumping bush cricket
Orthoptera	Tettigoniidae	*Pterophylla*	*camellifolia*	Common true katydid
Orthoptera	Tettigoniidae	*Scudderia*	*furcata*	Fork-tailed bush katydid
Orthoptera	Tetrigida	*Tetrix*	*ornata*	Ornate pygmy grasshopper

AMPHIBIANS AND REPTILES

Genus	Species	Common Name
Lithobates	*sylvaticus*	Wood frog
Lithobates	*clamitans*	Green frog
Lithobates	*catesbeianus*	American bullfrog
Pseudacris	*crucifer*	Spring peeper
Acris	*blanchardi*	N. cricket frog
Hyla	*chrysoscelis*	Copes gray tree frog
Lithobates	*sphenocephalus*	Southern leopard frog
Lithobates	*pipiens*	Northern leopard frog
Anaxyrus	*americanus*	American toad
Plethodon	*cinereus*	Red-backed salamander
Eurycea	*cirrigera*	Southern two-lined salamander
Desmgnathus	*fuscus*	Northern dusky salamander
Plethodon	*dorsalis*	Northern zigzag salamander
Plethodon	*glutinosus*	Northern slimy salamander
Ambystoma	*opacum*	Marbled salamander
Eurycea	*longicauda*	Longtail salamander
Ambystoma	*jeffersonianum*	Jefferson salamander
Ambystoma	*maculatum*	Spotted salamander
Ambystoma	*tigrinum*	Tiger salamander
Notophthalmus	*viridescens*	Eastern newt
Ambystoma	*texanum*	Smallmouth salamander
Plestiodon	*fasciatus*	Five-lined skink
Chelydra	*serpentina*	Common snapping turtle
Terrapene	*carolina*	Eastern box turtle

Genus	Species	Common Name
Ophheodrys	*aestivus*	Rough green snake
Cotalus	*horridus*	Timber rattlesnake
Diadophis	*punctatus*	Ring-necked snake
Storeria	*occipitomaculata*	Red-bellied snake
Agkistrodon	*contortrix*	Copperhead
Pantheropus	*spiloides*	Gray rat snake
Thamnophis	*sirtalis*	Eastern garter snake
Carphophis	*amoenus*	Midwest worm snake
Nerodia	*sipedon*	Northern (banded) water snake
Coluber	*constrictor*	Black racer
Lampropeltis	*triangulum*	Eastern milk snake

SPIDERS

Family	Genus	Species
Agelenidae	*Agelenopsis*	*emertoni*
Agelenidae	*Agelenopsis*	*pennsylvanica*
Agelenidae	*Agelenopsis*	*potteri*
Agelenidae	*Agelenopsis*	*utahana*
Agelenidae	*Coras*	*juvenilis*
Agelenidae	*Wadotes*	*calcaratus*
Agelenidae	*Wadotes*	*hybridus*
Anyphaenidae	*Anyphaena*	*pectorosa*
Anyphaenidae	*Wulfila*	*saltabundus*
Araneidae	*Acanthepelra*	*stellata*
Araneidae	*Araneus*	*bicentenarius*
Araneidae	*Araneus*	*marmoreus*
Araneidae	*Cyclosa*	*conica*
Araneidae	*Eustala*	*anastera*
Araneidae	*Mangora*	*maculata*
Araneidae	*Mangora*	*placida*
Araneidae	*Metepeira*	*labyrinthea*
Araneidae	*Micrathena*	*gracilis*
Araneidae	*Micrathena*	*mitrata*
Araneidae	*Micrathena*	*sagittata*
Araneidae	*Neoscona*	*arabesca*
Araneidae	*Neoscona*	*crucifera*
Araneidae	*Ocrepeira*	*ectypa*
Araneidae	*Verrucosa*	*arenata*
Cheiracanthiidae	*Cheiracanthium*	*inclusum*
Clubionidae	*Clubiona*	*sp.*
Clubionidae	*Elaver*	*excepta*
Corinnidae	*Castianeira*	*cingulata*
Ctenidae	*Anahita*	*punctulata*
Cybaeidae	*Cybaeus*	*sp.*
Dictynidae	*Emblyna*	*zaba*
Dictynidae	*Lathys*	*immaculata*
Gnaphosidae	*Drassodes*	*neglectus*
Gnaphosidae	*Drassyllus*	*fallens*
Gnaphosidae	*Gnaphosa*	*fontinalis*
Gnaphosidae	*Herpyllus*	*ecclesiasticus*
Gnaphosidae	*Micaria*	*longipes*
Hahniidae	*Cicurina*	*arcuata*

SPIDERS (*continued*)

Family	Genus	Species
Hahniidae	*Hahnia*	*flaviceps*
Hahniidae	*Neoantistea*	*agilis*
Hahniidae	*Neoantistea*	*magna*

Halonoproctidae

Halonoproctidae	*Ummidia*	*tuobita*
Linyphiidae	*Agyneta*	*barrowsi*
Linyphiidae	*Agyneta*	*semipallida*
Linyphiidae	*Bathyphantes*	*alboventris*
Linyphiidae	*Bathyphantes*	*pallidus*
Linyphiidae	*Centromerus*	*latidens*
Linyphiidae	*Ceraticelus*	*fissiceps*
Linyphiidae	*Ceraticelus*	*sp.*
Linyphiidae	*Drapetisca*	*alteranda*
Linyphiidae	*Frontinella*	*pyramitela*
Linyphiidae	*Islandiana*	*longisetosa*
Linyphiidae	*Lepthyphantes*	*turbatrix*
Linyphiidae	*Mermessus*	*maculatus*
Linyphiidae	*Pityohyphantes*	*costatus*
Linyphiidae	*Styloctetor*	*purpurescens*
Liocranidae	*Agroeca*	*sp.*
Lycosidae	*Allocosa*	*funerea*
Lycosidae	*Gladicosa*	*gulosa*
Lycosidae	*Gladicosa*	*pulchra*
Lycosidae	*Pardosa*	*lapidicina*
Lycosidae	*Pardosa*	*milvina*
Lycosidae	*Pirata*	*alachuus*
Lycosidae	*Pirata*	*sedentaris*
Lycosidae	*Piratula*	*insularis*
Lycosidae	*Piratula*	*minuta*
Lycosidae	*Schizocosa*	*crassipes*
Lycosidae	*Schizocosa*	*ocreata*
Lycosidae	*Schizocosa*	*saltatrix*
Lycosidae	*Tigrosa*	*aspersa*
Mysmenidae	*Maymena*	*ambita*
Oxyopidae	*Oxyopes*	*salticus*
Philodromidae	*Philodromus*	*imbecillus*
Philodromidae	*Philodromus*	*rufus*
Philodromidae	*Tibellus*	*sp.*
Phrurolithidae	*Phrurotimpus*	*alarius*
Phrurolithidae	*Phrurotimpus*	*borealis*
Phrurolithidae	*Scotinella*	*redempta*
Pisauridae	*Dolomedes*	*albineus*
Pisauridae	*Dolomedes*	*tenebrosus*
Pisauridae	*Dolomedes*	*triton*
Pisauridae	*Dolomedes*	*vittatus*
Pisauridae	*Pisaurina*	*brevipes*
Pisauridae	*Pisaurina*	*mira*
Salticidae	*Chinattus*	*parvulus*
Salticidae	*Colonus*	*puerperus*
Salticidae	*Colonus*	*sylvanus*
Salticidae	*Eris*	*militaris*

SPIDERS (*continued*)

Family	Genus	Species
Halonoproctidae		
Salticidae	*Hentzia*	*sp.*
Salticidae	*Maevia*	*inclemens*
Salticidae	*Pelegrina*	*galathea*
Salticidae	*Pelegrina*	*proterva*
Salticidae	*Phidippus*	*audax*
Salticidae	*Sassacus*	*sp.*
Salticidae	*Zygoballus*	*rufipes*
Segestriidae	*Ariadna*	*bicolor*
Tetragnathidae	*Leucauge*	*venusta*
Tetragnathidae	*Tetragnatha*	*elongata*
Tetragnathidae	*Tetragnatha*	*versicolor*
Theridiidae	*Argyrodes*	*sp.*
Theridiidae	*Crustulina*	*altera*
Theridiidae	*Cryptachaea*	*porteri*
Theridiidae	*Dipoena*	*nigra*
Theridiidae	*Enoplognatha*	*caricis*
Theridiidae	*Faiditus*	*globosus*
Theridiidae	*Latrodectus*	*variolus*
Theridiidae	*Neospintharus*	*trigonum*
Theridiidae	*Parasteatoda*	*tabulata*
Theridiidae	*Pholcomma*	*hirsutum*
Theridiidae	*Phylloneta*	*pictipes*
Theridiidae	*Robertus*	*frontatus*
Theridiidae	*Steatoda*	*triangulosa*
Theridiidae	*Theridion*	*albidum*
Theridiidae	*Theridion*	*cheimatos*
Theridiidae	*Theridion*	*fronduem*
Theridiidae	*Theridion*	*murarium*
Theridiidae	*Theridula*	*opulenta*
Theridiidae	*Thymoites*	*marxi*
Theridiidae	*Thymoites*	*unimaculata*
Theridiidae	*Yunohamella*	*lyrica*
Theridiosomatidae	*Theridiosoma*	*gemmosum*
Thomisidae	*Misumena*	*vatia*
Thomisidae	*Tmarus*	*angulatus*
Thomisidae	*Xysticus*	*ferox*
Thomisidae	*Xysticus*	*fraternus*
Titanoecidae	*Titanoeca*	*brunnea*
Uloboridae	*Hyptiotes*	*sp.*
Uloboridae	*Uloborus*	*sp.*

AQUATIC SPECIES

Order	Family	Genus	Species	Common Name
Amphipoda	Gammaridae	*Gammarus*	*sp.*	scud
Coleoptera	Dryopidae	*Helichus*	*basalis*	long-toed water beetle
Coleoptera	Dryopidae	*Helichus*	*striatus*	long-toed water beetle
Coleoptera	Dytiscidae	*Acilius*	*mediatus*	predaceous diving beetle
Coleoptera	Dytiscidae	*Agabus*	*sp.*	predaceous diving beetle
Coleoptera	Dytiscidae	*Agabus*	*sp.*	predaceous diving beetle
Coleoptera	Dytiscidae	*Heterosternuta*	*wickhami*	predaceous diving beetle
Coleoptera	Dytiscidae	*Hydaticus*	*sp.*	predaceous diving beetle

Order	Family	Genus	Species	Common Name
Coleoptera	Dytiscidae	*Hydroporus*	*sp.*	predaceous diving beetle
Coleoptera	Hydrophilidae	*Cymbiodyta*	*sp.*	water scavenger beetle
Decapoda	Cambaridae	*Cambarus*	*sp.*	crayfish
Decapoda	Cambaridae	*Orconectes*	*sp.*	crayfish
Diptera	Chironomidae	*Chironomidae*	*sp.*	midge
Diptera	Tipulidae	*Hexatoma*	*sp.*	crane fly
Diptera	Tipulidae	*Tipula (Nippotipula)*	*sp.*	large crane fly
Ephemeroptera	Heptagenidae	*Heptagenia*	*sp.*	flatheaded mayfly
Ephemeroptera	Leptophlebiidae	*Paraleptophlebia*	*sp.*	prong-gilled mayfly
Hemiptera	Corixidae	*Sigara*	*sp.*	water boatman
Hemiptera	Gerridae	*Aquarius*	*remigis*	water strider
Hemiptera	Veliidae	*Microvelia*	*sp.*	smaller water strider
Isopoda	Asellidae	*Lirceus*	*sp.*	sow bug
Megaloptera	Sialidae	*Sialis*	*sp.*	alderfly
Odonata	Cordulegastridae	*Cordulegaster*	*obliqua*	arrowhead spiketail
Plecoptera	Chloroperlidae	*Alloperla*	*sp.*	green stone fly
Plecoptera	Perlidae	*Acroneuria*	*sp.*	golden stone fly
Plecoptera	Perlidae	*Agnetina*	*sp.*	common stone fly
Trichoptera	Lepidostomatidae	*Lepidostoma*	*sommermanae*	bizarre caddis fly
Trichoptera	Limnephilidae	*Ironoquia*	*sp.*	northern caddis fly
Trichoptera	Limnephilidae	*Pseudostenophylax*	northern caddis fly	
Trichoptera	Phryganeidae	*Ptilostomis*	*sp.*	giant casemaker
Trichoptera	Phyganeidae	*Oligostomis*	*ocelligera*	giant casemaker
Trichoptera	Psychomyiidae	*Psychomyia*	*flavida*	net tube caddis fly

FISH SPECIES

Genus	Species	Common Name
Chrosomus	*erythrogaster*	southern redbelly dace
Semotilus	*atromaculatus*	creek chub
Percina	*sciera*	dusky darter
Etheostoma	*spectabile*	orangethroat darter
Pimephales	*notatus*	bluntnose minnow
Rhinichthys	*obtusus*	western blacknose dace
Campostoma	*anomalum*	central stone roller
Moxostoma	*sp.*	redhorse sucker
Campostoma	*anomalum*	central stone roller
Catostomus	*commersonii*	white sucker

MAMMALS

Genus	Species	Common Name
Odocoileus	*virginianus*	white-tailed deer
Procyon	*lotor*	raccoon
Lynx	*rufus*	bobcat
Canis	*latrans*	coyote
Vulpes	*vulpes*	red fox
Neovison	*vison*	mink
Mephitis	*mephitis*	striped skunk
Didelphis	*virginiana*	Virginia opossum
Scalopus	*aquaticus*	eastern mole
Sorex	*fumeus*	smoky shrew
Blarina	*brevicauda*	short-tailed shrew
Sorex	*longirostris*	southeastern shrew

MAMMALS (*continued*)

Genus	Species	Common Name
Sorex	*hoyi*	pygmy shrew
Sylvilagus	*floridanus*	eastern cottontail
Glaucomys	*volans*	southern flying squirrel
Tamias	*striatus*	eastern chipmunk
Tamiasciurus	*hudsonicus*	red squirrel
Sciurus	*niger*	fox squirrel
Sciurus	*carolinesis*	gray squirrel
Microtus	*pinetorum*	woodland vole
Peromyscus	*leucopus*	white-footed mouse

APPENDIX 2

Ecoblitz Participants

Beyond the ecology experts highlighted in this book, the Indiana Forest Alliance's multiyear forest inventory required the dedication of many individuals. While we could not profile all involved, Indiana Forest Alliance (IFA) is sincerely grateful to all those who assisted with this effort, shedding light on the complexity of life in the forest and documenting the value of the Morgan-Monroe/Yellowwood Back Country Area as a storehouse of life.

Special recognition is given for the contributions of:

- Tim Maloney, former senior policy director of the Hoosier Environmental Council, who helped conceive of the Ecoblitz, served on many of the survey teams, and cochaired the entire Ecoblitz census with IFA's Jeff Stant.
- Dr. Tim Rice, who helped lead teams of students from St. Joseph's College in the herp surveys, donated and provided the fish shocker for the fish survey, and took part in bird surveys.
- Ron Kerner, who put in many hours identifying and photographing fungi throughout the Ecoblitz area.
- Steven Dunbar, David Mow, Kevin Tungesvick, and Dr. Collin Hobbs, who walked through all types of terrain for miles across every one of the six zones in the Ecoblitz area more than once to identify vascular plants and continually update a burgeoning list of finds.
- Drs. David LeBlanc and Darrin Rubino, who put in many hours bushwacking across the forest to take tree cores and saw "cookie" profiles from logs, respectively, and Jerome Delbridge, who extensively participated in the forest characterization surveys.
- Ross Carlson, who led the macroinvertebrate surveys for two years and reported on those surveys, and Dr. Richard Miller, who assisted in those surveys.

- Dr. Jeff Holland and Michael Brattain, whose surveys for two years identified 172 beetles in the taxonomic group containing the highest number of insect species found in the Ecoblitz.
- Jim Jean, who participated in many of the surveys and whose knowledge of the woods and unrelenting effort located an Indiana bat maternity roost that biologists were previously unable to find.
- Heather Millbrath and Nick Asher, who participated from the beginning to the end of the herp team's three years of surveys, and Geoff Keller, who lent his expertise participating in surveys of the herp, bird, and bryophyte teams.
- Brad Jackson, Lee Casebere, Donna Yates, Derek Coomer, Nancy Lightfoot, Scott Evans, Joe Bailey, and Jess Guin, who put in many hours over three years on the bird surveys.

Experts, Team Leaders, and Consultants

First Name	Last Name	Survey Teams/Expertise	Affiliations
Bob	Ball	Aquatic macroinvertebrates team/ stream biology	Indiana Department of Natural Resources, retired
Jeffrey	Belth	Butterfly team leader/lepidopterist	Author of *Butterflies of Indiana: A Field Guide*
Leslie	Bishop	Forest characterization and spider team leader/arachnologist	Professor emeritus, Earlham College
Aimee	Bjornstad	Small mammals and bat survey, 2014	Assistant, Orbis Environmental Consulting
Robert	Brodman	Herp team leader/herpetologist	Professor of biology, St. Joseph College
T. Travis	Brown	Bird team/research biologist	Senior ecologist, West Inc.
Ross	Carlson	Aquatic macroinvertebrate team leader/stream biology	Office of Water Quality, Indiana Department of Environmental Management
Roger	Carter	Herp team leader/herpetology	Hoosier Herpetological Society
Lee	Casebere	Bird team/ornithology	Division of Nature Preserves, Indiana Department of Natural Resources, retired
Linda	Cole	Bryophyte team leader/bryology	Self-taught expert on mosses and liverworts, Brown County
Angela	Chamberlain	Small mammals survey assistant to Dr. Whitaker, 2015/mammalogist	Mammalogy Research Associate, Indiana State University
Angela	Dämm	Bird team/ornithology	Assistant to 2017 cerulean warbler survey
Jerome	Delbridge	Forest characterization team/tree expert	Certified professional arborist, Tree-Centric
Steven	Dunbar	Naturalist with vascular plant, insect, and bryophyte teams	Formerly with Indiana Department of Natural Resources
Brian	Foster	Spider team/arachnology	Laboratory manager, Indiana State University
Rod	Goforth	Bird team leader/ornithology	High school teacher, New Albany
Jeffrey	Holland	Beetles team leader/entomologist	Professor of entomology, Purdue University
F. Collin	Hobbs	Vascular plant team leader/ botanist	Assistant professor, Department of Biology, Huntington College

First Name	Last Name	Survey Teams/Expertise	Affiliations
Jim	Horton	Herp team leader/herpetology	Hoosier Herpetological Society
Brad	Jackson	Bird team leader/ornithology	Indiana Breeding Bird Atlas leader, high school teacher
Michelle	Jean	Bees and bats/entomology and mammalogy	Assistant, Environmental Solutions & Innovations Inc.
Robert	Jean	Bees team leader/entomologist	Environmental Solutions & Innovations Inc.
Geoff	Keller	Herpetofauna, bird, and bryophyte teams/expert in ornithology and herpetology	Frog preserve owner, Brown County, and recorder of bird calls and songs in the Cornell Ornithology Laboratory's Macaulay Library
Ron	Kerner	Mushroom team leader/mycology expert	Hoosier Mushroom Society
Leroy	Koehn	Moth team leader/lepidopterist	Self-taught expert and owner of Leptraps Inc.
David	LeBlanc	Forest characterization team/dendrochronology	Professor of ecology, Ball State University
James	Lendemer	Lichenologist	Curator, New York Botanical Garden
Mike	Litwin	Fish team leader/fisheries biologist	U.S. Fish and Wildlife Service, retired
Megan	Martin	Bat team/mammalogist	Environmental Solutions & Innovations Inc.
Justin	Maxwell	Forest characterization team/dendrochronology	Associate professor of geography, Indiana University
Dick	Miller	Aquatic macroinvertebrate team leader/limnologist	Professor of biology, Butler University, retired
Marc	Milne	Spider team/arachnologist	Associate professor of biology, University of Indianapolis
David	Mow	Plant team leader/botanist	Indiana Native Plant Society
Glené	Mynhardt	Insect team leader/entomologist	Associate professor of biology, Hanover College
Tim	Rice	Herpetofauna and fish teams/herpetologist and fish	Professor of biology, St. Joseph's College
Paul	Rothrock	Plant team leader/botanist	Associate research scientist emeritus, professor emeritus, and curator emeritus, Indiana University Herbarium
Darrin	Rubino	Forest characterization team/dendrochronology	Professor of biology, Hanover College
Don	Ruch	Plant team/botanist	Professor of biology, Ball State University, past president, Indiana Academy of Science
David	Rupp	Bird team leader/ornithologist	Owner/operator, IndiGo Birding Tours
Steve	Russell	Fungi team leader/mycologist	Founder, Hoosier Mushroom Society, and Ph.D. candidate, Purdue University
Jeremy	Sheets	Small mammals survey, 2014/mammalogist	Orbis Environmental Consulting
Angie	Shelton	Spider and vascular plant teams/ecologist	Research scientist at the Research and Teaching Preserve, Indiana University Bloomington
Dale	Sparks	Mammalogist	Environmental Solutions & Innovations Inc. and Indiana State University
Carl A.	Strang	Singing insect team leader/entomologist	Ph.D. wildlife ecology, Purdue University, naturalist, DuPage County, Illinois
John	Taylor	Consultant to forest characterization team	Restoration ecologist, Ball State University

First Name	Last Name	Survey Teams/Expertise	Affiliations
Zach	Truelock	Herpetofauna team/herpetology	Volunteer
Kevin	Tungesvick	Plant team leader/botany	Senior ecologist, EcoLogic Inc.
John	Whitaker	Small mammals survey, 2015/ mammalogist	Professor emeritus, Indiana State University, founder of Center for Bat Research, Outreach, and Conservation, Indiana State University, author of *Mammals of Indiana* and numerous other publications on mammals

Indiana Forest Alliance Staff, Board, and Other Organization Leaders and Volunteers

First name	Last name	Role/team
Paula	Albers	Moths
⁂ Lacey	Alison	Herpetofauna
Catherine	Anders	Volunteer
Gary	Arbeiter	Birds
Nick	Asher	Herpetofauna
Giorgia	Auteri	Bats
◆ Zoe	Bachmann	Intern/insects
Joe	Bailey	Photographer/birds
Bob	Barber	Birds and butterflies
⁂ Tressa	Bartholomew	Herpetofauna
* Kristen	Becher	Volunteer
Alan	Belth	Butterflies
Sandy	Belth	Butterflies
Charlie	Bookwalter	Birds
* Mary	Bookwalter	Planning committee/birds, forest characterization, herpetofauna, insects, singing insects, and vascular plants
Michael	Brattain	Beetles
Austin	Broadwater	Bats
◆ Audrey	Brockman	Insects
Jack	Brubaker	Volunteer
** Paul	Bryan	Planning and site setup/birds and bats
Sam	Bryan	Produced maps of listed species locations/birds, herpetofauna, and bats
** Samantha	Buran	Planning committee, assistant to multiple teams/forest characterization
Alisha	Burcham	Birds
Grant	Burcham	Birds
⁂ Rose	Calhoun	Herpetofauna
* Vince	Caristo	Bryophytes
Holly	Carter	Herpetofauna
Jeremy	Caseltine	Herpetofauna
⁂ Alison	Chandler	Herpetofauna
⁂ Kristi	Chelius	Herpetofauna
Don	Clifford	Dendrochronology work on logs/forest characterization
* Natalie	Colbert	Volunteer
* Charlie	Cole	Birds

First Name	Last Name	Role/team
Myron	Cole	Bryophytes and vascular plants
Dana	Conner	Volunteer
Derek	Coomer	Birds
♦ Jordan	Craven	Insects
Erin	Crone	Hoosier Environmental Council (HEC) intern, assisted different teams/bats
Wendy	Croning	Birds
Megan	Cross	Moths
Denny	Currutt	Moths
Sadie	Dainko	Birds
✳Inga	Dainton	Herpetofauna
Nathan	Damm	Birds
* Angelo	Datillo	Birds
Jessica	Davis	HEC intern, drafted survey data collection forms
✳ Danielle	DeFries	Herpetofauna
Patty	Denison	Birds
Celina	DeVries	Herpetofauna
✳ Dana	Dolhide	Herpetofauna
Jeremy	Downs	Birds
Theresa	Duemler	Birds
Chad	Durant	Volunteer
✳ Chris	Ellington	Herpetofauna
✳ Logan	English	Herpetofauna
✳ Eyup	Erdogan	Herpetofauna
Dana	Ericson	Vascular plants and other
Scott	Evans	Photographer/birds
** Jason	Flickner	Staff and board, planning committee
Danielle	Follette	Vascular plants
Falon	French	HEC staff, cooked and brought food
Michael	Fulton	Bats
✳ Dalton	Good	Herpetofauna
✳ Megan	Gramhofer	Herpetofauna
Elizabeth	Grubb	Forest characterization
✳ Jordan	Guimond	Herpetofauna
Jess	Gwinn	Birds
Pat	Hammond	Herpetofauna
Gillian	Harris	Birds
♦ Zoe	Henry	Intern/insects
Ben	Hess	Vascular plants
Andrew	Hiday	Volunteer
Joe	Hiscox	Birds
Mark	Hoard	Dendrochronology work on logs/forest characterization
Kaitlin	Hosson	Volunteer
* Bill	Hurley	Herpetofauna
Mary	Hylton	Herpetofauna
Jeff	Hyman	Forest characterization and spiders
** Eric	Jagger	IFA intern from Manchester College/bats
Barbara	Janiak	Volunteer

First Name	Last Name	Role/team
* Jim	Jean	Planning committee/bats, bees, beetles, birds, insects, moths, small mammals, and vascular plants
Maya	Jenkins	Volunteer
Doug	Johnson	Forest characterization
Sarah	Johnson	Bats
Rebecca	Jordan	Spiders
＊ Mary	Keenan	Herpetofauna
＊ Payton	Kellenburger	Herpetofauna
＊ Vickie	Kennedy	Herpetofauna
Sharlene	Kipfer	Vascular plants
Bob	Kissel	Birds
Ashley	Kissick	Purdue University graduate student/beetles
Betty	Koehn	Moths
Josh	Kroot	Bats
**Anne	Laker	Photographed surveys
Art	Laker	Bats
Emily	Lessig	Insects
Nancy	Lightfoot	Birds
Joe	Lindsey	Volunteer
Ulla	Linenthal	Vascular plants
Rebecca	Lorenz	Volunteer
Julia	Lowe	Sierra Club Hoosier Chapter volunteer/forest characterization
Tim	Luttermoser	Purdue University graduate student/beetles
** Myke	Luurtsema	Planning committee/survey manager and stand-in leader for different teams
Heather	Mackinnon	Volunteer
Andrew	Mahoney	Birds and other
* Elizabeth	Mahoney	Birds, spiders, and other
Sandra	Malcolm	Volunteer
Tim	Maloney	Senior policy director, Hoosier Environmental Council, Ecoblitz cochair, planning committee/birds, bats, and other
＊ Katie	Manika	Herpetofauna
＊Anastasia	Marsh	Herpetofauna
Laura	Martin	Volunteer
Maria	Mastale	Volunteer
* Curt	Mayfield	Planning committee/bats, birds, forest characterization, herpetofauna, insects, and singing insects
Robert	McInteer	Dendrochronology work on logs/forest characterization
** Sandy	Messner	Assisted with planning and survey setup
* Joan	Middendorf	Birds
Heather	Millbrath	Herpetofauna
Leah	Milne	Spiders
Suzanne	Mittenthal	Bryophytes
** Audrey	Moore	Planning committee, spearheaded lunch and supply production, report editing and layout/plants
Donovan	Moxley	Volunteer
＊ Rick	Mullis	Herpetofauna
＊ Jenifer	Munson	Herpetofauna
＊ Jessica	Nagel	Herpetofauna

First Name	Last Name	Role/team
Bev	Ohneck-Holly	Volunteer
Bill	Okie	Dendrochronology work on logs/forest characterization
✳ Joel	Pearson	Herpetofauna
Kara	Phelps	Volunteer
Gareth	Powell	Beetles
Bowden	Quinn	Director, Sierra Club Hoosier Chapter/forest characterization
Crystal	Rensker	Vascular plants
Aleah	Roadruck	Bats
Kelly	Rockhill	Birds
✳ Allison	Roller	Herpetofauna
* Mary Kay	Rothert	Planning committee/forest characterization and other
✳ Evan	Saberhaus	Herpetofauna
Bob	Sander	Volunteer
Rosemary	Sauer	Birds
** Rae	Schnapp	Planning committee/forest characterization, birds, and other
Dale	Schoentrup	Herpetofauna
Clayton	Schulte	Volunteer
* Dave	Seastrom	Planning committee and meetup site preparation
Jim	Shackelford	Vascular plants
Cheryl	Shearer	Other
* Dave	Simcox	Forest characterization
Gavin	Simon	Bats
Allie	Skalnik	Volunteer, report writing and analysis
♦ Amelia	Smith	Insects
Karen	Smith	Birds and vascular plants
Megan	Smith	Volunteer
✳ Jessica	Sobers	Herpetofauna
** Jeff	Stant	IFA executive director, Ecoblitz cochair, lead organizer of surveys
Judy	Stewart	Bats
* Todd	Stewart	Bats
✳ Sydney	Strang	Herpetofauna
✳ Nathan	Stroup	Herpetofauna
♦ Samuel	Stryker	Intern/insects
Dennis	Tibbetts	Volunteer
Tom	Tokarski	Volunteer
Connor	Treacy	Volunteer
Michael	Trudeau	Volunteer
✳ Rebekkah	Vail	Herpetofauna
✳ Hanna	Van Meter	Herpetofauna
♦ Keaton	Veldkamp	Intern/insects
✳ Jacob	Villalpando	Herpetofauna
Elizabeth	Wagner	Insects
Todd	Wall	Volunteer
Kevin	Weinberg	Vascular plants
✳ Ethan	Weisgerber	Herpetofauna
✳ Marissa	Whitaker	Herpetofauna
Graeme	Wilson	Spiders
Donna	Yates	Birds

First Name	Last Name	Role/team
Dawn	York	Birds
Ryan	York	Birds
Tom	Zeller	Planning committee, site setup, birds and other
Shaun	Ziegler	Vascular plants

* IFA board member

** IFA staff member

❋ St. Joseph College student of Drs. Brodman and Rice

♦ Hanover College student or intern of Dr. Mynhardt

The Ecoblitz was truly a community effort. The entire Board of Directors and staff of IFA played some part in this census. I am grateful to every person—experts, volunteers, staff, and board—who gave their time in service of increasing knowledge about this forest.

—Jeffrey N. Stant, Co-Chair, Yellowwood/ Morgan-Monroe Back Country Area Ecoblitz, Executive Director, Indiana Forest Alliance

CONTRIBUTORS

JOHN A. BACONE received his bachelor of science degree from Eastern Illinois University with a double major in botany and zoology and a master of science degree in forest ecology from the University of Illinois. He was the first full-time professional naturalist at Turkey Run State Park. He then served as Central Illinois Regional Ecologist on the Illinois Natural Areas Inventory. He retired in 2019 after 40 years as Director of the Division of Nature Preserves, Indiana Department of Natural Resources.

LESLIE BISHOP, Professor Emerita of Biology at Earlham College, led the Ecoblitz spider team and served as a consulting scientist for the Indiana Forest Alliance from 2016 to 2019.

ANNE LAKER is a freelance writer and poet living in Indianapolis. She served as Director of Communications at the Indiana Forest Alliance (IFA) from 2016 to 2019, where she helped tell the story of IFA's Ecoblitz, and developed campaigns to engage Hoosiers in forest advocacy. In the fall and spring, she can be found primitive camping in the Hoosier National Forest.

JUSTIN MAXWELL is Associate Professor of Geography at Indiana University. His research bridges climate science and ecology by using dendrochronology to understand how past ecosystems responded to a range of climate and environmental factors, such as drought, precipitation, and temperature. He also uses dendrochronology to understand how climatic extremes impact forest ecosystems.

Deidre Pettinga has more than 30 years of experience in marketing, from both theoretical and applied perspectives. She holds a Ph.D. in media psychology and taught marketing at the University of Indianapolis for 20 years. In addition, she has served as Chief Marketing Officer for a national association and worked for a variety of for-profit and nonprofit organizations. From 2021 to 2023, she served as Director of Operations and Communications for the Indiana Forest Alliance. She has been published in a number of academic journals and coauthored four books on K–12 educational marketing.

David Rupp is the owner and guide for IndiGo Birding Nature Tours, which offers customized tours in Indiana and around the world. He has an M.S. in environmental science from the University of Idaho and a B.A. in biology from Goshen College.

Steve Russell is the president and founder of the Hoosier Mushroom Society, a scientific/educational nonprofit. He is a Ph.D. candidate at Purdue University with a focus on botany, plant pathology, and molecular biology. He and Hoosier Mushroom Society member Ron Kerner led the Ecoblitz fungi team in 2014, 2015, and 2016.

Rae Schnapp spent her childhood climbing trees and hunting fossils near the Meramec River in Missouri. She attended college at Southern Illinois University and earned her master's degree there working on plant responses to environmental stress. After earning her Ph.D. from Purdue University, she worked on crop improvement at the International Institute of Tropical Agriculture in Ibadan, Nigeria. Returning to Indiana, Rae served as Water and Agriculture Policy Director at the Hoosier Environmental Council for more than a decade. She worked as Conservation Director at the Indiana Forest Alliance from 2016 through 2023, coordinating Ecoblitz taxonomic surveys in the Nebo Ridge area of the Hoosier National Forest, researching forest policy issues, and advocating for forest protection. Rae is the Wabash Riverkeeper and is especially interested in the role of forests in watershed protection and carbon sequestration.

Karen Smith, engaged by the beauty, wildness, and mystery of the natural world, is an advocate for forest preservation, nonviolence, and simple living for the sake of the earth and our fellow creatures. She resides in Bloomington, Indiana.

Jeffrey N. Stant has served as Executive Director of the Indiana Forest Alliance (IFA) since 2013, directing scientific research and outreach campaigns. Mr. Stant has decades of experience integrating science-backed research with public outreach. He led the campaign that enacted federal legislation establishing the 12,953-acre Charles Deam Wilderness in the Hoosier National Forest (HNF) in 1982. While serving as Executive Director of Hoosier Environmental Council from 1985 to 2000, Mr. Stant also directed a seven-year campaign that produced a management plan for the HNF considered an ecological model for other eastern national forests. To see the progress that IFA is making under Jeff's leadership in protecting and restoring forests in Indiana from the depths of inner-city Indianapolis to the state forests and the Hoosier National Forest visit: www.indianaforestalliance. org or follow IFA on Facebook, Twitter and Instagram.

Emma Steele is a writer and community organizer born and raised in Fort Wayne, Indiana. She served as Outreach Coordinator for Indiana Forest Alliance from 2021 to 2023. Growing up with a deep love for the natural world, she studied geology at Indiana University Fort Wayne and now carries that love into her adult life as an avid birder, rock hound, and hiker. Emma is passionately midwestern with an intense appreciation for Indiana's nature. When she is not enjoying the wonders of the midwest herself, she is in her community advocating for climate action and conservation of the land she loves.

MAIN INDEX

Page number in italics refer to illustrations.

SPECIES INDEX

FOR INDIANA UNIVERSITY PRESS

Lesley Bolton *Project Manager/Editor*

Tony Brewer *Artist and Book Designer*

Dan Crissman *Editorial Director and Acquisitions Editor*

Anna Francis *Assistant Acquisitions Editor*

Anna Garnai *Editorial Assistant*

Samantha Heffner *Marketing and Publicity Manager*

Brenna Hosman *Production Coordinator*

Katie Huggins *Production Manager*

Dan Pyle *Online Publishing Manager*